Get Your Pitchfork On!

Get Your Pitchfork On!

The Real Dirt on Country Living

by Kristy Athens

 process self-reliance series

Get Your Pitchfork On! The Real Dirt on Country Living
© 2012 by Kristy Athens

Get Your Pitchfork On!
is the seventh volume of the Process Self-Reliance Series

Process Media
1240 W Sims Way #124
Port Townsend WA 98368

processmediainc.com
getyourpitchforkon.com

Design by Gregg Einhorn

ISBN-10: 1934170348
ISBN-13: 978-1934170342

10 9 8 7 6 5 4 3 2 1

Contents

Acknowledgments

This book may never have happened if it weren't for my grandmother, Marian Eberle Athens. In October 2009, after my husband and I were devastated by having to sell our country homestead, she welcomed me to visit for an entire month. Grandma is also a writer, and she understood the value of sequestering oneself to focus on a project. My aunts, Edie and Betty, took me on tours of the Wisconsin countryside, giving me family history as well as rural perspectives to add to my own. I had left for the Midwest with little more than an outline and returned with 60,000 words.

During March and April of 2010, I added another 45,000 words as an Eastern Oregon Writer-in-Residence. The experience was invaluable in its giving me time to write and also in re-immersing me in rural culture. The kind folks in Harney County, Oregon, invited me into their schools, their homes, their barns and—in some wonderful cases—their hearts. I shall always be indebted, especially to Kate Marsh, Carolyn Koskela, Terry Keim, Nancy and Matt Fine, Peg and Tom Wallis, Diane and Walt Rapaport, Jen and Dean Schulze, and Fran and Rich Davis. Thanks to Rick Bombaci, who kept the flame burning as the executive director of Fishtrap, the residency's sponsor, and to Peggy C. Ross for flexibility with my work schedule.

Thanks to Julie Jindal, Lea Ryan, Jim Tindall, Stephanie Irving and Julie Schlemmer Hamilton for their input on horses and pasture, and for their support. Thanks to Andrea Woloschuk for letting me put her on speakerphone as the pickups roared by and the leaf-blower raged. To Karen Kudej and Monica Burke for their thoughtful responses. Thanks to Lisa Wolf and Anne Sheeter for taking me hiking with their llamas. To Glory Schulze for introducing me to her pigs, Fern, Olivia and Girl. To Masie Custis, D.V.M., for entertaining my litany of animal-related questions. Peter Mehringer for sharing his sordid tale of dashed country dreams. And John Mayo, Eileen Fordonski, Sue and Jim Wanner, and Kristin and Nick Walrod. And all of the good people of the Hood River/White Salmon area. The bad ones, too, I guess; I also learned from them.

Thanks, hugs and kisses to everyone who volunteered to read draft chapters— Elizabeth Quinn, Meg Daly, Fritz Bogott, Tara Keairnes, Edie Phillips, Sue Wanner, Amanda Wineman, Linda Peck Athens, Angie Reynolds, Joan Chantler, Gardner Johnston, Pam Markus, Christina Cartier, Jodi Charrier, Stephanie Lanning, Chris Hamilton, Julie Jindal and Jon Rombach (as well as aforementioned Harney County-ites Terry, Nancy, Peg, Diane and Jen). In July 2010 I got one more week, at a residency called Soapstone, to hone the draft. Their comments and questions made this a better book.

Early remnants of this book, in the form of personal essays, were published by *Portland Monthly Magazine* ("Acres and Pains" in October 2006) and *Northwest Palate* ("How to Dress a Quail," July/August 2008). Ali McCart at Indigo Editing fine-tuned my book proposal. Chelsea Rose and Tyler Davis recommended Process Media to me, and vice versa, for which I will be eternally grateful. Thanks to Process's Adam and Carrie for their careful readings.

And, of course, thank you to my family and to Mike Midlo—for everything.

Introduction

So, you want to move to the country. You're tired of the crush of humanity, the incessant noise, the homeless people digging through your recycling bins. You want your own little piece of paradise in the sticks. Do you think you can handle it? Let's face it: Contemporary urban people don't know how to do much with their hands. Most can't operate an espresso machine, let alone a chainsaw. This isn't their fault; they simply never needed to learn. If you are going to make it in the bucolic rural heaven of your dreams, you are going to have to ramp up your skills—fast.

If you're like me, you grew up in the suburbs of a large city in the final third of the twentieth century. You spent your twenties living in that or another large city. You now own a house there and fantasize about living in the country. You think that it will be satisfying and character-building. You are right. You think it will be "fun." You are wrong. Or, partly wrong.

Ten years ago, my husband Mike and I lived in a little house in Portland, Oregon, across the street from a nice neighborhood park. We had fixed up the house and planted a garden. We planted fruit trees in the yard. We trained hops to climb the garage.

This should have satisfied us. We could take any of four different bus lines into Portland proper. People picked up our refuse and took it somewhere else. Water came to our house clean, and went away dirty. Friends thought nothing of stopping by for a visit. The grocery, post office, restaurant—even a movie theater—were all within walking distance. Yet, we drove around the Columbia River Gorge every weekend and imagined life on one of the homesteads tucked off the road.

Neither Mike nor I had a background in rural existence. Though some of my great-grandparents farmed in the Midwest, I had not known them; the relatives I know live in cities, or at least towns. Mike and I were not interested in becoming *farmers* per se, just living a little more connected to the land. We had done the suburban thing; we'd done the urban thing. We wanted to see what this rural thing was all about.

My interest in "rural" writ large probably stemmed from an awareness of organic farming that developed as a young adult. Growing up, I had eaten a *lot* of processed food. So do most Americans currently. This story has garnered plenty of attention in recent years—people in the United States have become so unfamiliar with the origin of food that they think nothing of grabbing a roasted chicken encased in a plastic sarcophagus from a display heated with warming lamps near the check-out stand in a big-box store. They have no concept of eating seasonally (which means you don't eat grapes in January because it's not okay to import them from South America). They don't know what vegetables look like when they're growing on a plant (for example, an artichoke is essentially a big thistle bud). Their main concern is how much something costs, meaning U.S. dollars and was it on sale—not "cost" in terms of environmental impact, how the workers who processed the food were treated, how much fossil fuel was used to transport it, and how the animals that became the food lived and were killed.

People my age were babies during the first wave of the back-to-the-land movement. Well, *the most recent* wave. As soon as the Industrial Age started gaining ground there were people who opposed it for its exploitation of resources (territorial and human), and its pollution, noise and greed. Utopian and communalist societies sprang up in rural areas as safe-havens from the clutches of capitalism throughout the 19th and 20th centuries—the back-to-the-land movement of the 1960s and '70s was only the newest.

During that time, a number of books were published to preserve the knowledge of yesteryear that was in danger of being lost. Books that continue to thrive include Carla Emery's *Encyclopedia of Country Living*, Storey's *Basic Country Skills* and *Back to Basics* published by Reader's Digest. They (and other classics, such as *The Whole Earth Catalogue*), showed those who endeavored to live a completely off-the-grid, self-sufficient existence how to skin an animal, how to build a house, how to make cheese. Those books remain immensely useful; *Get Your Pitchfork On!* is intended to supplement, not replace, them.

Unlike the back-to-the-landers of the 1970s, my generation wants the organic, natural pleasures of rural life without sacrificing the culture and convenience of urban life. In other words, we may hawk our garden produce at a farmer's market but we are not about to give up good coffee or *The New York Times*. Additionally, thanks to high-speed Internet, we tend to stay connected to and bring our work with us from cities. Unlike the '70s crowd, we have no intention of "dropping out." We want to eat our cake—baked from scratch with local, organic ingredients, and using sustainable power—and have it, too.

That's why *Get Your Pitchfork On!* is more than a how-to about farming for beginners. Between the aforementioned books and the Internet, you don't need me to tell you how to deliver a calf (thank heavens; it's not pretty). But you may be wondering about pitfalls when purchasing rural land; how to start a Montessori School; when (and how, and why) to get involved in small-town politics.

Once Mike and I moved to our seven-acre parcel in the Columbia River Gorge in 2003, I finally rued ignoring the opportunities that I had as a younger person to learn how all this stuff was done. As a suburban teenager, I was profoundly uninterested in any domestic art, but especially gardening. I could have taken all of my Grandma's canning supplies when she sold her house, but at the time I couldn't have cared less. Why would one preserve food? There's plenty in the store.

So, on the farm, I learned. I improved my gardening skills; I bought a canner; I slaughtered a couple chickens. We had the help of many, especially our neighbors Jim and Sue. We asked a lot of questions, made a lot of mistakes, and kept going. It was an adventure, after all.

In the beginning, we relied on Portland's economy—Mike's job and all my free-lance clients were there. I tried to find writing and editing jobs in the country, and learned that while people were happy to have my skills available to them, they weren't willing or able to pay a city rate for them. This was something I hadn't considered. We couldn't afford to buy a tractor and didn't have time to donate to other people's projects, which is how you barter for the use of someone else's tractor. This was also something we hadn't considered. As time wore on, the number of things we hadn't considered started to pile up.

In 2009, Mike and I faced the reality that we were in over our heads. The 70-mile commute to Portland hadn't worked out; the job prospects in our community were unsatisfactory. The house and outbuildings required maintenance that we could neither do ourselves nor hire out. Our beloved dog had been killed on the highway bordering our property. Fighting against pests and pestilence had made growing crops more exasperating than rewarding. We had made many friends but I, being nonconformist and outspoken (a dangerous combination), had made a few enemies. We reluctantly sold our home in July to two retirees from Alaska—people who had both time and resources to keep the place up as it deserved—and retreated to the city.

In those six years Mike and I learned many things about rural life—the good, the bad and the chainsaw. Though the experience was stressful and ended sooner than we intended, we cherish it. We plan to do it again, smarter the next time.

I began to accumulate notes and research for *Get Your Pitchfork On!* when Mike and I were still in it for the long haul. The prospect of selling our farm was not on the radar. You, the reader of this book, can benefit from our experience: In addition to learning from our successes, you'll also learn from our mistakes. And the stories of dozens of other people I interviewed, who live in towns all over the United States, as well. I'm not trying to dissuade you from following your dream—my hope is to give you the tools to make it a reality.

Section One

Land

Land

After all the expensive massages, lavender footbaths and boxes of herbal tea that I had acquired as an urbanite, I loved that in the country all I had to do to relax was look around me—the sun setting over the Cascades; the trickle of water flowing through the woods; the juncos shuffling around in the snow looking for fallen thistle seeds and leaving little footprints on the deck. Sitting and looking at my land was all the relaxation I needed.

I loved knowing that I was responsible for the upkeep of one little corner of the Earth. Those trees over there? Mine. I didn't feel ownership of them, but stewardship. They were under my purview for a few years of their long lives; I wanted to take care of them as best I could.

You may never have breathed air so pure it's nearly perfumed. I have, and it's a heady experience. Breathing is such an unconscious thing that when it becomes consciously pleasurable you can't get enough of it!

Living in the country will likely engender an appreciation for astronomy that you didn't know you have. The night sky in the city is like a watered-down, warm soda—washed out by light pollution of all but the brightest stars and planets. On a clear night in the country, you will marvel at what you see. Watch an astronomy website or maybe even your local newspaper for meteor showers, like the Perseid in August. Get to know the planets: Venus burns bright blue; Mars really looks reddish. A friend once brought on a visit extremely powerful binoculars, through which we could see not only Jupiter but three of its moons. Remember the Milky Way? It's still there, waiting for you to strain your neck looking up at it.

The only clear nights that you won't be able to see the stars are when there's a full moon—and a country moon is just as magical. In the city, you can't appreciate the way it bathes everything in a blue glow because everything in urban areas is lit with yellow, incandescent lights—between the streetlights, house lights and car headlights, it's amazing anyone can sleep. And when the moon is new, you will experience darkness you never realized was possible. I have lain in bed, eyes wide open, literally unable to see my hand before my face. It's disorienting and thrilling.

Chapter 1
Buying

Before you go real estate-shopping, figure out what is most important to you—particular trees? Open area for a garden? A year-round creek? Amazing views? What are the things you're willing to put up with? In our case, the property was very similar to what we'd been discussing, and we could afford it. But, as we sat on the back deck chatting with one of the sellers (it was "for sale by owner"), we were a little distressed about the traffic noise. The property was bordered on the east by a state highway. Even though the house was a couple hundred yards from the road, and a wall of Douglas fir trees blocked our view of it, we could still hear the cars just fine—and on a Saturday afternoon in good weather there were a number of them.

"You don't even notice it after a while," the seller said. I'm sure she was being truthful, but six years later I was definitely still noticing it.

As a buyer, you need to understand that the best home sites in any area were claimed decades ago. You are unlikely to find the perfect piece of land with the perfect house on it unless you have unlimited financial resources, and maybe not even then—the descendants of owners of perfect spots rarely let them out of the family. So, work out your must-haves and your compromises ahead of time, and be ready to re-negotiate them as you tour real properties and see what's actually available.

Once you own some land, you are responsible for everything on it, whether you were the source of it or not. So, make sure that there aren't, for example, old car batteries buried in shallow graves in your woodlot. Find out as much as you can about previous owners via your real estate agent, county records, local newspaper and library archives, any neighbors you can get a hold of, and any other means in your power. You do not want to purchase someone else's sloppy decisions, illegal maneuvers (there are a lot of those, believe it or not) or bad luck. Blindly, at least—if there is an issue that you feel you can deal with, go for it.

Make sure you can get a building permit for bare land, unless you plan to just camp on it. Then, make sure there is a suitable "building site" (i.e. a flat area large enough to build on). If the building site isn't where you want it, you'll either have to live with it or spend a lot of money to hire someone with a bulldozer to move it.

An interesting and sometimes exasperating thing about buying in a rural area is that your bank will only loan you the money for the house; the land itself is not valued. So, if the parcel is listed at $300,000, but your home appraisal only comes in at $175,000, your bank will only loan you $175,000. Another complication to pricing real estate in the country is that comparable sales ("comps") are difficult to acquire— there are so many variables in country property, and chances are that no recently sold property is exactly like yours. Therefore, appraisals are fairly, "fluid," shall we say. When we applied for a loan for our farm, we basically let the appraiser know what we needed our house to come in at, and the appraiser made it happen. A rather shoddy system, but that was the system.

One way people circumvent the financing issue is to start small: Live in a trailer or yurt while you build the guest house; then live in the guest house while you build the big house. One friend was so comfortable in the garage he had built, with its temporary kitchen, bedrooms and bathroom, that he almost didn't feel compelled to build the main house! His wife and children thought otherwise. Other friends of ours had two kids under the age of five in an Airstream trailer—they couldn't get the main house up soon enough!

If the seller is claiming that the land is "dividable," and you have intentions of dividing it, find out why she didn't divide it herself. It may be that there are a lot of bureaucratic hassles and fees associated with it. Or, maybe the subdivision/s failed a "perc" test, which verifies that a septic field would drain properly.

Some buy property in the country and work on it over a few years while keeping their life in the city. These weekend warriors then have the freedom to fix up a dilapidated old farmhouse without living in the middle of the construction. If your finances allow, consider keeping your house in the city as a rental after you move to the country, as extra income (and just in case things don't work out…).

Realtor Versus FSBO

When we found the farm that we wanted to buy, we were a little reluctant to get involved because it was a FSBO ("for sale by owner"). The sellers had gone this route because they didn't want to pay real estate agents the several-thousand-dollar commission. The negotiations were a little awkward, as the sellers were moving to an adjacent lot and would be our neighbors, which made dickering on the price and terms an extremely careful exercise in diplomacy.

Its status as a FSBO is, however, probably the reason we found the place at all, because buyers' agents ignore them. If you go it alone, hire a title company to make sure there aren't any claims to the property that your seller hasn't disclosed.

Regardless of whether you hire a buyer's agent or not, you should do your own research. No one cares more about your future than you do. In addition to the

Multiple Listing Service (MLS), watch the local classifieds section in the newspaper and real estate websites. Find out if there is a local Internet Service Provider—their website may include a locals' classifieds section, which is where Mike saw the ad for our farm.

Make sure your house is priced appropriately. This may never be an issue again in our lifetimes, but just in case: If you're buying in the middle of a real estate boom, you might consider waiting. I know more than one person who ended up having to sell their house after a couple of years, for various reasons, and because they'd bought too high their house was no longer "worth" what they owed on it. This is called a "short sale," and it isn't pretty. When all is said and done, you no longer have your house but may still owe money on it. And your credit rating is toast.

If you want to circumvent the lending industry altogether, you might be able to set up a contract-for-deed, also known as a "land contract" or an "installment sale agreement." This simply means that instead of borrowing money from a bank or mortgage company, you are essentially "borrowing" it from the seller of the home. You make payments directly to him or her, just like you were paying a mortgage. The advantages of this are avoiding all the closing fees that traditional financers charge (though there will still be some filing fees). You don't have to come up with a big cash down-payment. The sale price of the home is usually lower than it would be under "normal" circumstances. There might be little or no interest charged.

Contract-for-deed sales require a lot of trust on both ends. The seller retains the deed of the property until it is fully paid off. While contracts-for-deed typically have shorter terms than amortized mortgages, paying for a house takes a long time. Your relationship will last years; any number of life events might upset this equilibrium. Or, worse—the seller might sell your contract to a mortgage company, and not necessarily a reputable one. You will have no control over this, and may find yourself having to make payments to a company that is trying to purposely cause you to default by randomly changing the due dates, etc. Most contracts end with a "balloon" payment—like a down-payment that comes at the end of the contract instead of the beginning. Some people successfully refinance their homes with a traditional lender before the balloon payment comes due.

All of the caveat emptor-type of advice goes double with a contract—both before closing on the contract for deed and before making the final payment, make sure the title for the home is "clear," meaning there are no liens (legal claims) on it. No unpaid taxes. Legally established property lines. Et cetera. Read on.

Topography

Think in three dimensions when you are learning about the lay of the land. Figure out where the sun rises and sets—for all seasons. It will follow a trajectory, back and forth, as summer and winter yield to each other. We lived in a narrow river valley; the high and low points on ridge to our east affected when the sun actually shined on our land. One particular high spot in that ridge caused the sun to rise a full forty-five minutes later. Make sure you don't purchase land in an east-to-west valley in which the sun never gets above the southern ridge in the winter! Unless you like being depressed. Remember that snow melts on south-facing slopes much sooner than on north-facing slopes.

Most counties now have access to Geographic Information Systems (GIS) technology that can answer questions you would have needed a helicopter for previously. This technology uses satellite images to create dozens of different maps of the parcel you're considering, from "viewshed" to wildlife habitat.

Potential Hazards

Is your property in a flood plain? Are there steep slopes on or near your property? What would happen if the slope collapsed? Many owners of houses built on the sand dunes of the West Coast are facing this issue—storm surges in the ocean and regular erosion undercut their homes, some to the point of their being condemned. A few homes in the Columbia River Gorge were inundated with rocks, mud and vegetation in 1996, as they had been built in a giant "alluvial fan"—a geologically known route for landslides.

If you live in the Plains states, there will be tornadoes. If you live near a river, there will be floods. If you live on the East or Gulf coasts, there will be hurricanes. If you live on the West Coast, there will be volcanoes, tsunamis and earthquakes. Learn about the topography of the area and what "events" have occurred in the past. Not everything is avoidable, but you should at least know the risks.

Water Features

Having water on your property is generally considered a boon. If there is a creek- or riverbank, lake or ocean beach, find out first of all what your frontage is: how long of a piece of shoreline do you own? How far out into the water does your property line go? If it's a major waterway, does the state claim ownership up to the line of "ordinary high water mark?" Note: In some parts of the United States, owning frontage does not mean that you also own water rights.

Any open water, especially if you have children or pets, can be a drowning hazard. If you have young children, or will have them often in tow of guests, how will you keep them out of the water? An irrigation ditch or a quickly moving stream is especially dangerous.

Find out if there are any big plans for the waterway. We lived uphill from Northwestern Lake, which was a one-mile dammed section of the White Salmon

River. It was a beautiful lake, but the dam was slated to be removed in order to restore the river as salmon habitat and, thereby, Native American fishing grounds. The initial breach occurred in October 2011—thousands watched via closed-circuit video as the entire lake drained in a mere forty-five minutes. In a few years no one will be able to tell that there ever was an aberration in the habitat. But first, there will be a "period of adjustment"—all of the cabins and homes that had docks on a lake, for one thing, now have docks on a dry bed of silt (near a beautiful river, of course).

Think about where water will go during heavy rain (or, better yet, visit the property during a rainstorm). Look for washouts and any new landscaping—as sometimes occurs with freshly painted houses, new landscaping might be hiding an issue.

Along those same lines, river and creeks sometimes change course. Lake levels change. What is the precedent in your area for dealing with the property lines that are made by the water?

Pond

A previous owner of our property took the south swale and dammed it in two places to make two small ponds, each with a drain sticking up toward the middle. The smaller was hardly more than a frog nursery, so narrow one could jump across it. The other was used as a trout pond. ("Swale" is a fancy word for "ditch;" real estate agents call them "seasonal creeks.")

Note: Because no one downstream from us was using our swales as a water source, we were pretty free to amend them as we wished. If someone had been, however, the previous owner would not have been allowed to build his push-up dams without permission from the holder of the water rights. Not that he asked anyone for permission.

During the summer, the swale dried up. The hazard with stagnant water is that it loses so much oxygen that the plants and animals in the pond die (except the mosquito larvae, of course). To keep the trout healthy, our neighbor had put a small fountain in the pond, which oxygenated the water. It was powered by an extension cord, which Mike and I didn't really think about until we'd been living there a week or two.

One day, we wondered where the cord came from, since the pond was at least fifty feet from the nearest building, the barn. We followed it from the pond into a Douglas fir, where it was draped in the August-dry branches and showed divots from having been chewed on by squirrels. It led to another cord that was woven through the fence and over the gate to the barn, where it terminated in an outlet under the roof of the lean-to. We unplugged that sucker faster than grass runs through a goose!

The last thing we needed was an arcing extension cord burning down our woods. The trout were eventually fished out by raccoons.

During Summer 2004, both ponds dried up. This gave us an opportunity to maintain the drains, re-securing screens over the tops to keep debris from clogging them. Once the water started running again, we saw that the drain on the smaller pond, while solidly constructed, was too small. One morning on a walk I discovered it overfilled, nearly breeching the land dam between it and the larger pond below it.

I had no choice but to wade in and try to unclog the drain. The water was so cold that my hands began immediately to ache. Thankfully, I was wearing knee-high boots that kept my feet dry. I felt around the area that I thought the drain should be, with no luck. Then, I spotted a tiny whirlpool. I followed it into the cold, brown water and felt around: there were the rocks around the drain, the drainpipe, pine needles—this must be it. As I pulled the pine needles away, the whirlpool grew and the sound of water crashing out the other end of the drainpipe intensified. I took a deep breath and plunged my numbed hands in. With every cold handful, the water moved faster until finally I could see the drain, and the water settled back down in its banks.

Channel Water

If you are fortunate enough to own property with river or stream frontage, you have something special. But keep in mind that, unless you own a water right, the water is there for you to look at, and not to remove for irrigation or any other purpose. If you live in a part of the country that irrigates via canals dug in the ground, be cautious with children and pets—the water in the canal can be moving quickly. In some parts of the country, these channels are being covered to make them safer and to minimize water loss via evaporation.

The more snow that falls in the winter, the more melted snow will come coursing through your property in the spring. And not necessarily where you want it. This is sometimes euphemized as a "water event." In our six years, we experienced some significant water events. Swales that meandered in winding paths straightened their routes, taking out good soil on the way. Places in the swale that once had a small dip were gouged out three feet deeper and three feet further back; we put big rocks and logs in to try to slow the erosion. Trees were weakened and fell. Our young fruit trees were completely swamped; Mike dug little trenches to try to help them drain. We were constantly monitoring the property to try to forestall further damage. Mother Nature was unmoved by our efforts.

Driveway

Is the driveway level and flat? If there are low spots, water will collect there. If it's paved and on a slope, water will pick up that much more velocity as it runs down the slope—figure out where it goes. If it's gravel, see that it has been re-rocked and leveled. Make sure there aren't ruts or washboard.

Snowfall is magical—it silences the usual noises, covers the trees in a sparkling blanket, and turns your field into a play land. But it can be a disaster when it's melting. If you have a gravel driveway that hasn't been recently leveled, chances are there will be significant mud and puddles. Not a big deal when you're marching around in your farm clothes and boots—another matter when you have guests who are wearing expensive, thin-soled shoes and are reluctant to step out of their cars.

If you're building on bare land and need to put in a driveway, it will have to be permitted to connect with the existing road.

Microclimates

Ask about the first and last hard-frost dates, especially if you plan to garden. As possible, find out about microclimates, which are small but significant variations in climate affected by elevation, slope, tree coverage and other factors. A friend of mine bought a house in August, maybe a quarter-mile out of a mountain town, and couldn't wait to plant her first garden the following spring, which was when she learned that the imperceptible rise in elevation to her house translated into snow melting two weeks later than it did in town.

We lived with a steep slope that rose several hundred feet on our east flank and dropped a few hundred feet on our west flank. The overall effect of this was cold air from the highest elevation on the east rolled down to the river to the west. Anywhere there was a little flat spot, such as our garden, the air stalled. This is sometimes called a "frost pocket." Not the best place to plant a garden. I never could get rosemary to overwinter.

View

Do you look forward to rising every morning and drinking your coffee while gazing at the tranquil, tree-covered hillside across the valley? Then you'd better find out what the hillside's owner's plans are for it, or you may wake one morning to a clear-cut or a housing development. Upcoming timber sales and development permits are registered with your county and often announced in the local newspaper.

The other thing to consider with a parcel that has great views: How did you get up there? Is it a steep, private road from which you'll be responsible for removing the snow? Are there a lot of trees that could fall and block it? Is it a road you can see yourself safely driving in the middle of the winter when you're in a hurry to get somewhere? As car commercials attest, driving a steep, curvy road is a lot of fun on dry pavement—and it's tense-to-terrifying the rest of the time.

Don't get so caught up in the view that you ignore other factors. For example: Our house faced (more or less) south, so we were disappointed when we saw that there was a beautiful, large deck on the north side of the house.

"Now, how dumb is that?" we thought, feeling that they should have put a deck on the front of the house, so one can look at the valley and watch the sunset. We made big plans to extend the porch on the front of the house all the way down to the southwest corner, where the dining room was, and then put in some French doors so we could dine more or less *alfresco*. Then, we could take advantage of the afternoon sun and get a cross-breeze going in the house.

After we'd spent a summer there, we understood. First of all, the prevailing winds came from the southwest and were very prevailing, indeed. We would have had to weigh the napkins down to keep them from blowing away. Possibly the plates as well. Any time our neighbors to the south used their gravel driveway (often), a giant plume of dust came straight at us.

And then, the sun. Its warmth was so welcome in cold weather…but when we would have had the French doors open, during the summer, the afternoon sun was nearly unbearable. Rather than opening the doors we would have been pulling drapes over them! The deck had been built onto the north side of the house with good reason—nice, cool shade.

Government and Municipal Considerations

Naturally, state and county laws will differ from one area to another—be sure to research your area.

Vehicle Licensing and Insurance

If you plan to leave a municipal area that required emissions testing on all vehicles, rejoice—you're now off the hook. Your vehicles will also be less expensive to insure (unless you are commuting to a city for work).

If you buy a trailer, it may require its own license. It will be licensed to one rig that can haul it, and there will be a limit to the gross weight you can haul with it. Check about farming license plates—if you plan to do a lot of hauling, it might be worth pursuing. These plates are more expensive than regular plates, but give you latitude as far as weights you can haul.

Taxes

What is the tax rate for your area? Is the community declining, stable or growing? When was the last time there was an assessment? How often are they completed?

Where we lived, assessments were only done every four years. After a couple of years, they decided to change it to every other year, and here's why: The Columbia River Gorge is a high-growth area. Washington is a 100-percent assessment state, meaning that homes are taxed on their entire assessed value. When our house was assessed in 2003, our resultant property taxes were $1,300. When our house was assessed in 2007, after four years of rising real estate prices, we were informed that our taxes were going up—doubling, in fact. The taxes of some homes in the area tripled or quadrupled. This, of course, did not go over well among the populace. So the county's tax assessor decided to change the system to perform assessments biennially to minimize the "sticker shock."

Tax rates are calculated, as they are in the city, per $1,000 of value. They can vary widely. In 2009 in New Mexico, the assessed rate could be as much as $48. In Greenville, Wisconsin, a former farm town that's been engulfed by growth around the city of Appleton, the 2010 rate went up three cents from the previous year, to a whopping $1.89. That makes a home worth $150,000 (which in Greenville is a fine home) have an annual tax bill of $283.30.

If you happen to be looking for property in a community like Greenville, bank those dollars, because it won't last forever. Greenville is currently in its boom period—farmers are selling their land to developers; developers are putting up exurb utopias with winding roads called "Pheasant Way" and "Pleasant View," and bike paths that lead to the school. Greenville's taxes are low because of its growing tax base. But, there will come a time when there is no more farmland to pave, and then, if Greenville's residents want to keep the bike paths and public landscaping maintained, they'll have to pony up for it.

"Farm deferral" is addressed in the Making a Living Chapter.

Zoning

Find out how your area is zoned, and whether that zoning is stable or being challenged. Where we lived, people were chomping at the bit to re-zone our Resource Land designation into something that allowed for lots smaller than twenty acres, so they could subdivide and cash in on the development in the area. While I was sympathetic to their economic needs, I had no desire to live in a giant subdivision—that's why I left the city! Many communities are struggling with this remain-pastoral-versus-stimulate-the-local-economy debate.

If you live near commercial farm operations, find out what the implications of that are. Living downwind of a mint farm might be kind of nice; a pig farm not so much. "Right to farm" laws exist because farming and ranching operations often have an impact beyond their boundaries—pesticide spray might blow in the wind; the sound of bird cannons or combines—often run at night—can be heard on neighboring properties. If a farm's normal activities have an undesirable impact on your household, you will not be able to challenge them. In open range, cattle are branded in the spring and left to fend for themselves in remote, open country for the summer, and then rounded up in fall. In such an area, it's incumbent upon you to build a fence around your farm to keep cattle out.

Check with city and county agencies to see if any public works projects are being planned (road-widening; sidewalks; etc.) that affect your land. Ask to see what conditional-use permit requests have been filed; these are requests by landowners who want to do something on their land that is not allowed by zoning. Ask multiple sources and cross-check their answers, for two reasons: one person in an agency may be unaware of things another person knows, and some people may not be completely honest with you.

If your property is located within a subdivision, or is subject to membership in a homeowners association, find out if there are covenants or other rules that limit its use. Ask for a copy of the bylaws and minutes to recent meetings, so you can see if there are annual dues and if the organization functions well.

Learn whether your property is in any kind of endangered habitat jurisdiction. For example, properties in the Columbia River Gorge that lie within a certain boundary and are visible from the river must be built and landscaped under certain rules so that they don't mar the scenery. You wouldn't want to buy an expensive parcel in this area with plans of cutting all the trees down and building a red-and-blue striped, four-story home.

Covenants

Sort of micro-zoning, a covenant is a set of rules and regulations that govern a neighborhood or subdivision. It can limit the size and number of buildings on your property (even their color!); how your yard can look (particular fencing material; no wind chimes; only roses in the front). They are rare in rural areas, but ask, just to be sure.

Environmental Health

People like to talk about the good old days, before there was pollution. They forget that in the good old days, everyone was burning wood or coal to heat their homes. This can create an enormous layer of fetid air, especially in densely populated areas. Watch Disney's *Mary Poppins* and you'll see what I mean. I get asthma just thinking about it.

Growing up, if we left a door open during the winter someone would holler for us to close it: "You trying to heat the whole outdoors?" In orchard country, farmers do just that. Early February mornings, Mike and I were often awoken by the drone of giant fans blowing in nearby orchards. The farmers were trying to protect their trees' buds from late frosts by moving the air to warm it up or, if they were really worried, they'd also light smudge pots—giant lanterns that run on propane. The next day, the Hood River Valley would have a thick haze of smoke floating over it.

My point is do some research about the area you're considering. Is there heavy industry or agriculture that will affect the air or water quality? Are they spraying pesticides or insecticides over fields or orchards? Spraying is usually planned for a day with no wind, but clouds of poison can still drift across lot lines…

Another concern is high-tension power lines. No one can argue that they're an eyesore and make disturbing buzzing and crackling sounds when you're near them. What many people who live near them insist, and the industry denies, is whether the electromagnetic field (EMF) surrounding the lines can cause cancer, Alzheimer's and other life-threatening diseases. You can see EMF activists on the Internet, holding up fluorescent light bulbs—which begin to glow by picking up electrons emitted through the air by the wires—to make their point. Of course, your cell phone, microwave oven and other electronic appliances also create an EMF. Studies are inconclusive. There is a frequency meter you can buy to measure the impact of wires at a particular site.

Conservation Easement

If you own a parcel that is popular with local animal and insect species, particularly rare ones, or that is part of a watershed or otherwise unique, you might consider granting a conservation easement (or "covenant") to a governmental agency or land trust. This guarantees the integrity of your parcel—and its nonhuman inhabitants—long after you cease to own it. The agreement stipulates various perpetual restrictions.

Such easements are generally donated, which qualifies them as tax deductions. Or, there is a "conservation lease," in which case the organization pays the owner a monthly "rent" until they turn over the property. These easements often result in reduced estate taxes and tax credits. If you're already conservation-minded, the restrictions that the easement brings—no further development of the parcel, for example—will have a minimum impact. You still own the land, and may still sell it or pass it on to heirs; the easement becomes part of the title.

Mineral and Timber Rights

Find out if someone else owns the mineral-extraction or timber rights. If a previous owner sold those rights to a third party, and that party decides to cash in on them, you may find yourself owning a clear cut or a festering hole in the ground.

Airspace

Because of the number of bridges and hydroelectric plants on the Columbia River, United States Air Force jets run practice defense missions. Our house happened to be beneath the flight path from the base, near Seattle. This meant that during certain times of the year a fighter jet or two might roar overhead at only a few hundred feet—so close we could see the numbers painted on its underside—frightening the animals and driving us to distraction. One flew so low that the percussion actually caused my heart to skip a beat. Mike contacted the FAA, whose representative assured him that there was nothing to be done about it. National security trumps hayseed annoyance.

There was a lot of flap in our area because of a local shooting range. Apparently, someone had moved within earshot (no pun intended) of the range and complained to various city officials about his weekend afternoons being ruined by the sound of dozens of rounds of rifle fire. Do your research before you move—if whatever is making noise was there before you were, you are unlikely to prevail.

Vegetation Control

If your property is bordered by roads, find out who owns them, for a variety of reasons, including to control vegetation. The vegetation along the side of a road may be cut or sprayed with herbicide—find out if this will affect your family or livestock. You should, depending on your area's laws, be able to submit a "No Spray" request (this is also true of areas that spray for mosquitoes). You must re-submit this request on an annual basis, and control the vegetation yourself. If there is a steep drop-off after the road's shoulder, this kind of maintenance might be dangerous.

On a side road that formed the northern boundary of our property, a county truck would occasionally come through with a fearsome tool—a giant buzz saw that hacked down a clear line through the brush along the road. The first time we saw them coming (they went down the opposite side of the road and then starting coming up on our side, Mike ran over there and asked them to spare one Douglas fir that would have been killed otherwise. They did.

Property Lines

If the existing owners don't provide a recent survey of your prospective property, have one done. Don't trust existing fences. Make sure the parcel was created legally. Learn if there are any setbacks or easements, and try to find out if there have been border disputes in the property's history. There should be "pins" at all corners— these are metal stakes that are driven deep into the ground by a licensed surveyor and sometimes topped with an orange plastic cap to make them easier to find. Some are made of brass. If the pins haven't been identified in a long time, you may need a metal detector and a GPS to locate them. Walk the entire property with the existing owner and your real estate agent so that everyone agrees on the boundaries.

A setback means that the state or county has acted on its right to eminent domain and basically moved your property line back ten, sixty, or more feet in order to make way for a municipal use, usually a road. It can also refer to the distance from a road that a building must be. An easement is an agreement with a neighbor to allow that person to use part of your property to access hers, usually in the form of a driveway.

If the property you are considering has an easement on a neighbor's property, make sure that easement is in good shape legally. It would be a shame to own some beautiful land that you can't access except by helicopter.

Find out whether your land is customarily hunted on. If so, decide whether you're going to continue to let people on your land to hunt. Laws regarding posting "No Trespassing" signs vary from state to state—in many places, land is considered open unless it's clearly marked otherwise.

If you decide to limit a hunter's access when he's already out there, do it gently—if he lives in the area, you don't want to get into a Hatfield-McCoy situation right off the bat. Remember, he's got a gun. You might even consider wearing blaze orange (hat, vest or jacket) during hunting season when you're out walking around.

Proximity

How far is the property from a hospital? Grocery? School? Gas station? Fire station? County seat? You will need to go to the county seat if you are renewing your driver's license or reporting for jury duty. The $10-per-day doesn't compensate for your time if you're driving forty miles. Well, it wouldn't compensate for your time even if you lived next door...

Neighbors

Mike was once visiting friends in Southern Oregon. He announced that he was going for a walk, and our friends began giving him detailed instructions about which side roads he could explore and which areas he should avoid. The reason? Many of their neighbors "grow" (a euphemism for having a marijuana plantation), and these areas have armed guards.

You want to try to get an idea of your neighbors' habits before you sign any papers. Does one of them breed guinea hens? Does one blare [insert type of music that you hate] all weekend when he's in his workshop? Someone near to us, I never even figured out who, used to rev the engine of a four-wheeler over and over, and then drive it around his yard in short bursts of acceleration, every afternoon at the exact time that I was in my garden.

What is different in the country is, ironically, distance and open space. When our neighbor called his dogs we knew it, even though he was the equivalent of a few city blocks away. If we had lived in the city in the same proximity, Mike and I would never have known he even existed—there would be so many people between us, making noise and doing their thing, that his bellow would have disappeared into the fray. As it was, nothing stopped it from coming straight across our field and into our ears. Sort of the trade-off for quiet most of the time.

Consider other neighbors as well, like the railroad. Trains can sound so romantic—if they're in the distance. If you are within a mile of railroad tracks, find out how often trains run and what the alert system is like. Many rural railroad crossings forgo the familiar striped crossbars and flashing red lights routine, but trains always blast their horn when going through a town. It's not a petite sound. I never knew what "hit the ceiling" looks like until I was surprised, driving alongside a set of tracks, by an engine blast from twenty feet away. You'd hate to buy a beautiful house only to learn that every night, for the rest of your life, you'd be awakened at 2 a.m. by the Nor-Wester bound for Philly. Or, conversely, you would have fair warning and learn to find it reassuring every night…

There are also animal neighbors. Especially if you're building on bare land, consider what animals have been using that land before you came along. It might be a good idea to put owl silhouettes in your windows, or apply flash tape outside of them, to try to alert birds to the new "road"-block. Check trees for nests before you cut them—you might be removing a critical nesting habitat. Give animals some time to realize you have moved into their territory and to find another route.

Utilities

Ask the current owners to show you where the underground lines are, and to tell you what the water and other utilities cost per month, including the heating bill in the winter (or, how much wood they stored). If there is a propane tank, find out how often they have it filled and how much that costs.

Mortgage companies will not loan money for a house that has a woodstove without a secondary, automatic (with a thermostat) heat source; we only used the backup heat to keep our house from freezing solid when we left for a weekend during the winter.

There is more about utilities in the Buildings, Inside and Out Section.

Bare Land

Consider in the price of bare land the cost of installing utilities. If you plan to use community utilities, find out where the nearest main lines are: electricity; telephone; DSL; natural gas. The shortest (read: cheapest) route to your house may be across another person's property, but only if that person gives you an easement to run the lines through. Running overhead power lines can cost $20,000 per mile. Underground lines, which may be required, cost twice that.

Does the city water supply come out that far? We were surprised to learn that we had a municipal water source, being six miles from town. It turned out that, when the pipes were laid back in the day, someone-of-authority's mother lived near our house and her son dutifully designed the water supply to come out that far.

If you plan to use environmentally sustainable utilities ("off the grid"), make sure the conditions are right to make your systems function correctly. There are more details below with each utility.

Make sure the land drains well by performing a percolation ("perc") test. If it's swampy you may have problems with your septic system.

If you plan to hire people to build a home for you, make sure their trucks can get to the building site. It may be too hilly, or too swampy—large equipment will sink right into the mud.

If you have more-than-household use planned for any utility, make sure it's available and that you can get a permit for it.

Find out if, once you've broken ground, there is a time frame in which you are required to finish building. A number of companies design kit homes and outbuildings, which are much less expensive than to hire an architect and build an original design. The buildings are delivered in pieces; you still have to hire a general contractor to construct them, even if you plan to do the work yourself. Make sure you're pre-qualified for a construction loan—you won't be able to finance this with a conventional home mortgage because there isn't a home on the property to serve as collateral. Once the home is built to a degree that satisfies a mortgage company, you can re-negotiate and get a better interest rate.

If your land is really out there, keep in mind that just because it's new to you doesn't mean it's been in a vacuum. Wildlife, hunters, and target shooters may consider your acres part of their usual route. A friend and her husband were out building their new dream house and found themselves ducking behind plywood sheets as bullets whizzed by. They went to complain to the neighbors, who shrugged, "Well, we've always shot here."

Domestic and Irrigation/Livestock Water

Confirming the property's water rights is crucial. Your domestic and irrigation rights may be separate rights. If there is any doubt about the integrity of the source of the water or the quantity to which you are allotted, don't buy the property.

Domestic water goes to your house and maybe a couple of spigots near your house. Irrigation is anything from a lawn watering system to four-foot-tall sprinkler heads to those massive aluminum structures that stretch hundreds of yards and wheel themselves across an entire field. Irrigation can be used for crops or livestock.

There are three sources of water—well, spring and surface. A well is a pipe driven through a hole bored in the ground to access a ground water that is pumped to the surface. Spring water rises naturally to the surface of the Earth from an underground source. Surface water is found in lakes and rivers.

Our house was on the municipal water system, which was nice because it was one fewer system to maintain. However, we did not have irrigation beyond our municipal limit. This meant that unless we punched a well, we couldn't farm the majority of our property.

Having water that comes to your house is just half the battle—what kind of water is it? Pour a glass from the kitchen tap and look at it, smell it and taste it. Water can have excess amounts of numerous minerals: sulfur, manganese, iron. It can have a fishy or swampy taste. Most issues with imperfect water sources can be addressed with a charcoal filter that intercepts the water as it comes from the main line into your house.

If you live in an area with a lot of limestone, you probably have dissolved minerals in your water. This is called "hard" water. It might taste all right—in fact, "mineral water" is bottled because of its healthfulness—but it may leave scale deposits on your dishes, shorten the lifespan of your plumbing and water heater, and render cleaning products less effective.

Because of this, some people install a water softener, which removes most of the minerals and adds sodium. It's good for your appliances and clothing, but it can taste a little weird, and it can have the opposite reaction to soap as extremely hard water—instead of feeling like you can't get any lather, you feel like you can't totally rinse it off.

Many homeowners with a water softener also install a charcoal or reverse-osmosis filter on a single tap in the kitchen that is dedicated to drinking water. This provides pure water with no aftertaste.

Remember to change your filters regularly—not only do they stop working after a while, but they also harbor bacteria.

Surface Water

There are two general traditions for determining water rights in the United States—"riparian" and "prior appropriation." Riparian means that if you own the land surrounding a body of water, you also own the water. If you own a portion of the frontage, you own a portion of the rights. Prior appropriation means first come, first served—if you applied for the right to pull water from a river in 1957 and a downstream neighbor applied in 1956, the neighbor gets her water first. And if it's a drought year and there isn't enough for both of you, you don't get yours.

In the West, prior appropriation rights have a colorful history. They've been fought and killed over for a hundred and fifty years. Chances are, you will not receive water rights with a moving body of water on your property. But, ask. If you do, you may plop a pump right into the water. You'll be able to use it for a certain number of gallons and/or certain times of the day. If you don't use your right, you'll lose it to someone down the line, which is why you'll sometimes see a field being watered for hours in the middle of the day.

In agricultural areas, most farms have water rights that transfer with the purchase of a property. They usually stipulate the area that may be irrigated (i.e. you may purchase a twenty-acre parcel but only have water rights for six acres) and/or the rate of water use (i.e. ten gallons per minute for three hours per day). If a property doesn't have water rights, you may apply for them with the state. But don't hold your breath; your petition could take years.

By way of example, the law in Washington State regarding water rights: A water right is necessary if you plan to divert any amount of water for any use from:

Surface water
- Lakes
- Streams
- Rivers
- Springs

Ground water
- If you plan to withdraw more than 5,000 gallons per day
- If you plan to irrigate more than half an acre of lawn or noncommercial garden

The gatekeeper to water rights is called the "water master." This person is the guardian of all records pertaining to water rights. This is someone to befriend.

Well Water

Because well water is less prone to contamination and its use less regulated (no monthly water bill!), many people prefer to punch a well. A growing problem is that there is a finite rate of replenishment of ground water; if too may wells draw from the same underground source, the water level drops and some of the pipes no longer reach the water. Think of straws in a giant Blue Hawaii cocktail. Water quality changes from one place to another; there's no guarantee that you'll find water at all, or that the water you find tastes good.

If you do order a well dug, someone will show up in a truck that is basically an enormous drill. A friend of ours asked his well-driller about "witching" a well—his father had insisted on walking the property holding a bent wire in each hand. When the two wires suddenly turned and faced each other, his father said, "Dig here." Our friend pointed out the spot and asked the well-driller if he thought there was anything to witching.

"Nope," said the man. "But, I wouldn't dig a well without it."

You want to make sure you get "sweet" (clear and lacking bacteria, iron, industrial pesticides and fertilizers, and other contaminants) water that pumps at least three gallons per minute. If the pressure is too high you'll need to have a regulator installed in order to protect your household fixtures.

Some neighbors tried to get away with punching a shallow well (one pays per foot of drilling). Their water was full of sulfur and they could only use it for bathing; it turned their daughter's blonde hair orange. They eventually tired of drinking bottled water and saved enough money to dig a new well, and the girl went back to being a blonde. You will have at least one filter on the water as it comes into the house; possibly also a filtered drinking water dispenser at the kitchen sink.

Research your well-drillers and be sure they follow regulations regarding capping the well. Despite the story I just told, a deeper well isn't necessarily better. It's all about hitting a good vein of water. Digging a well is an art.

Because it's fighting gravity, a well has a pump on it to drive water into the storage tank that is connected to the house's fixtures. The pipe to the storage tank from a submersible pump (in a four-inch well) is underground and has just a short pipe sticking out of the ground. The pump for a two-inch well is above ground and needs to be protected from the elements, either in a minimalist box structure or in its own small building, called a pump house. Here's the caveat about having a well: if the electricity goes out, so does your water—no pump. If you're expecting a storm, fill some buckets.

The water quality of a well should be tested once per year. If you're on municipal water, the city should send you a report of its quality testing. If you live in a farming community you can pretty much assume there will be excess nitrogen in the water, which is a byproduct of all the fertilizer that's dumped on conventionally farmed fields. The Environmental Protection Agency's 2007 standards allowed for 10.0 mg/liter. Water with excess nitrogen must be treated.

Septic System

Note: There is more about maintaining an existing septic system in the Buildings, Inside and Out Section.

In nature, animals defecate all over the place. Their feces are transformed into humus by insects and bacteria. Humans used to have similar habits, until they started living in big groups. Various strategies have been employed over the millennia, all with the basic premise of "get it out of here."

In the modern city, buildings are connected to one giant sewer that brings wastewater (both "black water" [toilet] and "gray water" [sink/laundry]) to a sewage treatment plant, which uses a variety of processes to return the water to a nontoxic state and then releases it into a body of surface water. In the country, each home has a septic system to treat its wastewater. The wastewater feeds into a two-chambered tank. Solids fall to the bottom of the tank, where bacteria break them down into smaller, more benign particles. Liquid floats; once it gets near the top of the tank it spills into a pipe, or over a barrier, that leads to the second tank. From there it feeds into a series of perforated pipes and seeps into the drain field. How well it seeps will depend on the type of soil you have; if you're putting in a new system, have a "perc" test (percolation) done.

Areas with compromised drainage due to heavy soil, a thin soil layer over bedrock, or a high water table may require a sand mound system. In this case, the effluent from the septic tank is pumped into a drain "field" that is above the natural soil level. If you're considering bare land that will require this system, keep in mind that it may cost $20,000, at least twice as expensive as a traditional tank-and-drain field system.

If it's not a legal requirement in your state, request that the existing owners have the septic tank cleaned and inspected—for a "fresh" start. Ask for a copy of the inspection report. Thereafter, how often you empty the tank depends on how much material goes into it. If you're a quiet two-person household, it could be ten years. If you're a six-person household that uses a garbage disposal, it might be two. Be sure you use a toilet paper that is septic-friendly, and ladies, please use the trash can for your "personal items."

I wasn't around for the septic inspection when we bought our farm, but I was there when we sold it. Mike and I had a rough idea of where the tank was located but we still had to dig around a bit to find the two lids; one for each tank. It was July, a time when the soil had set up like stone. If we had done the inspection in May we might have been able to dig around with shovels; instead, we had to order a backhoe. If you hire a backhoe to find your lids, make sure that you have someone who's very good at what she does—a sloppy or inexperienced backhoe operator can destroy your lids rather than uncovering them.

Note: Before you uncork your septic perfume bottle, close all the windows on that side of the house. We didn't, and it took a couple of hours for the smell to dissipate.

The backhoe driver finally found the lids. Meanwhile, the inspector had arrived with his giant vacuum and tanker truck. My heart sank as they opened the first tank (the "business end")—the lid was coated with slimy muck and roots. The tank was full of murky, foamy brine. It looked and smelled horrible.

Well, the sale's off, I thought. The inspector pulled the roots away from the lid, looked around for a minute, got up and brushed his knees off, and said, "Looks good!" I couldn't imagine how a septic tank would be if it looked bad, so I asked him. As he fished around the bottom of the tank will a long, flanged auger, he told me that the good ones are made of concrete, the bad ones metal. "After a couple years, a metal one becomes Swiss cheese," he said. "I was supposed to empty a failing metal tank once and I told the Realtor, 'If I empty that out, it will collapse.' The water pressure was actually holding the walls up."

Other ways a system can fail: A leaking tank sends untreated sewage into your land and, possibly, the ground water. Clogged drainage lines will eventually back up and cause the appliances in the house not to drain. If your system fails, an entire new one must be installed. This means digging up a huge section of your yard, extracting muck-encrusted pipes and then replacing the system. Tens of thousands of dollars. A failed septic system is an enormous problem.

Trees are attracted to the concentrated nutrient slurry. Their roots can do a lot of damage to the tank and the lines, so it's best to not have any trees near the system.

"What do you do with this...stuff...now?" I asked the tank inspector. He said that he dumps his loads at a sewage-treatment plant, which costs 13 cents per gallon. I made a joke about just dumping it over a cliff, and he said that some people have done that, and get fined if they're caught.

"I went up to drain the toilets at Lost Lake once," he said, "and on the way down a forest ranger pulled me over. He was convinced that I had dumped my load illegally.

"'Tell me where you dumped it,' he said. He wouldn't believe me!

"Finally, I told him, 'Why don't you stand here in front of the drain, and I'll turn the spigot on, and we'll see if anything comes out.'"

Services

Find out where on the priority list the roads abutting your house are on the snow-removal list. If the power is knocked out, how soon do they restore your home? If your house is on a main road, both of these things will happen quickly. If you are one of three families on a road that is miles from the thoroughfare, you'll be waiting a while, possibly days. Utilities are generally restored in the order that puts the greatest number of households back on line first. If your house is on a private road, the county will not plow it at all.

Is there garbage service to your house? If so, you'll still need to take your cans to the end of the driveway. If not, you'll have to haul it to the dump (nowadays euphemized as "transfer station") yourself. For Mike and me, this turned out not to be a big deal at all. First of all, between the non-packaged food from our garden, and the chickens, dog and compost taking all of our food scraps, we really didn't create a lot of garbage. Except at Christmas, when people sent us elaborately wrapped packages buried in piles of Styrofoam chips, or when we were in the middle of a home-improvement project, we would fill our two big rolling-cans just four times per year. One load of trash (read: whatever will fit in the back of the pickup) cost $5.18 to dispose of. (Klickitat County is home to an enormous landfill, so we got a deal.)

We live in an area that recycles: If we stored those materials separately from the garbage, we could take recycling to the same dump for free. They took everything except printer cartridges and fluorescent light bulbs. We were not allowed to recycle metal wire (we had some old baling wire and barbed wire to offload) because it snarls up the processing machinery.

Be nice to your Dump Meister. If he likes you (Mike), he'll help you fish out your keys when you accidentally throw them into the dumpster along with your trash. If he doesn't like you (Kristy), something like this might be more likely:

You'll pull in to the transfer station. No one else will be there. You'll pull in front of the recycling station—not a customary parking area—because no one else is there. Dump Meister will hoist himself from his rickety office chair in the office and amble over to your pickup. He'll scratch his beer gut with both hands; you may have woken him from a nap.

"Hi!" you'll say cheerily, hoping to start this off on a good footing.

"Gotta move yer rig." Dump Meister will say. Scratch, scratch.

"Why?"

"It's The Rules."

"But no one else is here," you'll reason. He'll only relent because you continue to unload your recycling and make no motion toward getting in the pickup. Instead, he'll "oversee" you as you toss glass containers into one of three bins: green, brown and clear. He'll go get a long grabbing tool and move some of the bottles that you threw from one bin to the other, even though you complied with the signage.

You will go over to the garbage area and dump your garbage. Then, you'll fish a handful of used toner cartridges from the cab of the pickup and walk over to Dump Meister to ask him where to put them to be recycled—near the batteries? The motor oil?

"Can't recycle that," he'll say, grabbing them from your hands and tossing them into the dumpster. "Rules."

"I would have taken them somewhere that recycles them!" you'll protest. Dump Meister will look at you like you're crazy, shrug and amble back to his office, scratching.

The next time you go there, with an armful of fluorescent bulbs, you'll be ready. When he grabs for the bulbs, you'll hold tight and yell, "Don't grab things out of people's hands!" The other patrons will look over, wondering why you're so upset. It's just the dump.

"It's The Rules," Dump Meister will say. Scratch, scratch.

Chapter 2
Maintenance

Woodlot and Yard

There are still natural areas in the world in which *lassiez-faire* is the proper management strategy, but your land is probably not one of those places. Whether you have five acres or 205, you will need to maintain it. This doesn't mean turn it into a golf course, it means control the balance of natural elements so native plants and animals can thrive in it. "Wild" doesn't necessarily mean "unattended to." Mike and I considered this a tremendous gift: On the surface of the Earth were seven acres that were entrusted to us! It was also a tremendous responsibility.

There are people you can hire to "grade" your woodlot, i.e. decide which trees should be cut in order to make the remaining trees more healthy. Because of the misguided fire-suppression efforts of the last eighty years, many forests are overgrown with unsuccessful young trees that would have been burned out in previous centuries. If you look in your woods and see, amongst mature, healthy trees, a lot of skinny stunted ones that are dead or sport a tiny tuft of living branches at the very tops, your woodlot needs to be thinned. The trees you cut will make nice poles for a project, can be sawn into lumber if they're a bit bigger or, if nothing else, can be cut into firewood. People have "portable sawmills" which make it possible to cut your lumber on site.

If your woods is not bordered or dissected by a road, you'll need to make a "skid road"—a trail on which you'll drag the fallen trees out of the woods. Skid roads cause a lot of damage, but the forest will recover after a year or two. Or, turn it into one of your access trails. Make sure, as much as possible, that you're not taking out the only trillium plant or other species. We had a number of plants and mushrooms that grew in only one spot.

Planting Trees

Orchard trees are covered in the Food Section; this bit is about trees that you plant to block wind, sight or sound. Even a single row of trees can be very effective for the first two things, less effective for sound. Look around you; is there anything you'd rather not see every day? In our case, we planted about twenty ponderosa pines trees along our neighbors' driveway and another dozen at the top of our pasture, where we could see a stop sign and traffic on the state highway.

Before you plant trees, look up—are there electrical wires? Don't plant trees under them. Look down—where is your septic field? Don't plant trees over it.

To plant a hedgerow, plant in a straight or staggered line, like a narrow zigzag. There are two strategies for starting the trees:

- Plant them in nursery pots or a started bed for the first year or so; then transplant into the ground.
- Plant straight into the ground. (When we did this, we put two seedlings in each hole and then pruned out the weaker one the following year.)

There are two strategies for planting:

- Plant many seedlings close (five feet) together; when they get bigger thin out the weaker ones.
- Plant seedlings in their permanent homes, *at least* ten feet away from each other. They will seem ridiculously far apart. Just wait a couple of years.

I was taught to plant in the spring rather than the fall because then the tree can grow some roots before it goes dormant, but others swear by planting in the fall. The baby trees will need to be watered for the first couple of years. Planting native species will decrease the amount of special attention you need to give them. All but the spikiest pines will also need protection from the nibbling lips of deer. Build a cage of chicken wire or netting around them.

You can also plant a secondary line of shrubs—once the trees grow and you've trimmed up the bottom branches for fire-abatement, the unsightly things on the other side will again become more visible through the bare trunks.

Fire Abatement

Wildlife management has changed a lot over the last century. Conservation, like all other Earth-friendly practices, came to the fore in response to the Industrial Age's focus on dominating the Earth and producing, producing, producing. "Maybe we shouldn't exploit *all* of the Earth's resources," said a few wise people, including naturalists like Aldo Leopold and John Muir. "Maybe we should manage it so that future generations can enjoy it, too."

Most people, especially businesspeople, ignored them. Management became science-based but extremely interventionist, leading to the fire-suppression movement of the mid-1900s (Smokey Bear). Even the people who agreed didn't quite get it right for many decades. Currently, the goal is to do the work of wildfire, which is essential to the ecosystem, without actually having the fire. Or to have a "controlled burn"—there are species that require the heat of a fire to complete their reproductive cycle. Additionally, scientists understand that to some degree, wildfire is impossible to stop. Most forest fires are started by lightning, not unattended campfires. To some degree, we have to let the wild forest experience fire—but hopefully without losing human lives or dwellings.

The first step in protecting your land and buildings is to clear a thirty-foot perimeter around them. Keep a green lawn around your house, and keep bushes and trees pruned and healthy. "Limb up" conifers: the low-hanging branches, especially ones covered in dead needles, and dead branches lying around beneath them are called "ladder fuel" because a small grass fire can easily climb a tree that way. Cut branches that are six feet from the ground, at the minimum. Clear away dead wood.

Wooden decks can harbor sparks and smolder, coming to life hours later. Can you replace it with a stone patio?

Don't assume that these precautions will guarantee your safety. There was a fire near our farm one year that climbed up a bluff so quickly, and got so hot, that people barely escaped with their lives. "I was going to go back in the house to get more stuff to put in my car," one man was quoted in the newspaper. "When the oak tree in my backyard exploded, I figured I'd better get out of there."

On the plains, grass fires can be just as damaging as forest fires. Remember that, just as the snowplows address heavily traveled roads first, fire trucks will defend more-populated areas before they'll come down a road with four houses on it. A woman I know lived in such a place in Oklahoma during a huge grass fire. Instead of fleeing, the neighbors, including a retired fire chief, dug in and defended their homes with "hoses, buckets, burlap, shovels, cars to block sparks, and bulldozers and tractors to create fire breaks."

Falling

Our property was a topographer's paradise, with a general downward slope from east to west but ups and downs throughout the property. Up a north-facing slope in the woodlot, a giant Douglas fir from our neighbor's yard crashed down-slope onto our property. It had a clear fall, thankfully—the only tree it took with it was the tallest branch of a vine maple.

But, we wondered: If the tree originated in our neighbor's property but fell into ours, whose tree is it? The answer: the part on our property becomes our tree. Look at a fallen tree as an opportunity—cut it up with your neighbors if possible. If their tree broke your fence, they should pay to replace it (and vice versa).

Logging remains one of the most dangerous careers in the world, despite copious safety measures that are taken. This was one of those times that I assured myself that I cannot and need not learn how to do *everything*. I happily paid a local guy,

Bruce, to bring firewood to our house, some of which needed splitting. No problem; we could do a little splitting. When you buy at least four cords of wood every year, you really appreciate a guy like Bruce.

That said, in the timberlands of Oregon and Washington, one can pay a few dollars for a wood-cutting permit and drive one's rig up a mountain road to cut. The best is "standing dead" wood, which is a tree that died without falling to the ground, recently enough that it's dried out some but not so long ago that insects and wood-peckers are all over it. Next best are recently fallen trees, and last are live trees, which need to "season," or dry out, in your woodshed for at least three months (preferably a year) before being burned.

The first thing to do when you're sizing up a tree to cut is how it's growing—does it lean? Twist? You need to predict where it's going to fall, so it doesn't fall on you, your friends or your rig. Try to identify a clear path, so it doesn't get hung up on neighboring trees or career off a big stump or rock. Are you on a slope? You don't want the tree to roll (or, maybe you do). Ideally, you direct the tree so that the cut end faces the road where your rig is. But conditions are rarely ideal.

If you're planning to go cut wood, get more information than I have in this book. Better yet, go out with someone who's done it before. There are a few country activities that can be deadly if they're botched, and this is one of them. I have more information about chainsaws further on in this segment.

The first cut is counter-intuitive to a novice—you cut a wedge into the tree in the direction you want it to fall. It won't, until you then make a cut into the back of the tree. Cut almost all the way through. When it starts to fall, move backwards as quickly as possible at a 45-degree angle to the direction of the fall—not directly behind the tree, which can kick backwards and send you straight to your eternal reward. As much as possible, don't turn your back on it. Get at least twenty feet away, behind a standing tree (a handy shield). A falling tree may not make a sound when it's alone, but you will know how much sound it makes when you're in its presence—a lot.

Next, you have to cut the branches off, and then cut it into logs, which is called "bucking." There are devices that can make this easier and safer, such as cant hooks and log jacks. These help you grab logs without using your hands (and subjecting them to being crushed), and get a log off the ground a bit, which makes it easier and safer to cut.

The rest of the road from tree to firewood is in the Buildings, Inside and Out Section.

Burn Pile

In the city, homeowners have cute little buckets with "Yard Debris" stickers on them, in which they deposit grass clippings, hedge trimmings and the odd branch that might fall into the yard. Out here, I could fill that bucket in about two minutes of raking pinecones. Not to mention the leaves, downed limbs and garden debris. Just as one's land is bigger in the country, so is one's pile of "yard debris."

Burn piles are banned in cities because of safety issues and pollution—imagine the smoky haze if everyone burned their leaves in the fall rather than composting them via their metropolitan yard debris program. People with asthma would never be able to leave the house.

A burn pile is not something on which you can throw a match and walk away, nor is it like the college bonfires you remember. A burn pile takes a lot more effort. As you clean up your land, start piling things in the right spot: at least fifty feet from any building but close enough that you can get a hose to it (this is often a permitting requirement, but if you burn your pile correctly you will not need a hose). It should also be at least fifteen feet from anything else that might burn, like fence posts or (look up!) an overhanging tree branch. And it should be somewhere that you don't mind killing the grass for at least a year—if you're smart you'll drop everything right on top of your worst stand of spotted knapweed.

Different areas have different requirements as far as what time of year you can burn (not usually during dry summer for fear of starting a wildfire), and how big a pile can be. You may also need a permit (where I lived, for example, one was not required to as long as the pile didn't exceed fifteen feet in height or diameter). If you can, put some large branches on the bottom to raise the pile off the ground an inch or two, so oxygen can get in there.

It's important to determine when to start the fire. Firstly, the weather conditions must be right: ideally the ground should be wet (either from spring thaw or a recent deluge), and there should be no wind, both for safety and so that you do not inundate a neighbor with smoke. If it's drizzly, so much the better. The goal is to have a burn pile and not a field, forest or house fire.

The other consideration is your time—a burn pile will go all day, and you need to monitor it nearly the entire time. So burn on a day that you have four solid hours to devote, and that you're not going out later so that you can check on it into the evening.

Starting a burn pile can be a bit tricky. Because you are eliminating recently living materials and not aged or kiln-dried wood, the fire may need a little coaxing with some two-by-four scraps. This may seem to not need mentioning, but I have seen it with my own eyes: do not burn upholstered furniture, wood products like oriented strand board or plywood, or heavily painted wood. The plastics involved will release toxins into the air. Along the same lines, do not burn poison ivy or poison oak—you will create a cloud of poisonous gas.

Determine any slight breeze and build a seed fire so that the flames will be blown into the pile (i.e., if the breeze is coming from the east start your fire on the east side of the pile). Build your fire at the base of the pile, using newspaper, kindling and small pieces of wood from your woodstove supply.

As the flames grow, pull dry pieces from your pile over the flames; you want the fire to continually feed into the next pieces. This may take a while. If you walk away from the pile for even a moment at this stage, chances are you'll return to a scorched dent in the pile and no flame. Coals are what keep a fire going, not flame, so until you get some hot coals you have to nurse it.

It may seem to take forever, and then, BOOM! Something dry will catch and flare into the sky, and you're off. Use a pitchfork to carefully pick up parts of the pile that are not on fire and drape them over the flames; fire goes up, not sideways (unless blown) so you have to bring the pile to the flame. After a while, there will be a sufficient bed of coals; that's when you can quickly run to the bathroom or get a snack. Otherwise, do not leave the pile unattended.

Another method for getting a burn pile going involves a great quantity of flammable gas: blasting it with a propane torch or actually pouring kerosene or diesel on the pile. I do not recommend this for a couple of reasons. It's dangerous to work with flammable gas and flames simultaneously. Secondly, you're wasting a resource that is mostly going to burn off quickly, without igniting the pile. Thirdly, it's an environmental hazard (though this is probably the weakest argument, as burning a pile isn't very environmentally correct anyway…). *Under no circumstances* pour gasoline onto a fire. Ever. The vapor is as explosive as the liquid.

Don't be surprised if a few mice or shrews rush out at some point—a nice pile of branches is great habitat for small animals (some people leave piles around for that express purpose). Burn the pile in early spring or late fall, when birds are not nesting. Stick a pitchfork into the pile and shake it around a bit before lighting the fire to give any critters a head's up that something is happening.

Once the pile is established, a great deal of ash will build up over the coals. When the flames seem to be simmering down, take your pitchfork and gently shuffle the coals around a little—this will introduce new oxygen into the pile and encourage a new flare-up.

When you have naught but a black, smoldering circle in the ground, you're done! To be most safe, water the ashes with your hose for a good five minutes so that the fire is completely out. If you had scrap wood in the pile, go back after a day or two and pick up any stray nails. (Caution: They will stay hot for a day—don't burn your fingers!)

Road Kill

If you live on a road, be prepared for the occasional carcass. Dead animals are, of course, taken care of by the Earth's scavengers—everything from buzzards and coyotes to beetles and maggots. Small mammals and birds are processed within a day or two.

Bigger animals are a little different. First of all, not every animal that gets hit by a car dies right away. Mike and I requisitioned a family rifle for this very purpose—if we had a severely wounded beast dragging itself down our driveway, we would have the means of putting it out of its misery.

Thankfully, that never happened, probably because we lived on a state high-way and cars were going pretty fast. While at least a dozen deer were killed on the road during our tenure, all but one was killed outright and removed within a few days by the county. The furthest that one ran (and that was probably nerves and adrenaline, not consciousness) was down the embankment and into a no-man's-land triangle of field next to ours.

Because the deer was not officially on our property, Mike and I planned to leave it to nature to dispose of it. Our neighbor Jim knew better. A big carcass like a deer's creates a LOT of death-stench, for at least a week, and the prevailing winds would have sent it pretty much straight into our living room. Partly out of kindness, and partly because it meant he would get to use a backhoe, Jim dug a trench and used the shovel to drag the carcass into the hole and cover it.

Noxious Plants

Plants have various strategies for survival; some grow impressive defense systems in the form of thorns or poison. Some, like dandelions, are ridiculously prolific. Some have been successful in making themselves Friends of Humans, such as marijuana and tomatoes. But remember: Not all plants are your friends.

Invasive Species

Nostalgia is to blame for much of the spread of invasive species in the United States—people from England, for example, brought ivy to the Colonies because it reminded them of home. The trouble with this is that the new species has no predators or other controlling mechanisms, so it runs rampant and overtakes the native species, on which other native species depend.

There were numerous invasive weeds where we lived, but the most annoying by far was tarweed. Left unabated, it grew a couple of feet tall and bloomed a nice yellow flower cluster, all of which was coated in a sticky sap. The first year at our farm, before we plowed the upper field and planted it in cover crops (triticale, clover and vetch), our dog would run through the field and return completely coated in muck:

the tarweed glue coated her fur and then the seeds of thousands of other weeds stuck to that.

In the southeastern United States, just say the word "kudzu"—and duck! This Japanese vine was introduced by the (rat-bastard Yankee) Soil Conservation Service in the 1930s as a fodder crop and a means of controlling erosion. Kudzu took the ball and ran with it, overtaking entire acres of land. I've seen it completely covering twenty-foot trees, abandoned buildings and cars.

Water hemlock is an extremely poisonous plant—even a small amount can be fatal. This plant is a parsley relative, so it grows that big cluster (called an "umbel") of tiny flowers, like parsley or Queen Anne's lace. It's called "spotted cowbane" in some areas. It's sometimes confused with the edible water parsnip, but its rootstalk is filled with pockets of poison. If hand-pulling, wear gloves and be sure you get the entire root.

Cheatgrass (also called "downy brome") and foxtail are insidious things that can seriously compromise the health of your livestock and pets. Both plants make a seed head that has a barb on one end. The barb catches on, say, your dog's paw and sticks to it. Then, it slowly works its way into your dog's paw, causing discomfort and infection. I read about a horse that died because his hay was infested with cheatgrass, which punctured his esophagus, and caused infection and swelling that asphyxiated the poor thing. Check your fields for these plants and, if you have them, monitor your animals and remove any seeds that are on them before they cause trouble.

If you have invasive plant species on your property, it is incumbent upon you to eradicate them. This may require physical removal; cutting or mowing specific parts of the plant at specific times of the season; burning; poisoning; or all of the above. Many plants have seeds that can lie dormant for years and then sprout, re-infesting an area you thought you'd cleared up. You might check with the local conservation district or university agricultural extension agency for advice about a particular plant.

Mike and I managed to keep our Scotch broom at bay by physically digging the new sprouts out. We launched some serious Himalayan blackberry attacks that left the stand a shadow of its former self, but were totally losing the battle against spotted knapweed and chicory. Short of a serious chemical or propane torch campaign, I don't know what would have stopped the knapweed. If you do apply an herbicide to a field on which you plan to graze animals, check the waiting period before it's safe to let them eat.

Invasives aren't limited to plants—mussels, mammals, insects and other species have also overstayed their welcomes. Where we lived in Washington, bullfrogs were insidious: ravenous beasts that were known to eat mice, birds and even bats! And, of course, bullfrogs eat the native frog species. Some of our friends were biologists and had been on government-sponsored bullfrog bounty hunts. Invasive animal species are included in the Wildlife Chapter.

Native Species

Stinging nettle's issue is right in its name. If you touch this plant, or even brush up against it while hiking, its nearly invisible hairs impale your skin and break off, depositing irritants. Ironically, this plant is harmless, delicious and chock-full of vitamin C when cooked like spinach; wear gloves to harvest. It also has medicinal and industrial uses.

Locoweed is a pea relative that grows mostly in the foothills and semi-arid desert areas of the western United States; it isn't dangerous to humans but is harmful or even deadly to ruminants. Poisoned cattle and other livestock may be found walking in circles, glassy-eyed and confused; some lose so much weight that they collapse or are taken by predators. Locoweed can also cause reproductive disorders and congestive heart failure. It looks a little like vetch or wild peas, but has a more upright, tuft-y growth, and usually—but not always—white flowers.

Poison Ivy, Oak and Sumac

It may be impossible to completely remove a noxious-but-native plant, such as poison ivy, poison oak or poison sumac. There may just be too much of it. If you have a dog that wanders, keep in mind that he may get it on his coat during his travels. Then you pet the dog and touch your arm or face, *et voilá!* You have infected yourself.

All of these plants are covered in an oil (urushiol) that, when it gets on your skin, soaks in and causes your body to fight it, resulting in horrendous, itchy, weeping blisters (which are, incidentally, not contagious). The worst cases require the use of steroids; those cases can last for weeks.

Most sumacs are not poisonous, and look nothing like poison sumac. Poison sumac is rare and grows in swampland. Poison ivy and oak are common. Western poison oak and poison ivy can have a shrubby appearance, or it can grow up tree trunks like a vine. Eastern poison oak grows in shrubs.

If you've been hiking or working on your land, and have been in a bunch of poison ivy or oak, the best defense is to wash everything carefully with soap. Take a shower, not a bath—you're dealing with an oil that would float on the surface of the water and re-infect you, possibly worse than your original exposure, upon rising from the bathwater. Use the coldest water you can stand—hot water opens your pores. There are soaps and ointments, usually containing pine tar, made specifically to "neutralize" the oil, but keep in mind that you're mostly rinsing and not washing—trying to coax the oil from your skin. Rubbing alcohol and witch hazel dissolve oil, and a spray antiperspirant that contains aluminum is also said to be effective.

Wash your clothes and shoes, too. And your dog. And the towel with which you dried him off. And your hands again. You might consider wearing gloves the next few times you have to use the toilet…just in case.

If you try to remove a plant, keep in mind that every bit of it—stems, leaves and roots—contain urushiol. Even in the dead of winter. Do not burn the plant; compost it or bury it. Do not go after it with a string trimmer, which will splatter bits of it all over your legs. Goats have been used to eradicate stands because they can eat it with no ill effects.

Tractors and Other Tools
Tractor
This purchase also warrants careful consideration. Questions to ask yourself:
- **What jobs do I need this machine to do?**
- **How flat is the terrain?**
- **How often will I use it?**
- **Will I use it at night?**

That first question is the main one. Do you just need to mow or are you looking for a full-fledged farm machine?

Before you answer "We just need to mow," like Mike and I did, I will interrupt and tell you that if you *don't* buy a tractor, you will end up either borrowing one all the time or hiring work done for you. No matter how strapping a pair you are, you will not be able to keep up if you try to do everything with a pickup, a wheelbarrow and two shovels. You will not be able to clear your driveway of snow in the winter. You will fall behind on maintaining your land. You will fall behind on maintaining your house. You will fall behind on maintaining your animals' quarters.

The reason Mike and I forwent a tractor is an understandable one—they cost as much as a car. When people get mortgages for homes in the country, the purchase price should include $30,000 for a tractor with implements. It's not necessary to buy a new tractor, especially if you're good with motors and welding equipment. Our neighbor bought a Ford 9N that was fifty years old! He then built a cab for it from sheet metal and fabricated a number of other improvements.

If you want a used but not decrepit tractor, make sure you check the usage gauge. The use of a tractor is not measured in miles, like a car, but in hours.

Unless you are going full-scale farm, which you're not if you're reading this book, you don't need a full-sized tractor, you need a compact tractor or a skid loader (the latter is usually referred to by the brand name "Bobcat"). All this terminology can be confusing: a front loader can be a stand-alone machine, or an implement attached to the front of a tractor. A compact tractor (still called a "tractor") has more tool attachments, but a loader maneuvers better. A loader has wheels; a track loader has tracks, like a tank. A mini track-loader lacks a cab to sit in and isn't as powerful, but doesn't weigh as much and thereby does less damage to the ground, which is important if you're doing landscaping and don't want to ruin the existing lawn, for example.

If you're the kind of person who likes to learn lessons the hard way and you decide on a lawn tractor, make sure it has a trailer hitch; then, at least, you can haul firewood and yard debris. We bought a new one because neither of us is mechanically inclined, though that turned out to work against us because the one we bought threw its belt all the time and was kind of a piece of junk. Ironically, one of its safety features—the engine turns off if the seat is not firmly pressed down—made it hard for me to use it because I didn't weigh enough. If I hit a bump, the engine would stall out on me. This feature was meant to keep small children from running the tractor but also kept this small adult from doing so!

There are a number of different brands of tractors, each of which has a "brand" color:

John Deere
Green

Kubota
Orange

Massey Ferguson
Red

New Holland
Blue

Case
Yellow

…and many, many others. The tractor-manufacturing world is similar to the automobile industry—some tractors are built in the United States, and some are built elsewhere. There are mergers and buy-outs, and similar models sold under different names. Some are built well and some aren't. Do your research. Brands like John Deere cost more up front but hold their value better.

Factors to consider when buying a tractor include its horsepower, visibility from inside the cab, whether it is four-wheel drive, whether the cab is heated and/or air conditioned, and whether it has remote hydraulics and a PTO (power take-off).

A PTO is a shaft, not unlike a drive shaft, that runs off the tractor's motor with the sole purpose of powering an implement that is connected to it.

Tractor Implements

A tractor with a PTO is the ultimate power tool. Some tractors are built to allow you to attach implements to the front or the back; they are called "versatiles" and are meant for larger-scale farming.

Implements include:

- **Auger:** Drills a hole in the ground, usually for fencing
- **Backhoe:** Digs trenches and moves rocks or dirt
- **Bale Spear/Fork:** Picks up and carries hay bales
- **Blade:** Pushes dirt or snow
- **Box Blade:** Levels and backfills graded areas (especially driveways)
- **Brush Hog:** Mower that cuts thicker/denser material (including brush with stems up to two inches in diameter)
- **Bucket:** Scoops up dirt or snow; also good for carrying large, heavy items like boulders
- **Cart/Trailer:** Carries nearly anything
- **Chipper/Mulcher:** Grinds up leaves and branches into chips or mulch
- **Cotton Picker/Baler:** Picks and bales cotton
- **Cultivator:** Digs furrows; comes in various shapes for various crops
- **Disc:** *See Harrow*
- **Drag:** Looks like a section of chain-link fence with spikes that stick down a few inches into the ground; dragged across a pasture to break up and distribute manure piles

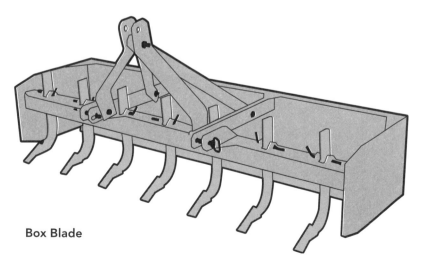

Box Blade

- **Fertilizer Spreader:** Distributes fertilizer evenly
- **Forks:** Makes your tractor a forklift; most often used to move large hay bales
- **Front End Loader:** Scoops dirt or snow (*see Bucket*) and lifts it (rather than pushing it, like a blade)
- **Harrow:** Spreads manure, covers seeds; comes in chain or disc models
- **Hay Rake:** Rakes hay into long rows, which a baling machine scoops up and turns into large bricks
- **Log Splitter:** Splits bucked logs into cordwood
- **Manure Spreader:** Distributes manure evenly
- **Mower:** Mows yard or grassy field; different models handle different needs
- **Post-Hole Digger:** *See Auger*
- **Rake:** Scoops up rocks in topsoil
- **Snow Blower:** Scoops up snow and shoots it a few feet away
- **Snow Plow:** Like a blade but angled to move snow to the side
- **Sprayer:** Sprays liquid product (fertilizer, herbicide) onto a field
- **Straw Tucker:** Anchors mulch into soil
- **Tiller:** Digs up a field and prepares it for cultivating or harrowing
- **Toothbar:** Added to a bucket (see above) to aid with digging

Repairs

If you own equipment, keeping it operational (not just the engine but all the other mechanisms as well) will be a constant battle. Prepare to bust some knuckles.

Repairing a tractor will often involve using a welder, but you can get away with making some repairs with "JB Weld," which many tractor owners consider the duct tape of farm equipment. JB Weld is an industrial epoxy that can bond non-stressed areas of a tractor, such as housings, fenders and such. It should not be used on moving parts or anything that will fly off the machine if the bond fails.

Chainsaw

One of my favorite city-meets-country moments occurred when our friends Karen and Monica volunteered to come out and help us with land maintenance. (This sort of invitation does not come often—take it when it does!). Our chainsaw was broken; they offered to bring theirs so we could limb up some trees in the woodlot. I was pleased to see they had brought eye protection and gloves. Then, they pulled their "chainsaw" from the trunk—a petite device with a ten-foot electric cord and a twelve-inch blade. Mike and I tried not to laugh. After the chainsaws we'd seen, it looked like a child's toy! More importantly, it had to be plugged in. We limbed up the edge of our woodlot as far as our orange and yellow rope of every-heavy-duty-extension-cord-we-owned would reach, and called it a day.

Choose your chainsaw carefully—it needs to be as big as possible but not so big that you can't operate it safely. By "big" I mean the length of the bar, the part around which the chain wraps—the longer the bar, the thicker a tree you can cut through.

Do not even consider buying a cut-rate brand. "You get what you pay for" comes into play often on the farm, especially here. Unless you have previous experience with chainsaws I wouldn't even recommend buying a used model—the safety features on a new one are superior to older saws. My uncle had a chain-saw accident in 1976, and nearly forty years later the divot in his calf muscle is still a serious health issue—it's never healed properly, has exposed nerves and gets infected often. He's had skin grafts and other surgeries on it, and is in constant pain. It's too easy to seriously injure yourself with a chainsaw, so start out with the safest model, as well as all the safety equipment you can buy.

Unless you want your ears bleeding at the end of the day, wear earplugs or "earmuffs" (not the kind you wore to marching band practice), or both. Anything with a two-stroke engine is loud but a chainsaw takes the cake. Also leather gloves, a heavy jacket, your toughest boots, and chaps (in some regions pronounced *shaps*). We had a pair of chaps that had been used in the Forest Service; they're made of Kevlar and they could save your life, or at least your leg and a lot of blood.

I can't speak to the merits of one machine over another because, first of all, I got away with almost never running the thing, and secondly the only saw we owned was a Stihl. But I will commend Stihl for its safety gear; we bought a helmet that had a facemask and ear-protectors built into it, and it was great.

Other Yard Power Tools

Another option is to have a tractor for the big jobs and a push mower for just around the house. If you have a piece of lawn, I would of course recommend a non-motorized model (otherwise known as a reel mower) to minimize your gasoline usage and noise pollution.

You will probably want a string trimmer, commonly called a "weed whacker." Newer models are coming out that have rechargeable batteries. If you get a gasoline model, be sure to wear earplugs. Wear eye protection either way.

It's possible to use electric devices near the buildings. Use only heavy duty extension cords for these jobs, never something meant for indoor use. If you're using more than one extension cord, tie the ends in a loose knot before connecting them; that way, if you happen to pull a little further than you should have, the knot will tighten rather than the cords separate. When re-winding an extension cord, make your first loop about two feet across and hold it in your palm (don't wrap it across your forearm). Give each new loop a quarter-turn twist, and it will coil up without kinks.

I've seen advertised brush mowers, which are basically giant push mowers intended to cut through nasty stuff rather than a grass lawn. A regular push mower can get destroyed in no time if you're trying to tame a field—the rocks and sticks, in addition to the tougher stems of mustard, chicory and lord knows what else you've got, will chip and dull your blades in no time. I've never known anyone who has one, though, so ask around before you buy it.

Pickup (Rig)

Do not even try to live in the country without a four-wheel-drive pickup truck, which I have already referred to as a "rig." You will haul wood, straw, feed, brush trimmings, compost, sand, garbage and recycling, tillers and other borrowed equipment, dead appliances and their replacements, sick pets. You will drag trees from your woodlot. You may need it to get around in the winter.

A good rig comes with a canopy. A what? I mean, a topper. Huh? I mean, a cap. *The fiberglass thing that covers the bed!* It's called different names in different regions. A bed liner is also a good idea—working rigs get pretty banged up. Some bed liners are like a big floor mat that can be removed; others are sprayed in. Consider a winch as well. A friend once got his burly four-wheel-drive 350 rig up our treacherously snowed-in driveway by hooking his winch to a tree at the top and then having it pull him up! Otherwise, he would have had to spend a couple of days at our house.

Storing Fuel

Flammable liquids can be extremely dangerous if they're handled carelessly. They should be stored in vessels specifically designed for this purpose, called "cans" (a gas can is shaped more like a squat, long-nozzled pitcher). Mark the cans (most store-bought cans are imprinted with the fuel type and also color-coded red for gasoline, blue for kerosene and green for diesel) and never put anything else in them. Cap them tightly so the fuel doesn't evaporate, and to keep water vapor from collecting inside. Keep a fire extinguisher near the cans and, for ultimate safety, put another extinguisher just outside that area (in case a fire prevents you from getting to the one near the cans).

Establish an area in an outbuilding that is the exclusive site for fuel cans. It should not be uphill from your house, as the gases are heavier than air—you don't want a leaking vessel to dump a cloud of flammable gas near your home. This area should be in a protected place so the cans are not at risk of being kicked over or otherwise compromised, out of the reach of children and out of the direct sun. Never near any kind of ignition source, such as an appliance with a pilot light. Need I add not to smoke a cigarette while working with these fuels?

Believe it or not, fuel needs to be fresh! Don't store it for more than a few months without using a stabilizing additive. The other reason to do this is that, in climates with distinct summers and winters, the fuel mixture that is sold at gas stations is adjusted for the change in temperature. Do not store gas-powered engines with fuel in them for long periods. For example, in the fall, siphon as much gas as possible from your mower and then run it until it quits. Conversely, keep the fuel in and start it every few months to keep everything operational.

If you plan to use a lot of fuel, you can invest in a larger storage tank—55, 100 or even 200 gallons. Just make sure you only store enough to last a few months, and use it up.

Gasoline

When filling a gas can at a gas station, place the can directly on the ground, not on your tailgate, so it's grounded. Static electricity can build up as you dispense the gas and spark, which could cause an explosion. Fill the can 95-percent full—you don't want a lot of room for vapor and you want to minimize spillage.

Diesel

Most tractors run on diesel, which is a little different from gasoline, and its engine is a little different from a gasoline engine. Without getting into too much detail, a diesel engine does not use spark plugs to ignite the fuel; it relies on compression. Diesel engines are more efficient than gasoline engines but have issues with cold temperatures. If the temperature drops below zero, diesel fuel becomes a gel that is difficult to ignite. It has a tendency to grow algae in storage, so be sure to filter it. Diesel fuel is also less volatile, with lower flammability and explosive tendencies.

Biodiesel

Whether biodiesel is here to stay in a large-scale way remains to be seen, but it is a viable alternative to petroleum. If you're really ambitious, you can build a biodiesel distillery at your farm and never have to run out again. Where we lived, biodiesel was even being carried by a few filling stations.

There are a couple of grades of the fuel: B-20 is 20 percent biodiesel and 80 percent petroleum diesel. This fuel can be put straight into a diesel engine with no adjustments and will run great.

In order to run on B-100, a few hoses need to be changed out and other adjustments made. Some people have a switch built into their engines so they can go from one grade to the other.

Hardcore users are the ones that end up in hippie-hipster documentaries, trolling the alleys behind low-end restaurants for vats of used cooking oil. I commend the positive impact on the earth that this represents, but if you have a farm you won't have time to harvest fuel in this manner. On the other hand, if you could arrange with a local restaurant for a regular pickup, it might be more feasible.

Gasoline-Oil Mixture
Power tools and other two-stroke engines run on a fifty/fifty gas-oil mixture. You can buy mixer oil wherever chainsaws and the like are sold, and then mix it up yourself. Never put this mixture into a gasoline engine.

Propane
If you have a gas barbeque grill, you've used propane. Many rural homes use propane to cook with, and sometimes for the furnace, water heater and clothes dryer. It can even power the refrigerator! Propane is efficient and relatively easy to use; the only hassle is having the tank refilled every once in a while, which just entails ordering a supplier to drive their truck out.

Your tank will most likely be buried or hiding behind some sort of short wall. Keep flammable materials away from it. If the tank is above ground and near the driveway, it may also have sturdy posts installed in front of it so that a car doesn't accidentally hit it.

Keep in mind that propane and natural gas are not interchangeable—you'll need an adapter kit to go from one to the other.

Liquified Petroleum Gas
LPG is a mixture propane and butane that is much more volatile and dangerous. It is used around the world as a heating and cooking fuel, and for cars. It is sold in pressurized tanks by a dealer.

Traditional Hand Tools
Of course, people have maintained their homes and land, and farmed, for many centuries longer than power tools have existed. So, what did they use? Traditional tools are effective, and many are a great workout! They just take more time. A woman I know says her father prefers to use a scythe to cut grass because "he likes to watch the birds, and not scare them." I've also heard wistful comments about the soothing "whoosh-whoosh" that a scythe makes, and the Zen-like state ones acquires with the repetitive motion.

Many of the implements used on a tractor started out being pulled by a team of horses or oxen, and most tools used in the garden are still non-motorized. There are dozens of hand tools that have been used, going back to stone hand-axes; here are a few:

- **Scythe:** Long, curved metal blade at the end of a pole that has one or two short handles, used for cutting tall grasses and grain crops
- **Crosscut Saw:** Saw with a handle at each end, used by two people for cutting trees
- **Axe:** Thick steel blade attached at a right angle to a handle, used for chopping small trees and cutting firewood
- **Hatchet:** Smaller version of an axe, used to cut branches and kindling
- **Sickle:** Smaller version of a scythe, used for smaller jobs

Fencing

I won't bother to quote Robert Frost; you know the drill. Fences are a vital component of property ownership; they help to delineate boundaries and keep animals where you want them. They can be eyesores, but are indispensable.

Different animals need different kinds of fencing. You may look at a property and think it's fenced, but if it's fenced for horses and you want cows, it's not fenced. Horses for the most part respect a regular four-foot wire fence. A cow on the other hand can push its way through anything—if you want to be sure to keep them in you need to add a well-voltaged electric wire that sits on brackets on the interior of the fence. Goats have quite the escapist reputation and require a bullet-proof fence. A goat will jump a fence if it can get up high enough, or sneak under it, or break a hole in it. Pigs need really strong fencing, or an electric wire set about six inches from the ground so they can't push their way out. Sheep are timid and the least likely to try to break out. But, any animal will try to break through a fence if it sees something it wants (typically fresh grass or a sexy mate) on the other side.

If you're really out in the country, you'll see miles and miles of fence. It boggles the mind to think that someone put all this fence in, and someone maintains it. When one of these fence lines crosses a small road or driveway, there may be a "cattle guard" rather than a gate. This is a wide steel grate that cars can drive over, but cattle refuse to walk on because their hooves would slip between the bars. Some are just painted on the road; the cows are afraid to test it!

And that's just keeping your livestock in. There are also fences to keep animals out: rabbit fence is wire fence that has smaller holes in it; it's usually buried a bit so they don't burrow under it. My garden perimeter was impossible to secure against rabbits, so I built small cages out of chicken wire and placed them around each plant—beans, brassicas and anything else rabbits get into. It didn't look pretty, but neither do a bunch of gnawed-off broccoli stumps.

The fencing to protect chickens is quite complicated unless you plan to use electric wire. Friends of mine have a simple, three-foot-high white picket fence with two strands of electric wire-tape: one a few inches from the ground to keep coyotes out and one a few inches from the top to keep raccoons out. Because the wire sticks out a few inches from the exterior of the fence, not the interior, they have to keep an eye on young children and visitors. And this method doesn't protect the chickens from raptors.

Mike and I were lucky enough to inherit a barn that had lean-to roofs added to it already, so all we had to build were the walls. We strung chicken wire between the posts, all the way up—raccoons will gladly climb a fence for a hot meal. On the bottom half we fortified the chicken wire with hog panels so that coyotes, dogs or curious children wouldn't push through the wire.

Whether you use electricity or lots of chicken wire, the base of the fence must be fortified with hardware cloth, which is crisscrossed strands of wire that make sort of a large, rigid screen. We took a strip of hardware cloth that was three feet wide and bent it at a ninety-degree angle the long way, so that there was a two-foot section and a one-foot section. We dug a trench that started at the bottom of the perimeter fence and went out a foot and down a foot, and laid the hardware cloth so that it overlapped and served as an extension of the fence and then came out toward us. We set as many big rocks as we could find on the mesh and replaced the dirt. Then, a raccoon, skunk or fox that tried to dig under the fence would just hit more fence.

Deer can easily leap over anything shorter than eight feet. Yes, eight. We did the first tier in regular wire fence and strung four rows of garden twine between the posts for the upper half—wire would have been more durable, but our garden fence was 300 feet long and wire was too expensive. I used jute twine because I wanted to be able to compost it rather than throw it in the garbage when it ran out; I had to replace the twine every spring. Nylon would have lasted longer, maybe two winters instead of one.

People get pretty inventive with fencing because to do it with proper materials is so costly. They'll use scrap wood, tree branches, old doors and windows, vodka bottles. I've heard of a couple who built a deer fence this way: For posts, they took ten-foot horizontal chain-link fence stringers, turned them vertically, capped them and planted them two feet in the ground with cement. For the stringers, they laced wire between the posts and then hung deer netting. Though stringers are rather thin for posts, the fence itself is so lightweight it probably works just fine. If you improvise your fence, just make sure it can stand up to the task you give it. Deer netting will keep deer out but not, for example, cattle.

Fence Materials

Fence styles that are popular in urban areas, such as cedar planks or white pickets, are generally too expensive to apply to a rural setting. You may see them around the house, but that is it. Types of rural fencing:

- **Chain-Link:** This is the interlinking thick-wire fence that is used in cities and towns alike
- **Woven Wire:** This is three- or four-foot height that comes in rolls of several feet in length; can be used with T-posts and wooden posts
- **Rabbit:** This is wire fence that has more wire at the bottom to make holes that are too small for rabbits to get through
- **Hog Panel:** These come in sections that are connected to the posts; this is very strong fencing that is easy to work with, but expensive
- **Cattle Panel:** Same as hog panel but even stronger
- **Chicken Wire:** This comes in rolls that are easy to work with. It's not particularly strong, so you may need to reinforce it in places
- **Netting:** This is plastic netting that has electrified wires woven in; good for fowl, dogs and rabbits
- **Wire:** Strings of barbed or regular wire; easiest and cheapest fencing but least effective alone; best used in conjunction with other fencing materials and for temporary, portable fencing
- **Electric:** Wire or a wire-laced tape (better visibility) is strung onto insulated holders that attach to the fence posts; requires weed and grass control so the circuit isn't compromised; minimally effective with fleeced animals; must be grounded
- **High-Tensile Wire:** Flexible but extremely strong, electrified wire

In addition to the perimeter fence, you'll need interior fences, called "cross-fencing," that delineate smaller pastures within your total land. This gives you the opportunity to move your livestock from one pasture to another, giving the fallow pasture a chance to re-grow. You'll also need "alleys," or "lanes," which are enclosed pathways from one pasture to another pasture, or to the barn, if they're not directly adjacent, and "catch pens," to isolate one or more animals for inoculations or breeding.

Make sure the fence is visible—you don't want a horse or a deer hung up on a fence because she didn't see it. If it's a wire fence, tie flash tape, plastic flagging, ribbons or anything, really, on the topmost line every ten or fifteen feet.

Posts

There are a few options: as with any fence, the factors involved are appearance versus cost. A cedar fence with copper caps on the posts is gorgeous, but do you have $10,000 to spend on fence? Maybe; if not, you might be able to compromise by using wire fence with nice posts, or building a fancy gate.

Remember, when buying posts, that you need an extra two feet in length to bury in the ground. Types of posts:

- **Rot-Resistant Wood:** Round or square, these look nice and are the most expensive. Most common species are cedar, Osage orange and black locust. Fence is attached with fence staples, burly two-pronged nails that are hammered around wires of the fence into the posts.
- **Treated Wood:** Usually made of Douglas fir, Southern yellow pine or poplar. Some are tapered at one end so they may be driven straight into the ground. Though this is changing, such posts used to be soaked in arsenic and other poisons—maybe not so great to put in the vicinity of your garden plants or children. You can also buy the treatment chemical and brush it on like paint to untreated wood of your choosing.
- **T-Post:** This is a thin but heavy, sturdy steel post with a flange at the bottom for stability. They aren't pretty but are the easiest to work with; they can be driven into the ground by hand or using the shovel on a tractor. Fence is attached with short lengths of wire that are wrapped around the fence and encircle the post. These posts cannot support a gate. The tops can be capped to avoid injury to yourself or to livestock. Some people intersperse the T-posts with some wooden posts to add overall strength.
- **Fiberglass:** This is a new technology. I don't know if I'd use it because, no matter what they say, fibers are eventually going to flake off. I've had a fiberglass shard under the fingernail before (no, I wasn't wearing gloves) and don't hope for another. But, fiberglass doesn't conduct electricity so it's good for electric fence.

If you like a rustic look, you could cut your own posts from your woodlot. We did this after two cedar trees fell in a storm. We used them as the posts of our gazebo and then cut Douglas firs (we needed to thin the stand anyway) for the beams and rafters.

Make sure your posts are set well, or the tension of the fence will pull the whole thing over. There are three tools for this job: a clamshell post-hole digger, a power-auger (similar in size and shape to a jackhammer), and an auger attachment for a tractor. If you are burying your posts in cement and live in an area in which the ground freezes solid over the winter, dig postholes that are wider at the bottom than the top, and stop pouring concrete before it reaches ground level. Otherwise, the posts will be pushed out of the ground over time—this is called "frost heave."

Gates

I recommend at least two gates into any one pasture or garden, keeping in mind that if you want to be able to get a tractor in, you'll need a ten-foot-wide gate. Few people build their own gates anymore—prefabricated panels are available at the feed-and-seed or hardware store. Don't forget to buy hardware: hinges and a closing mechanism, which can be as simple as a length of chain and a carabiner. A mechanism that requires only one hand to open is advantageous. Don't forget to amend the design if you plan to be able to open the gate from the back of a horse.

The framework for the gate needs to be reinforced, especially if it's a heavy, ten-foot-wide tube gate. On the eight-foot-tall garden fence, we used a crossbar for the people gates but not the rig gates, to avoid any clearance issues. Instead, we ran a rope across the top—a visual deterrent for a deer but removable for a pickup.

Gates on electrified fence need pieces that separate from each other (sold with other fencing materials) so you can get in or out. When the gate is in use, the circuit will be broken. Or else, bury the line under the gate. But then the gate isn't electrified.

Tools

For wire fence, you'll need a fence-puller or come-along, a tensioning tool, claw hammer and wire-cutter. You would benefit from a crimper and set of sleeves, but they're not mandatory. We had a friend's grandfather's antique fence pliers, which cut wire and had pincers that closed around a fence staple and then used leverage to pull it out—invaluable. Sometimes the oldest design is the best design.

If you're driving T-posts by hand use a setter ("pounder"), which is a strange-looking tool—a heavy steel tube that's closed on one end and open on the other, and has two handles opposite each other on the sides. Set the post in the ground as far as you can by hand, and then slide the setter over the top of the post and start pounding! Lift the setter up, but not so far up that it comes off the post, and then drop it down as fast and hard as you can. While you're driving the post, make sure it's straight. Mostly for aesthetic purposes, try to get them all the same height.

The fence needs to be pulled taught before it's attached to the posts or it will sag. This can be done with a fence-puller, which is a come-along-type of mechanism. Rolls of wire fence include strands that are thicker—and thereby stronger—than the rest of the wire. These are the ones you want to pull on. Our neighbor, Jim, showed us how to use a pickup or tractor to stretch fence (instead of a fence-puller), which was much easier than using a fence-puller. First, we set our posts. We leaned a roll of fence on the first post and attached it. We unrolled the fence and set it loosely against the posts. Then, we wove a T-post through the end of the fence, chained it to the pickup and carefully pulled forward so there was tension on the fencing. We put the brake on the truck and attached the fence to the posts. If we'd had a tractor we would have used it instead.

Corners

Anywhere wire fence ends in a gate or turns a corner, that junction needs to be fortified to stand up, literally, to the pressure of the stretched fence attached to it. Even if your fence is a simple T-post affair, you'll want to build the corners with burly, naturally rot-resistant or treated wood posts with a diameter of at least six inches.

In most areas, where one can bury posts, the corner is built with a design that's sort of a right isosceles triangle, except the long edge is not connected. The three sturdy posts compose the actual corner. On the short sides, the posts are held together with wire cross-braces that are tightened so that the whole corner becomes one sturdy unit that can last for years.

For areas not conducive to burying posts, the "box" is a set-up of four posts at least as tall as the fence, one or two feet across from each other, wrapped with woven wire fence and filled with rocks.

Odd Terrain

I spent just as long setting one particular end-post as I had the whole rest of the fence. The reason: The fence ended at the top of an embankment that was about fifteen feet high, made entirely of fill material. Our house had been built on a slope in the 1930s, and to create a level building site the men brought in truckloads of crushed rock. I had to run this fence up the edge of the fill area and terminate it at the top, where there was an existing fence for the yard.

Whether I dropped a few feet below the level of our yard or hiked up the embankment, I had to dig my feet in to try not to slide. I hauled the post-hole digger up there, stuck it in and laughed—it practically bounced off the rocks. I ended up having to loosen and dislodge each rock individually. A jackhammer might have come in handy but it would have been unsafe to operate it on that slippery slope.

If you have a dip in the terrain, it's going to create a gap under your fence—not a big deal if you're keeping deer out; a problem if you're keeping rabbits, goats or chickens out.

Attire

Forget New York's "Western-inspired" clothing ads—fashion has no place on a real farm. The things you wear have two purposes: 1) Protect you from the elements, and 2) Protect you from *seriously* hurting yourself. You're going to hurt yourself—that's unavoidable—but the goal is to not lose any appendages, eyeballs or large hunks of flesh.

Country people have two sets of clothes: farm clothes and town clothes. They mostly wear the farm clothes, which are more beat-up. Town clothes are new, or at least in good shape. There is no place on a farm for most city clothes: high-heeled shoes (though some women insist on wearing them to church and special occasions); white shoes or clothes (or anything white, really); thin, sensitive fabrics. Country things need to be tough—jeans, boots, sweatshirts—and not expensive (except the boots) because you're going to hack on them, and you can't be worrying if you catch a sleeve on a nail, or pop a button.

From the bottom up:

Boots

There are a couple variations, but regardless of the task the role of the boot is to give you solid footing for what you're doing and protect your feet. Since you're going to spend a lot of time in them, they must be comfortable as well. Wear the right type of boot for the job:

- **Wood-cutting or other work in the forest; tractor or other machinery work: lug-soled boots.** They need to lace up at least over your ankles, and can go as high as your knee. Brands include Westco, White, Danner, Red Wing, Wolverine, Rocky Boots and Georgia. Farm machinery manufacturers like John Deere and Caterpillar are even getting into the act. These boots are not light-weight, nor should they be if you're going to be kicking around big hunks of wood and crashing through brambles and other underbrush.
- **Mucking out the barn, gardening or other "farm" chores: rubber boots.** I had two pair: rubber shoes* for hot weather and knee-high boots for the rest of the year, or when I was doing a big job and didn't want a bunch of debris building up in my shoes. My brand of choice was Muck Boots; Mike preferred XtraTufs, which is what fisheries people wear. Other brands: Workmaster; Monarch/LaCrosse; Ranger; Northerner; L.L. Bean.

    It's also feasible to buy cheap, plastic knee-high boots at a discount store, but you must know this by now: "You get what you pay for." Cheap boots are fine if you're walking up the driveway to get the newspaper, not so fine if you're digging garden beds for six hours.

*Note on rubber shoes: Crocs are not good for this role. In the barn, you'll end up with a bunch of wood chips or straw poking you in the arch because they got in through the holes. And you can imagine what happens in mud.

- **Old-school farmers in dry climates wear cowboy boots for everything;** I find other boots more comfortable and warmer, but you could give them a try. They are the best, obviously, for riding a horse; the toes and heels are designed to keep your feet in the stirrups, or to slide out quickly. Switch to rubber boots when mucking out the barn, though—urine can disintegrate the stitching of cowboy boots.
- **Unless you're doing very light work, there is no place for sandals or flip-flops on a farm** except in the house, or in the car on the way to the beach. A friend once stopped by for a visit while my chickens were roaming around but left abruptly, because the hens were attracted to the freshly manicured toes peeking out from her sandals.

Clothes

Again, if you're doing light work you can get away with wearing shorts and a T-shirt. Otherwise, you will be grateful for those sleeves! Working on a farm might seem like a good way to work on your tan, but if you're smart everything will be covered up. Sorry.

My most prized article of town-demoted-to-ranch apparel was a pair of Liz Claiborne leather pants. They used to be quite the fashion statement, but over the years leather starts to look worn and there's not much that can be done to perk it up. Leather is fantastic as a work pant—just as tough as heavy canvas. I wore them any time I was in the woods or fighting Himalayan blackberry. Liz would shudder.

You'll need a farm-use-only jacket that you can wash or just leave dirty—it's going to get all sorts of debris and dirt on it. Mine was wool—in fact, it was my old high school letter jacket! Sometimes, I got nostalgic for high school and snuck behind the barn and slammed a two-liter bottle of Sun Country cherry wine cooler, just for old time's sake. Kidding.

If you buy a brand-new jacket, try Carhartt or Filson. They make other things, like pants with double-thick knees, and pants lined with flannel. Dickies, Arborwear and Blaklader are other brands. Blaklader also makes kilts, as does Utilikilt. Yar!

Gloves

Must. Be. Worn. For nearly everything. There are many times that you will set out to do something—grab a couple pieces of wood; pull some weeds; cut a little kindling. You'll think, "Oh, I'll just do it," because your gloves are in the garage and fetching them would take an extra minute. On the not-so-bad end of things, you'll fill your fingernails with dirt or get a splinter. On the bad end, you might lose a finger. Take the time to get your gloves. We had multiple pairs so they were lying around all over. A few types of gloves (this is another "you get what you pay for" item):

- **Leather work gloves:** The Mack-daddy of gloves. Double-palmed. Make sure they fit—you're impairing yourself if you're flopping around in too-big gloves. Many manufacturers are finally making gloves that fit women's hands.
- **Cotton gloves:** These were fine for gardening when there was no alternative, but I find today's high-tech designs far superior to bulky cotton that dries slowly.
- **Rubber gloves:** Good in wet weather or for nasty jobs but don't breathe, so your hands come out of them smelling like a sewer.
- **Nylon back/rubber front:** These are my favorite for gardening unless it's early spring and too cold. The rubber is form-fitting so you hardly lose dexterity and the back breathes so your hands stay dry inside. I have also used a variant on this design with the nylon part made from hemp! My only criticism is they stop at the wrist, so dirt does sometimes get inside.

Nothing is quite as unsettling as sticking your hand in a glove and realizing you're not the only occupant. To keep spiders and earwigs out of my gloves, I stored them in an old ceramic casserole dish. Any covered or sealable container will do—even a locking plastic storage bag. I still squeeze all the fingers of my gloves before I put them on, so if something is in there at least it will be dead when I find it.

Hat

Most farmers wear a "seed cap" or baseball-type hat with a brim to keep the sun out of their eyes.

I recommend a straw hat with a full, wide brim that keeps the sun off your ears and the back of your neck as well. If you live in a windy place, make sure it will cinch tightly under your chin. It should fit snugly but not be jammed on. You have to be conscious of the hat for a while after you start wearing it—every spring, after my wool work hat went into storage and my straw hat came out, I was constantly knocking the brim into things (like when I poked my head in the chicken nests to see if there were eggs).

Section Two

Buildings, Inside and Out

Buildings, Inside and Out

Buying a country house entails the same sort of research and preparation as buying a city house—have the home inspected by a professional who takes you with her and explains things as she goes along (ask around for recommendations). The same anti-romantic advice I gave about buying land applies here: figure out your must-haves and compromises ahead of time, and be ready to re-negotiate them as you tour real properties and see what's actually available.

What used to be "mobile" or "trailer" homes (which actually were mobile—set on wheels with a tow hitch) are nowadays called "manufactured homes." These are mobile in the sense that they were built in a factory and then brought to the home site, but they are loaded onto a flatbed truck rather than towed. "Modular" homes are partly built in a factory, and then assembled and often sided on-site. Some of the newer ones are quite nice—you wouldn't know it wasn't a regular house. Most are "double-wide" and can have cathedral ceilings, tile countertops and high-end appliances. And, newer homes are the only ones in the country that will have lots of electrical outlets and more than one bathroom, unless another was awkwardly wedged in somewhere long after the house was built.

A regular house, built on-site of dimensional lumber, is called "stick-built." If you're considering a proper, original farmhouse, be cautious. While old farmhouses are far and away the most picturesque, you are not buying this building to photograph—you need to be able to live in it comfortably.

The trouble with old farmhouses is that they precede modern conveniences. I once visited such a house in Wisconsin, built before running water had been introduced to the area. Its sole source of heat was a woodstove in the kitchen. In the 1970s, a bathroom had been tacked onto the other end of the house. You can bet that the heat hardly made a dent in the cold of the un-insulated, glorified lean-to that was the bathroom. I'm not just talking about a chilly toilet seat; the family who lived in that house struggled for months every year to keep the pipes from freezing. If they failed, it was back to the original outhouse—which in January would have been ten kinds of nasty.

A friend owns an 18th-century stone farmhouse in New York. It is a thing of rustic beauty. But, the masons couldn't have comprehended the notion of how one runs wiring or heating ducts through stone walls (ditto log homes), nor how one insulates. A house overrun with rodents was common at the time. Think about it: a stone wall is like a fancy mouse-and-chipmunk condominium. And warm, since the inside is being heated. Snakes and insects like it, too.

If the farmhouse you're looking at has more than one story, check for subfloors; the floor may be just a series of tongue-in-groove planks. A subfloor makes a house warmer and quieter, and keeps dirt from the overhead story from filtering down, through the floor, to the lower story.

If the house has stairs, chances are they would not stand up to modern building code, which requires handrails and dictates how steep the stairway can be, how wide the steps must be, how deep the treads, and many other things. Make sure that you're comfortable with the stairs, especially if you have young children or will use the stairs with laundry, grocery bags and the like in your arms. When you get older, stairs might become especially prohibitive.

Chapter 3
Maintenance

A house is really an amalgamation of systems. As the owner of a house, you are responsible for each. There are two ways to interact with these systems: maintenance and repair. If you ignore maintenance, you will soon find a lot of repair in your future.

People who successfully live in the country are either handy or wealthy (ideally, both). Those who are handy know the basics of:

- **Carpentry**
- **Electrical wiring**
- **Plumbing and, while we're at it,**
- **Small engine repair**

Otherwise, you'll find yourself living in squalor or hiring out a lot of work. And that's if you can get someone to come to your house. The carpenters, electricians and other skilled laborers who are responsible and good at what they do get hired for big jobs, usually new construction and major remodels—the people who pick up the nickel-and-dime handyman jobs that you need done are either desperate for work or new to the area, the ones mentioned above who are taking extra jobs on the weekends, or stoners who show up late, work for an hour, say they're going to lunch and never come back. Most of them will do a great job; ask around for recommendations.

While an incorporated repair outfit will likely take credit cards, these folks prefer to be paid in cash so they don't have to pay taxes on it (called "working under the table"). However, I always wanted to write them a check so I could claim it on my taxes as an expenditure. If you're planning to write a check, tell them in advance. You may have to pay a little bit more to make up for it. A "cash rate" is for cash only.

Roof and Gutter

In the West, where wildfires are common in the summer, most people have roofs made of sheet metal. Imagine an enormous fire near your home that is throwing baseball-sized sparks dozens of feet in the air—would you want those fireballs falling onto shingles that are soaked in tar?

We liked this roof. Although we had to live with its color (white, which was a practical choice because it reflects the sun's heat in the summer) it was virtually maintenance-free. It was built at a proper pitch, so we didn't have to go up on the roof and remove snow during the winter. The gutters were a different story.

We had quite a bit of gutter, probably 140 linear feet on the house, eighty on the garage and a little on another outbuilding. There was a beautiful mature maple tree that was, by today's construction standards, too close to the house and made a lot of gutter maintenance necessary. We decided to buy a product made of aluminum that covers the gutters in a large mesh that keeps debris out. It worked pretty well that first year on the leaves, though the helicopter seeds slid right through the mesh.

One morning, Mike and I were lounging in bed—it was Saturday, it had snowed quite a bit the previous week, and we were enjoying being snug and warm. Suddenly, we heard a thunderous, thumping crash and felt its percussion through the floor. We both shot out of bed and looked out the window, hearts racing. It was what we thereafter called a "roof avalanche"—a major portion of the snow that had been piled on the roof let go at once, slid down the metal roof and crashed onto the ground right outside our bedroom. Whenever it happened after that, we'd still startle; it was arresting to say the least.

The first year, a roof avalanche pulverized the bushes I had unwittingly planted in its path and made a twisted mess of the nice aluminum gutter-cover we had installed that fall. A friend of mine owned a small building in town, and a roof avalanche there completely destroyed a cedar fence that separated his building from the dentist's next door. Another friend had divots in her lower roof from ice blocks falling from her upper roof.

If there were a period of freeze-thaw-freeze, water would build up under the enormous blanket of snow on the roof, especially where there were two planes meeting in a valley. Held by surface tension, the snow would extend down a bit from the edge of the roof and into the gutter. If you weren't on top of this, knocking it off every couple of hours, and the temperature plummeted, the water/snow would freeze and expand. The first couple of years, the damage was minimal. One year, however, ice dams snapped the brackets that held the gutter to the roof, bent the gutters themselves, and broke apart the joints at the corners and at the drainpipes. Total gutter devastation.

I have a friend who lost not only her gutters this way, but also the fascia boards to which they were attached. If you have this situation, it might be worthwhile to ditch the gutter thing, and just build French drains around your house. You could try gutter-heater cables, but I would still put my money on the snow.

Septic System

Nothing will make you more aware of what you pour down your sink than having a septic or gray water system, because instead of going vaguely "away," as city effluent does, whatever you put in your pipes ends up in your own soil, and eventually in your own groundwater, from which your own well is drawing. If you happen to be one of those totally irresponsible people who pours motor oil and paint onto the gravel driveway or down the sewer, well, finally you'll get your comeuppance.

In order to keep your septic system healthy, pour a bacteria-slurry (available at the hardware store) down there on a regular basis. Use environmentally friendly soaps and detergents. Do not flush condoms, tampons or anything other than septic-friendly toilet paper. If you have a garbage disposal in your kitchen sink, use it sparingly if at all (compost instead; see Food Section). Don't drive over or park on the drain field; if the ground is soft you may compact the soil or even crush the lines.

You need to manage the "load" of your system. This means spacing out big-water-use events, like showering, doing laundry and running the dishwasher. Fix leaking toilets and faucets. If you have a big party, rent a portable toilet and post a sign on the bathroom door asking guests to use it.

Critter-Proofing

Human homes are so darn comfortable that lots of critters like to live in them: mice, rats, bats, insects, spiders, squirrels, and so on. A friend once had an enormous nutria squatting in her basement. I do not recommend sharing your home with anything except your pets and the occasional spider. To keep animals out, you need to seal up the exterior. This means caulking every seam. Covering every vent with hardware cloth. Sealing every crack in the foundation. Making sure your storm windows and screens fit your windows properly.

However, some designs may be impossible to fortify, such as homes made of stone or logs. Don't make things easy for critters by leaving food or unwashed dishes out overnight. Make sure your dry goods are in jars and on shelves that they can't reach. You'll be able to tell if mice have been around if you spy little black turds. Mice feces are only a few millimeters long; rat feces are about a quarter-inch and much fatter. Set traps! Get some cats! Don't shoot coyotes (they eat rodents)!

If you find you have a squatter, such as a skunk under your front porch, first try to lure him out, or wait until he leaves to hunt for food, and then close up the entryway.

Second strategy: live ("box") trap and relocation. This may be illegal to do yourself without a permit. Move the animal at least five miles away, or it will find its way back. A friend once dabbed nail polish on a mouse to test this, and released it one mile away. Saw it the next day.

Third strategy: shoot it. Keep in mind that with a skunk, the latter two strategies will result in a lot of stink.

Sump Pump

If your house's basement or crawl space is below the area's water table, or on a slope that directs rainwater and snowmelt toward your house, you may need a sump pump to protect your belongings and foundation. This is a pretty simple system that pumps water away, either to a non-threatening area of your yard or into a drywell. Some are manual, meaning you need to pay attention and turn them on, and some automatically respond to the water level. If you need to move a lot of water, I'd recommend a back-up system.

Check this pump at least once per year to make sure it's functioning properly. If you live in an area that freezes, you may have to adjust the discharge part of the system.

Wood Heat

I find few things as comforting as a wood fire. Furnaces heat the air; woodstoves heat all the *things*. Winter mornings on the farm, I'd open a cupboard to get some dishes out and feel a little gush of warm air. The cupboard was warm. The dishes were warm. Everything was warm.

The warmest room was the living room (sometimes up to 90 degrees!); the next rooms were about eight degrees cooler, and our bedroom about eight degrees cooler still, which was perfect. We had a one-level house and ran a ceiling fan pretty much all the time in the living room, which helped to move the air around. The only thing that was slightly inconvenient was that all the interior doors had to stay at least halfway open, or that room wouldn't get any heat. I am a heat junkie and never minded the extreme heat in the living room; it was a little much for Mike at times.

Today's modern woodstoves recycle the byproducts of combustion, making the stoves both more efficient and environmentally friendly than older models. But, they are expensive. Most people I knew had an older-model stove in their house (and an even older one out in the garage). I wouldn't recommend having a stove older than twenty-five years in your home—they don't have catalytic converters (let alone the even more efficient dual-chamber), their dampers may be broken and their welds cracked, which means the wood will burn faster than it needs to, and some toxic compounds might leak onto your house.

While fireplaces are beautiful to look at, they are an efficiency disaster—most of the heat goes right up the chimney with the smoke, and when there's no fire they draw existing heat out of the house. You're much better off filling in your fireplace with an insert, or closing off the fireplace and installing a freestanding stove in front of it. You should be able to run the stovepipe up the existing chimney. Don't necessarily buy a giant stove—it's better to have a full firebox in a small stove than a smoldering fire in a big one. Smoldering fires pollute more than a clean-burning fire and create excess creosote build-up in your stove and chimney.

Some stoves have one opening and some two, one in front and one on the side. Open the front to build a new fire and to clean the door (if it's glass). Use the side door after the fire is going. Stoves that are made of cast iron heat up faster but also cool down faster. Stoves that have stone built into them take longer to heat up, but then radiate heat for hours after the fire is out.

Even if you have a brand-new stove, install a carbon monoxide monitor in your house. We bought one that was combined with our smoke alarm, but in retrospect that might not have been the best idea since carbon monoxide is a heavy gas, so it probably would have asphyxiated us long before it built up high enough to reach the ceiling, where the alarm was mounted.

If you have small children, you'll need to either block off the room in which the stove is located, or build or purchase a gate that surrounds it. And teach them to steer clear of it.

Put a cast-iron kettle or other vessel, filled with water, on the stove to add humidity to your house. To keep it from boiling dry requires daily attention; I was in the habit of pouring extra water from water glasses in there. As I ran water to wash dishes and waited for the hot water to make its way through the pipes, I captured the water in a pitcher and used that in the kettle as well.

Ceiling fans, as I mentioned, can help move the air around. Another option, best if your stove is at the far end of the house, is a little fan that rests right on top of the stove. Convection from the fire makes it run. They are expensive little buggers but extremely efficient. They stop when they come in contact with anything, so they're not a finger-chopping-off hazard (but they can get hot).

Acquiring

There are different ways to get wood: (in order of easiest to hardest, and most expensive to cheapest):

- **Delivered to your house already split**
- **Delivered in rounds**
- **Delivered in unbucked lengths**

- **"U-haul":** You take your rig to the farm or clear-cut and load rounds or slag (clear-cut waste material), cut and/or split yourself
- **"U-cut":** You get a wood-harvesting permit from the landowner (often the U.S. Forest Service or Department of Natural Resources), and fell, buck and haul the trees yourself; cut and split yourself

You can also scavenge wood, such as mill-ends if you live in an area with a logging operation, but this should be considered supplemental to your main wood source. If you have a sufficient woodlot, you can cut trees from it.

The standard measurement of wood is the cord, but our wood was always called a "load," because the average pickup can't hold an entire cord (which is a stack of split wood that measures four by four by eight feet). Some people just fill the bed of the truck; some add plywood walls so the pieces can be stacked higher. Ask questions of wood-haulers to try to get a good idea of how much wood you're getting.

Whether wood heat is a cost-savings is debatable. Depending on the size of your house and how well it's insulated, you're looking at three to ten cords of wood. We spent around $500 buying wood (approximately four cords) delivered to our house every summer. It would be much cheaper if you cut it yourself, but only if you don't factor in the value of your time.

Make sure you buy enough; you can use the extra the following winter (use it first). You don't want to start looking at your woodpile in March and projecting: If it took us a week to get through this much, that means that…uh oh. You start rationing the wood a little—maybe not such blazing fires; maybe not during the day; maybe waiting an extra hour at night before starting a new one…

Recent campaigns discourage people from moving firewood from one place to another. The reason: the wood may be carrying pest insects and deadly pathogens. You wouldn't want to be responsible for decimating your woodlot by bringing in some borer-beetle from the next valley over! What constitutes one "place" varies depending on the region, but the Nature Conservancy suggests within a fifty-mile radius.

Splitting

Note: Felling trees is covered in the Land Section.

If you have cut wood from a local woodlot (perhaps even your own!), you felled the trees (a fellow who fells trees is called a "faller"), and then bucked it into lengths appropriate for your stove with a chainsaw. If it's dry (though there are a few species that should be "green," such as live oak), it's time to split the rounds into halves or quarters so that they'll:

1) Fit through the door of your woodstove

2) Burn more easily—it's the same principal as shredding cheese to expedite its melting (increased surface area)

3) Not roll around and ruin your careful placement within the stove

Mechanical wood splitters do this most efficiently. While all matters involving processing firewood are dangerous, a mechanical wood-splitter is right up there. It is imperative that you plan ahead, so your system is seamless and everyone involved is paying 100-percent attention. Locate the emergency shutoff.

My dad has a manual wood-splitter, which uses hydraulics to force a log apart. He pumps a pedal with his foot a half-dozen or so times, and *voila!* The piece snaps in two. It might be better than going to the gym! But not practical if you have more than one cord. Make sure you get the top-of-the line model; my dad's has broken twice. There are also models that use their own leverage, good if you need to minimize wear-and-tear on your body.

Mike and I split a small portion of our wood by hand, which was fun, and which was plenty. Splitting a half-dozen pieces makes one feel like she's working hard, doing Farm Stuff. If we'd had to split our entire winter supply, we would have rented or purchased a gas-powered splitter.

Shortly before we moved to our new country home, my grandma offered to buy us a housewarming gift. We were at the hardware store at the time, and I remembered that we needed an axe so we could split firewood.

"Don't you mean a maul?" Grandma asked. A splitting maul (the name should have been my first clue) looks sort of like an axe, but instead of a narrow head it has one with sides that bulge out. The effect of this is to drive the two halves of a piece of wood apart—rather like using a wedge.

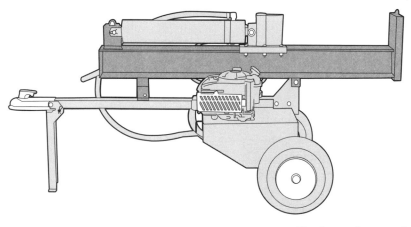

Mechanical Log Splitter

But I thought I meant an axe and, unfortunately, insisted on it. She shrugged her shoulders and bought me an axe. Which we never used, because who is going to cut down a tree with an axe when there is a chainsaw? I can't imagine how long that thing must have sat in the hardware store until my poor grandma purchased it.

On a day that you're feeling frisky don some protective eyewear, gloves and boots, and head out to the woodshed. Examine your maul; if it's showing any signs of loosening, fix it immediately. Stand a log squarely on its end, and size it up. The log should be dry and cracked (called "checks"); examine the checks and see which to exploit. Even a faint crack could get bigger inside the piece. Turn a big crack away from you so that when you hit it with the splitting maul, the crack you make will join the crack that already exists and make a bigger crack. If you're good at this, you can split a piece with one hit.

I was not particularly good at this and—let's be fair—I only weigh 115 pounds. It usually took me at least two hits, sometimes embarrassingly more. In any case, make sure the log is on level ground. Face the log squarely, with your feet apart and your dominant hand holding the handle near the maul and your other hand holding the handle a little more than halfway down the handle. In what you want to be one motion, throw the maul-end up to the side and over your head (in front of you, not all the way back) and then snap down with both hands as quickly and decisively as possible. Do not look at or think about anything other than the exact spot that you want the maul to hit. Just like in baseball or golf, you are not hitting the log, you are hitting *through* the log.

Occasionally, I hit a piece with everything I had and the maul barely made a dent. This usually meant that the piece wasn't dry enough, or there was a branch that I couldn't see. Branches form when a tree is young; as the trunk expands it adds layer over layer on top of it, so a branch sticking out of a tree actually penetrates the trunk quite a ways (these are the knots in milled wood). Other reasons a piece may be un-splittable: the wood is twisted; the piece is a fork of two branches; both ends were bucked at an angle. We either saved those for really cold nights when we needed a huge piece or, if they were completely intractable for the stove, burned them in an outdoor fire during a party.

Storage

It is imperative to build a weatherproof shed or lean-to for your wood—having a woodpile covered with a tarp will not cut it, except in arid climates. The best shed has three sides to protect your wood from the blowing rain and snow. Ours was lined on the inside with scrap pieces of sheet metal (roofing material)—that way we could chuck pieces of wood around and not worry about smashing through the walls. The floor was covered in old plywood, which limited (but certainly didn't eliminate) the number of bugs and vermin living in the woodpile, and gave the stacks a straight foundation. Old pallets work well also. The front of the shed was just dirt and woodchips, which is where we split wood—if we tried it on the plywood everything would bounce around dangerously.

Kindling

Some of the best kindling we ever had was when we asked one of our carpenter friends to save the ends from the Douglas fir flooring that he'd been laying. That wood was bone dry—when you hit it with a hatchet, pieces flew across the wood-shed as though they were just *waiting* for the chance to be free. If you can't score anything like that, then just take a short piece of firewood and chop it into smaller and smaller pieces. Small branches work well but don't fit together nicely in the kindling basket the way cut lumber or firewood does. Make sure they're truly dried out; green twigs are not good for anything but toasting marshmallows.

I've seen other fire starters, including pinecones dipped in wax and—an inge-nious use of local materials in orchard country—small wax-coated drinking cups filled with dried cherry pits in wax and stapled into a brown paper sack. I'm reluc-tant to introduce wax into my chimney, since we light fires every day for months, but those worked well to start outdoor fires. Fatwood is a type of wood that contains a huge amount of sap, which makes it burn hot. Use it sparingly.

You can scavenge wood from construction and de-construction sites—old fencing, old shakes, old paneling are all great, dry hunks of wood. But watch for nails.

Do not burn coated paper (anything full-color and shiny), plywood, or wood that's been painted or treated for rot-resistance.

Lighting

Before starting a fire, make sure that if there is a damper, it's open—if it isn't your room will fill with smoke really fast. What happens next is personal; everyone has her own "perfect" fire set-up. Mine is this: two smallish (five to seven inches in diameter) pieces of wood paralleling each other by about six inches. In the between-space I put two crumpled full sheets of newspaper on the bottom and lay a handful of kindling sticks on the newspaper (parallel to the wood). Then I put two bigger pieces perpen-dicular, maybe one or two more on top of those if it's really cold (we have a big stove). Some people call this "log cabin style." The other popular type is "teepee," which I don't prefer because it requires too much hand-holding.

Before lighting the fire, start a draught through the chimney by lighting a small sheet of newspaper and holding it up to the area right below where the chimney starts. This heats the air in the stove and, since heat rises, it creates a small current that goes up the chimney.

I light the fire and keep the door open a crack in order to pull the air through quickly, which serves the same purpose as a bellows—blasting some oxygen in there to get things going. Until there are coals, your fire depends on drawing oxygen. Once it's roaring and has a life of its own, I close the door.

Don't get in the habit during the off-season of putting anything on the woodstove except the aforementioned kettle of water. Or else, this will happen: you'll light a fire, go out to dinner, and return to a house full of smoke and a molten wax-mess on the woodstove because you left a candle on it. Not that I would know.

Wood Type

The first year we moved into our house there was a fair amount of wood in our shed, and some friends also gave us their wood, maybe a cord, because they were moving to town and wouldn't need it. About half of it was oak and half Douglas fir. When we started building fires in October, we burned the oak because it was near the front of the pile. It was difficult to get the pieces going, which made us worry that our woodstove was broken—a big problem since we hadn't planned to use the electric baseboard heaters at all. But the oak would eventually burn, and burn hot and long, so we weren't sure what the deal was.

As winter pressed on and we started burning the fir, we noticed that while the fires were easy to start they weren't nearly as hot, and burned out hours before the oak fires did. Finally, Mike did some research and learned that different wood burns at different temperatures. We eventually worked out a good system: We had fall and spring fires in fir, and saved the oak (and maple and fruitwood) for winter, with some fir reserved to get those hot fires going.

How hot a particular type of wood burns is measured in British Thermal Units (BTUs). Other factors when harvesting your wood are how easy it is to split, how easy it is to start in a cold stove, how much ash it produces, how much it sparks (mostly affects fireplaces) and what kind of fragrance it has when it burns. One type of tree in our area, grand fir, is called "piss fir" by the loggers for that last reason.

Cedar is pretty weak as a heat-generator but boy, does it smell wonderful. Douglas fir isn't bad, either. Fruitwoods also smell terrific and burn pretty well as a secondary wood (hard to start cold). But a neighbor once pointed out that fruitwood from commercial orchards may not be that good to burn, as the trees have been sprayed for years with pesticides. Something to consider.

- **Best starter logs:** Pine, cedar, spruce, hemlock, cottonwood, poplar, aspen
- **Moderate logs:** cherry, tamarack, walnut, sycamore, elm
- **Best overnighters:** Oak, maple, ash, beech, birch, apple, hickory

If you live in a part of the country that doesn't grow a lot of starter wood, split smaller pieces of the hardwoods.

Whatever you burn, make sure it's "seasoned," which means it has sat, cut, for at least six months but preferably longer. If you burn "green" or wet wood you will get fewer BTUs from the fire and more creosote build-up in your chimney.

Most woodstoves have a thermometer and draught control built in somewhere, which help you monitor your fire. There is an optimal temperature range you want to keep—too low and your fire burns inefficiently and pukes smoke (and thereby, creosote) up the chimney. Too high and you risk breaking welds in the stove and chimney, and you'll burn through your woodpile twice as fast as you need to. You can control this to some degree by adjusting the draught control down after the fire is going well. You don't need a roaring movie fire; you need a slow but steady fire.

Chimney

If you have fires often, you will need to clean your chimney a couple of times per year—once in late summer or early fall, before heavy usage begins, and once snuck in during an unusually warm day in the spring (well before you actually stop using it). "Safety first" is the name of the game: Use a climbing harness, a helmet, gloves, protective eyewear—as much as you are willing to wear. This is a two-person job—one on the roof and one on the ground.

The tools are rather simple: a ladder, a sweeping brush, which is a round brush made of steel bristles on a very long handle; a wrench, screwdriver or whatever is required to remove the cap from the chimney (if you don't have a cap on your chimney, get one today); and a rope or other means of lowering these items to the other person. The chimney brush should be the same diameter as the chimney, usually six or eight inches.

Meanwhile, the other person will have separated the chimney from the stove (in the house) if that's possible and secured a garbage bag around the end of it. This way, all the creosote and junk that gets scraped from the chimney goes straight into the garbage bag and doesn't fall into your stove or go flying around the house. This person will also intercept the chimney cap, which was lowered from the roof, and scrape all of the creosote from it using a wooden-handled brush with steel bristles. Wear gloves and eye protection, and perhaps even a mask, as little pieces of gunk will go flying in every direction.

Compost note: Wood ashes from the stove are good for the garden and should be added to compost. Creosote from the chimney and ashes from a charcoal grill are toxic, and should be bagged and put in the garbage.

Sap

Once you've gotten sap onto something, it's hard to get off. There are dozens of remedies out there to try; what works for you might be a magic formula consisting of the type of sap you're dealing with, the type of product you're using, the humidity and lord knows what else. Experiment.

In my experience, dealing with Doug fir sap, it mostly has to wear off. But there are some ways to expedite that process. The last thing you want to do is wash with soap and water—sap is impervious to both. There are two strategies: If you have sap on your hands, take advantage of its sticky properties and coax it to stick to something else. Rub a few squares of toilet paper across the sap—the thin paper bonds and disintegrates, making a sticky, paper-y mess that you can scrape from your palm. Oil (vegetable oil, peanut butter) also works, but then you've got an oily mess on your hands instead of a sticky one.

If you find sap on furniture or clothing, freeze it with an ice cube and then carefully chip away at it with a sharp blade or your fingernail. There are a variety of solvents—nail polish remover, mineral spirits, WD-40 and the like—but you run the risk of bleaching out the area.

Chapter 4
Other Utilities and Services

Other Heat Sources

When people get tired of the effort and mess required of wood heat, they replace their stove with a pellet stove or propane gas fireplace. Or, if they're *really* tired of it, they'll actually have a furnace or heat pump installed. A furnace can run on natural gas, propane or oil. In the Pacific Northwest, many people use electric baseboard heat because our darn dammed rivers provide relatively cheap electricity.

I have mixed feelings about pellet stoves. On the one hand, they combust wood-industry waste material, as well as corn, sunflower husks and other things that would otherwise be composted at best. A pellet stove can be connected to a thermostat; it heats quickly; the hopper only has to be loaded occasionally; there is virtually no mess. But—and in my mind it's a big but—the feeder runs on electricity, so if there is a power outage it can't be run (or you have to fire up a generator). I would own a pellet stove if I also had a regular woodstove or fireplace as a back-up.

A heat pump is an amazing device. It cools—and heats!—a house using the temperature of the Earth. It's more efficient than a furnace because it merely transfers heat rather than creating it. However, if you can't put it in an out-of-the way place, get used to listening to it; it runs constantly instead of turning on and off like a furnace. While some pumps are being developed for cold climates, they work best in a moderate climate.

There are three types of heat pumps:

- **Air-Source:** This system consists of two units, one inside and one outside, which are connected through an exterior wall of the house. The indoor unit is as large as a furnace; the outdoor unit is a little smaller than a standard free-standing air conditioning unit. The outdoor unit should be protected from high wind.
- **Ground-Source:** This system has one large unit in the house that is connected to an underground closed- or open-loop pipe circuit. Installing this type of heat pump requires excavation next to the house.
- **Absorption:** This is a single unit powered by something other than electricity (usually natural gas, propane, solar power or geothermal

energy). Absorption units are used on commercial buildings and some large homes.

Electricity

Many small communities run cooperative electricity companies. This means that the company is "owned" equally by everyone who is a customer. The board of directors is voted on and the overhead is kept low. If the co-op sells excess electricity to other markets, shareholders may even receive a payout!

In most rural areas you have to read your own electric meter—the houses are so far apart it would take all day for someone to read twenty meters. The company will instruct you on how to read your meter and report your usage.

Communications

Unless you're in an extremely remote area, it's no longer an issue to get regular telephone service. The question is, do you want a landline? This question has pretty much become moot in the city, but is still something to consider in the country. While most young people have cellular telephones, many do not (and will probably refer to their phone number with four digits, since everyone has the same area code and prefix). If you're trying to fit in with the community, you really don't want to make a neighbor have to call you long distance.

Secondly, your cell phone may work in town but not at your house. Or, not in your house. Mike and I lived up a twisting, narrow and deep valley that blocked all but the most intrepid radio waves. In our area, metal roofs were the norm, further blocking a cell signal. For the first couple of years in our house we could use our cell phones in one corner of the house; we had to face east; we couldn't move. Our calls dropped half the time anyway.

As is true in the city, one can get Internet service over telephone wires, a cable or from a satellite. At least, in theory. Before you commit to purchasing a house, make sure this is the case, and confirm how much it will cost. If a local service provider has run a high-speed line near your house, it should be no big deal to connect to it using the old copper. If they haven't, find out when they plan to.

There are still "low-speed" Internet providers as well. If you have one, you may be accountable to FAP, or Fair Access Policy. This means you're limited in the amount of content you can upload or download at any one time. If you're a freelance graphic designer, or someone who likes to watch on-demand movies, this will be an issue.

Satellite connections are not foolproof either. In order to get either Internet or television, the dish on your house needs an unimpeded southern exposure. If your house is well oriented, it faces south; this means that you either slap a big blemish (in my opinion) on the front of your house, or put it in a less-than-ideal location and risk a less-than-ideal signal. Our dish was in just such a less-than-ideal location and often got misadjusted by snow and strong winds. And if you're in the trees, you're out of luck. The nice thing about dishes is that they are now quite small—about one foot across, rather than those behemoths people used to set up in their yards that were as big as a swimming pool. If you can, put it somewhere that you can clear snow from it with a broom. As one friend said, "No one wants to climb up on a snowy roof because they lost the Internet or the Super Bowl."

A word about locally run Internet Service Providers: If you have one, give them a shot! It's nice to know that, if you were to have a problem with their service you can drive to their office to chat about it. If you go with a corporation with a national headquarters thousands of miles from your house, you'll just be on hold on an 800-number a lot. And, that will be on your cell phone, since if your Internet is out your landline is out as well. Oh, and your cell phone doesn't work well inside your house? Bummer.

Postal Service

House-to-house delivery routes are becoming more and more rare as the postal industry contracts in response to the prominence of email, text messages and social websites. If you live on a rural route, your mailbox will probably have to be on the main road, not down a driveway which, where we lived in the mountains, meant that in the winter we would have had to dig the mailbox out every time a snowplow went by. Though I had been looking forward to walking up the driveway to get the mail, we decided instead to rent a post office box. This meant we only got our mail every other day or so, when we were in town on another errand.

If you do keep a mailbox on the road, install one that locks—identity-thieves love the convenience of trolling a lonely country road for checks and other goodies. Another challenge is to mount it in such a way that nothing can destroy it—not a snowplow, herd of cows, or carload of teenagers with a baseball bat (yes, that still happens). Strategies I have seen: encasing the box in a stone pillar or wooden box; hanging it from chains; attaching it to a large spring. We lived in whitewater-rafting country, so one mailbox was encased in an old kayak that stood on end. This doubled as a landmark to show visitors where their driveway is.

When I used to write letters to rural relatives as a girl, I was innocent of the significance of a post office box. Why would I send it to their P.O. Box if I could put their street address on there—that would save them the effort of having to go to the post office to fetch it. I didn't understand that there was no home delivery. In most small-town post offices, the employees will recognize the name or figure out whose mail it is, and put it in the box. If they're getting cranky about it, they'll write a note on the letter. When you make a catalogue order or sign up for something, be sure the person entering your data understands not to send any item or correspondence to your street address.

Some post offices are nothing more than a bank of sixteen locked boxes protected by a roof enclosure. Our post office was a small building; the lobby (where the boxes are) was open twenty-four hours per day. The retail counter had more limited hours; open until 5:30 p.m. during the week and not at all on the weekend. If we received a package, we either got a claim slip in our box, which we took to the retail counter during business hours, or we got a small key with a number on it. Our post office had lockers (similar to the ones at the roller-skating rinks and public pools); we simply inserted the key to claim our package.

Package Delivery

United Parcel Service (UPS) and FedEx go everywhere, right? Yes and no. Some properties are so remote, especially during the winter, that there may be a significant delay. Overnight delivery is unlikely.

Both companies refused to come to our house because of our dog, which was loose and went ballistic whenever one of them came down the driveway. The drivers were (understandably) unwilling to get out of the truck. The fact that they shunned us was rarely a problem, because we didn't order many things to be delivered, but be advised—some companies refuse to ship things to a P.O. Box.

If all is copacetic, remind to the company from which you're ordering something to deliver the package to your street address and bill the invoice to the P.O. Box. You'll get used to it.

Newspaper Delivery

I highly recommend taking the local newspaper in order to get to know your community. The newspaper of the nearest large city and *The New York Times* are probably also deliverable to your new house, but *The Times* may not arrive the day it was published. As with the mailbox, if you have a delivery box that's on the road, you will need to maintain access to it.

Locator Landmark

Make sure that your house number is well marked, with reflective numbers, at the top of your driveway. You want to make it as easy as possible for a fire truck, ambulance or delivery service to find you. Some people add a landmark, which can be easier to spot than house numbers, especially for friends who are visiting, and especially if they're arriving at night. What usually happens is something like: "Is that their driveway? It's…I can't tell yet…oh, @!!%?!, that was it." Turning around on a country road can be dangerous as well as inconvenient. Some people put giant, fancy gates over their driveways; some hang flags or whirligigs; others put some kind of sculpture there.

Chapter 5
Winter and Storm Preparedness

Note: This bit is directed at those buying property in areas of the United States that have snowy winters, but the parts about losing electricity are valid for everyone.

I'm guessing that you did not buy your farm in the middle of winter. You probably bought it in May, when the irises were in bloom, calves frolicked and birdsong filled the air. Chances are you did not even consider what your driveway would look like in December. Or January. Or February. Or March.

But, here it is, December. Three feet of snow fell over the weekend, and even your trusty rig is balking at making it up the driveway. Now, you can't:

- Get to your garage
- Exit the driveway
- Get your firewood into the house
- Get to your barn

And, oh! You forgot to go grocery shopping before the storm hit, and you're out of chicken feed as well.

So, let's back up and pretend it's still September. The first thing to do is assess your property and make a plan. If the composter is buried, what will you do with your kitchen scraps? How much feed do you need to store for your animals? How long is your driveway—could it be shoveled or will it need a plow? What will you do if a tree falls? What if your electricity goes out? If you have children, the need to be ready for winter intensifies.

Critical Systems

The first things to consider are the essential systems within your house: water, electricity and heat. In fall before a hard freeze, empty and turn off any water systems that are not in the house unless they are protected from freezing, including outdoor spigots and irrigation systems. So long as your home remains heated, there should be no problem, but follow the pipes and make sure none ventures through a wall into an unheated crawl space—if it does make sure it's wrapped with insulation and/ or heat tape (requires electricity).

Having a fireplace or woodstove makes a power outage a pleasant adventure rather than a crisis. You can even cook on it!

Losing electricity in this day and age is a big deal; merely having a couple of candles and a transistor radio on hand is not sufficient. First of all, if you diligently filled a freezer with garden produce and/or meat, your investment is in serious danger. Do not open freezers unless the power's been out for a couple of days—then it's time for emergency measures. If it's well below freezing, move your frozen goods outside to a place that is impenetrable to dogs, raccoons, and anything else that would love to share your bounty, until power is restored.

Secondly, if you have a well with an electric pump, guess what? You no longer have fresh water. If this is the case, store water ahead of time in large containers—you may need it for drinking as well as cleaning and flushing the toilet (though if you're desperate you could melt snow on the woodstove). Thirdly, no electric accessories on your wood stove, such as fans and a feeder mechanism on a pellet stove, will work. Fourthly, loss of power will interrupt your Internet connection and your land-line phone if it's cordless.

Generator

Many people avoid this issue by owning a generator, which turns propane, gasoline or diesel into electricity. This works well but can be loud and, well, uses a lot of propane, gasoline or diesel. Newer models are quieter and much more efficient. You could limit its use to an hour or two at a time to pump the well, keep the refrigerator cold and take care of necessities. A generator should never be run inside the house.

There are two kinds of generators: "portable" ones are smaller and have outlets into which you can plug appliances. They are used in primitive situations, like a building site that doesn't have electrical hook-up yet, and can be used in an emergency with an extension cord that runs into the house. A "fixed" generator is professionally installed into your home's electrical service, so it can take over if the grid is down. A fixed generator needs to be hooked it up properly, with a separate breaker, so that it doesn't energize parts of the power grid and endanger the poor linemen who are working overtime to restore power to your area (called "back feeding").

If you're serious about self-sufficiency, choose a fixed generator. You'll need to be aware of your typical usage, so you buy the right size for your household's needs. Propane and diesel are preferred to gasoline because of the shorter shelf-life of gasoline, and its propensity to "gum-up" an engine if it's not used regularly. In any case, make sure you change the spark plugs and run it every six months, hooked up to the electrical, so it stays in good working order for the day you actually need it. Never re-fuel a generator that has been running and has a hot engine, and always keep children away from it.

Getting Out

The next major consideration is access to the outside world—if you're more than a mile from town; cross-country skiing for groceries becomes pretty un-viable. Options for driveway maintenance include:

- Putting a plow on a pickup
- Buying a snow blower
- Putting a snow blower attachment on a tractor with a PTO
- Using a tractor with a plow or blade
- Hiring someone who already owns a plow

All of the vehicles mentioned above must be four-wheel-drive and usually also need traction chains. A hand-held snow blower is not good for gravel. A plow-for-hire should cost $20 to $75 per trip, depending on how long or tricky your driveway is, how much snow is involved, and its condition (dry snow is much easier to deal with than wet). Don't worry, you'll still be doing plenty of shoveling—from the house to the barn, to the garage, to the woodpile...

Chapter 6
Sustainable Power

The best green power is conservation. It's a good idea to explore conservation strategies before investing in green-energy infrastructure. As one friend put it: "You must
be prepared to basically own and operate a private energy company." None of the
following options, except passive solar, are "plug-and-play"—be prepared to manage and maintain the systems you install. So, start by decreasing your energy needs
and go from there.

At this point in time, very few farmhouses remain in their original state; most
have undergone remodeling. Therefore, it's easier to "corrupt" the original design in
order to take advantage of energy-efficient retrofits. If your home happens to be on
a registry of historic places, you'll have limits to what you can do.

Green power options are the same in the city as they are on the country. Rebates
exist on the local, state, regional and federal levels but are always changing—do your
homework so you can save as much money on installation as possible.

The easiest conservation efforts are to upgrade various parts of your home:
windows are expensive but also one of the biggest culprits in energy-inefficiency.
You can really geek out on glazing (glass)—depending on your climate, maybe you'll
use heat-rejecting glazing on the south-facing windows and high R-value glazing
on the east and north windows. New window technology also makes them easier to
clean; they just fold open into your hands!

Energy-efficient models of appliances like front-loading clothes-washers and
-dryers, freezers, refrigerators and dishwashers can save you money on heating
water and also use less water, putting less pressure on your septic or gray water system. And then there are the ever-popular compact-fluorescent (CF) light bulbs and
aerated showerheads. Make sure there is a recycling program in your area before you
buy a bunch of CFs; they contain mercury and should not be thrown in a landfill.
The least sexy but easiest and cheapest efforts are insulating the attic and floor above
a crawl space, and caulking cracks and joints.

One term you need to know: "R-value." This is a measurement of insulation power; the higher the number the better insulation is provided. Insulation
keeps homes warm in winter and cool in summer, minimizing the heating or air

conditioning bills. You may need less insulation (lower R-value) if you live in a moderate climate; check the local building codes.

Solar Hot Water

If you're ready for a more involved system, consider starting with a solar hot-water system. A sustainable-energy guy I know considers solar hot water to be the perfect green system for the novice—it's the cheapest to install and easiest to manage. These systems can either directly heat the water that you use for washing, or provide ambient heat to the house using hydronic tubing.

Considerations include whether you live in a climate that experiences freezing; whether the water in your area is "hard" (has lots of minerals dissolved in it) or "soft;" how much water your household uses; and whether you have direct sunlight on a south-facing rooftop.

If you live in an area that has no chance of freezing during the winter, you can install the simplest system, which drives water through a system of pipes that connect a heater unit on the roof and a storage tank in the house. They can also run straight into your hot water tap, which can be a scalding hazard when the water exceeds 105 degrees or so.

Areas that freeze use a closed system of tubes filled with propylene glycol (non-toxic antifreeze) or another liquid. The tubes extend onto the roof to heat the liquid and then pass through the water storage tank to heat it via a heat-exchanger.

Hot areas have the opposite problem—the fluid in the system can rise to temperature of 400 degrees! This can create air pockets of gases coming out of solution, and cause the antifreeze to break down. A "drainback" system can help by draining the panel when not in use. This system requires a larger pump and a separate tank for the antifreeze reservoir.

If you inherited an aging "draindown" system with a home you've purchased, you'll have to be diligent in freezing climates. These systems require manually draining the rooftop part of the system when a freeze is imminent.

Hard-water homes are better off with a closed-loop heat exchange or drainback system.

Solar Electricity

There are two ways to harvest electricity from the sun: using batteries for storage or connecting directly to existing electric utility lines ("grid-tie"). The latter allows you to sell excess electricity—your meter can actually run backwards on sunny days! If at the end of the year you have sold more electricity than you've purchased, you'll get a rebate from the utility company.

If your home isn't already tied into the power grid, it's probably not worth the expense of running the wires in. In this case, you store extra power in a bank of large batteries. Batteries have become safer than the original systems of the 1970s; they are sealed so they can't boil dry and explode. However, they still need to be stored in a fortified room or separate building that has ventilation.

Either way, you will collect this electricity using photovoltaic (PV) panels that are installed on a south-facing roof or on a stand somewhere on your land. The roof-top installation is far less expensive; its disadvantage is that your roof's pitch may not provide ideal solar-collection and it is stationery, so it collects less in the morning and afternoon. A stand can be adjusted to just the right angle; there are even stands that follow the sun from east to west, maximizing the panels' daily absorption rate.

Engineers have made great strides in the past decade on PV panel design. They are now much, much thinner than the original models—some are even shaped like, and installed like, regular asphalt shingles. Their maintenance has been reduced to almost nothing. The systems are expensive, though, even with every penny of incentive money you can find. At this point, you just plain have to want to do it (and have the $30,000 to spend).

Before committing to a system, you'll do a site review and also a system-load review. You'll be paying attention to output in terms of voltage and wattage, because there will be times during low-sun periods that you can't run the television, the dishwasher and the vacuum all at once. Make sure you include all the loads you don't usually consider, such as water pumps and the chest freezer in the basement, and any expectations for increased loads (for example, your kids may not require a lot of extra electricity now, but what about when they're teenagers, with laptops and cell phones and two showers per day?). Add on a little bit to account for "ghost loads," meaning all those green lights and time read-outs on your appliances. Things like modern televisions and computers also use electricity even when they're just sitting there, so that they turn on right away when you want them to (remember how the television used to have to "warm up?").

Water and Wind Turbines

These electricity generators require specific conditions in order to work well. Micro water generators use the power of gravity pulling water down a slope to generate electricity. Factors include a water source that has the proper slope or a waterfall that runs enough water year-round to power the generator, and possibly a water right and special permits. The system will need a bypass to accommodate high-flow periods, such as after a storm or during spring thaw.

Small wind turbines have been controversial for years. They do a fine job of generating electricity but can be loud, and deadly to birds and bats. More recent models are quieter and have bypass mechanisms for high-wind situations. One of the tricks of this kind of system is not having it so close to your house that it impinges on the aesthetic enjoyment of your grounds, but not so far away that you have to pay thousands to run the power to your house.

Passive Solar Heat

This great technology really works best on a new build, but bits of it can be incorporated into an existing house that is oriented toward the south. The basic premise is to harness the power of the sun without adding mechanical systems. You know how, on a hot summer afternoon, you draw the drapes on the west side of your house, and in the winter you open them wide? That's a simple passive-solar technique. Add some dark-colored tile or rock flooring, upright plastic tubes full of water as a heat-sink, and you're doing half the heating or cooling job, taking pressure off your furnace or other heat source.

Passive solar really works—so well, in fact, that you need a way to block the sun altogether during the summer. You could install blinds, a long overhang that blocks all but low-angle (winter) sun, or use plants. Friends of ours grew hops in front of their solar wall—the vines grew up during the spring and leafed out in the summer, just in time to diffuse the most intense sun. Then, they died in the fall and were cut down, revealing the entire wall during the winter months.

Geothermal Energy

Those with the good fortune to have on their property a spring that is heated by the molten core of the Earth may be in for more fun than just bathing in it under the moon—one could heat an entire house with it! Depending on the site and other factors, you may be able to run the water through pipes in the floor of your house. This is easier to do on a new build than a retrofit.

I once stayed at a hot springs resort that had, when they put in concrete walkways, lined them with tubes of hot water. Brilliant! There was snow on the grass, but the walkways were clear.

Another option is to install an open-loop heat pump, which uses the constant temperature of the underground to heat either the water or air in your home.

Chapter 7
Alternative Building Materials

Many of the world's inhabitants live in dwellings made of natural materials for an obvious reason—it's what they had to work with. Leaves, dirt, branches; nearly anything can provide at least a temporary shelter. Many natural-building techniques can stand up to modern tastes and building codes, and have enjoyed a rebirth, compliments of the environmental movement.

Earth-based buildings have thick walls that make them fantastically well insulated and sound-proof, as well as rodent- and insect-resistant. And fireproof—even straw bale walls are more fire-resistant than a stick-built home because of the lack of oxygen in the compressed bales.

While the building techniques listed below are best used in dry climates, there are dozens of exceptions—cob originated in rainy old England.

All structures need a level building site. Natural buildings are finished with earthen plaster, stucco or tile. This enhances durability and makes the walls less likely to rub off on you (especially nice if you've built a bench).

Be sure the home you plan to build is insurable (required if you want a mortgage), and get an estimate on cost.

Adobe

These structures are made of mud bricks that are dried in the sun; they've been used to construct some of the oldest buildings in the world. The most basic models are extremely inexpensive but do not hold up during seismic activity without additional reinforcement. Building codes are beginning to catch up with this ancient skill, creating more strict parameters about where and how adobe structures may be built.

Because the medium is bricks, adobe designs are at once organic and mathematical. The basic form is a box, but adobe craftspeople add arches, coves and patios that feature curved walls and swooping archways.

Straw Bale

I've never been on a straw-bale building site, but I imagine it must be somewhat like playing with giant LEGOs. Because of the thickness of the walls and the extra-long overhang, straw bale is impractical for small outbuildings and has special design considerations for large buildings (particularly with plumbing, heating and electrical systems).

Straw bale walls are so sturdy they sometimes carry a building's vertical load! These walls can support lots of built-in nooks and niches, which can be fun. Straw bale has been tested and found to perform well for seismic activity. In wet climates, buildings require a good foundation and roof overhang.

Cob

A finished cob structure is beautiful and slightly otherworldly—its sleek, earthen-colored organic forms can swirl in rounded archways and curved walls that other construction cannot imitate. Cob is somehow more friendly than concrete and—if done correctly—just as sturdy. Cob homes in England have stood for centuries.

Notice I wrote a "finished" cob structure. I know of more than one un-finished cob structure, usually because the people who started it didn't realize just how long it would take, and they ran out of materials or gumption.

If you are interested in cob, start small—maybe a bench or a short accent wall. And get your friends to help. Have a cob party! It's good, clean, dirty fun.

Cob is made of dirt, straw (which acts as a structural stabilizer, like rebar in concrete), and a little water to get everything going. If you were planning to dig a trench for a separate project, this would be a good opportunity to use that dirt. Otherwise, keep in mind that you either need to bring in dirt or make a big hole somewhere on your property. Ditto sand or clay—if your dirt is too sandy, you'll add clay, and vice versa.

The footing should be bordered in big rocks and then filled with little rocks and gravel. Even though it's weather-resistant, it will need a roof if you live in a rainy climate.

Make a pit somewhere, a place where you will mix the cob ingredients, not too far from your building site. Shovel out a few scoops of mud, about half as much sand, a few handfuls of straw that are broken into four- to six-inch pieces, a little water and—march! Stomp up and down on the pile with your feet to mix it. Bare feet work better than shod ones.

One way to expedite the process is to shovel everything onto a tarp that's about eight feet across, then fold the ends onto each other to get the initial mixing going. Or, use a tractor. But you're still going to need to get in there with your feet.

Once the mixture is a consistency like pie dough, take a big handful and kind of throw it back and forth from one hand to the other. Work it this way for a few minutes to make sure everything is mixed together, and then throw it into the structure. You cannot lay it into place; you must blend the different cobs into one monolith.

As your bench, wall or building takes shape, smooth the sides and check to make sure it's straight and level. No sense building a lumpy structure when an elegant one is within reach.

Rammed Earth

Ever build a sandcastle? This is yet another variation on the natural-building theme, with motorized tamping tools used to compress layers of soil, sand and sometimes a little Portland cement into a form, creating a kind of concrete. Rammed earth is the ultimate passive solar material—the 18- to 24-inch-thick walls of the entire home are a heat sink! It's great for areas with warm days and cool nights.

Chapter 8
Other "Green" Ideas

Composting Toilet

This appliance can be a lifesaver—a way to add a bathroom in a room or an outbuilding that is not connected to your septic system. A composting toilet can be as simple (and gross) as a bucket, with sawdust or lime to sprinkle over the "deposits," that is later dumped into an underground pit, or as complicated as an electric toilet that bakes the fecal matter into a safe, benign powder.

Because the electric models need a place to store the matter, they can be taller than a regular toilet and can make some noise when operating. Most people build a small platform around the base if the toilet didn't come with a small step for the front. Some have a small flushing action and some no flush at all.

Other models look like a regular toilet and flush the excrement to a storage tank located beneath the toilet (so they won't work for basements).

Composting toilets accelerate aerobic decomposition by heating and injecting oxygen into the pile. Some models can even accommodate extra kitchen scraps. Some are heated using solar power.

Gray Water System

A true gray water system is more complex than one would think. The basic premise of this system is: unlike the water that drains from your toilet (called "black water"), the water that exits kitchen and bathroom sinks (excluding garbage-disposal use), shower and laundry is dirty, but not contaminated. If one uses an environmentally friendly soap, this water can be recycled in the garden.

The thing with installing a gray water system is you pretty much have to do it under the radar—most county codes forbid them, even if engineered by a professional. But, by all means inquire where you live and see what their policy is. Our house had an unpermitted gray water system, and moreover it was not a good system.

Inspecting the land before buying our house, Mike and I found two two-inch pipes running out of the ground and into the swale, and assumed they were run-off from the gutters (When inspecting a potential house to purchase, never assume anything!). After we moved in, we realized that it wasn't the gutters draining into the swale; it was the kitchen and laundry.

Now, we didn't know much about gray water systems but we did know that they were supposed to be underground affairs. Also, we intended to plant crops where the sink water was pouring out. (Oh, yes—there were the bits of cheese I had just washed off our dinner plates.)

I went to the irrigation supply store and bought some perforated pipe, the ribbed, black plastic kind. I bought a six-foot length of four-inch pipe and some gravel. It was a nice, September day—a good day to be outside digging.

In order for this contraption to not stick quite so far into the garden, I needed to bring the length of the pipe up toward the house a bit. I dug up the entire pipe for ten feet, cut it with a hacksaw, dug a deep trench, dumped the gravel, laid the perforated pipe in the trench and around the cut-off pipe ends, tried to cover the pipe in gravel (it mostly slid off) and buried the whole shooting match.

Problem solved!…For about two months. The pipe filled with grease, soap and who-knows-what, and the drains backed up. I went back to the irrigation supply store, and this time asked for advice.

"You can't really have a gray water system like that," the guy said.

"I know," I said, "but that's what we have."

He shrugged and led me to what looked like a giant corn dog, which was perforated pipe wrapped in a mesh bag that was filled with Styrofoam pellets. "The Styrofoam helps to wick away the water," he said. "Make sure you dig a deeper hole."

I could tell he thought I was doomed, but we didn't have the money to have these pipes rerouted to the septic line. I shoved the giant corn dog into the bed of my pickup and bought more gravel.

Naturally, this November day was not sunny at all. In the cold rain, I dug until I found my perforated pipe, nasty and full of gunk. Dislodging it was a lot harder than installing it. Fetid water squirted out at all angles and soaked me. Then, I had to keep digging. And digging. I widened and deepened the trench. I poured in gravel, then carefully laid the giant Styrofoam contraption in the hole and begged it to last the winter. Being a cynic, I marked with bricks where the pipes ended and the corn dog began, in case I had to locate it again in January.

Luckily, we didn't. Not wanting to take a chance, we regularly poured a (purportedly nontoxic) chemical down the drains that broke down grease and soap scum, and that seemed to work. We just had to refrain from washing four loads of laundry in a row while also running the dishwasher.

But—back to a proper gray water system that has as its goal the watering of plants. The two things that are supposed to be addressed before the water filters into the watering system are temperature and grease. Your plants will not benefit from being steeped in 100-degree water. Nor can they process grease or excess soap.

Therefore, you need to "treat" your gray water before you send it off to your garden. There are numerous plans online, but here are the gray water basics:

- Never drink gray water nor wash produce with it.
- Never water lawns or gardens via sprinkler, nor use any other surface application.
- Use gray water on lawns and ornamental plants, not food-bearing plants.
- Run gray water through a holding tank and a sand filter before pumping it into a planter or landscaping.

Rainwater Catchment

In my mother's house in a small town in Wisconsin, there was a cistern in the basement in which, she and her sisters believed, lived monsters. Theirs was a concrete tank, but everything from a toilet tank to a covered reservoir constitutes a cistern.

Household cisterns fell out of favor in the middle of the twentieth century in the United States, when everyone was busy modernizing everything. But—terrorizing small children aside—cisterns make a lot of sense, whether you're collecting the precious dew on a desert morning in Arizona or storing ten gallons per hour during a downpour in the Pacific Northwest. They take water that would otherwise be "wasted" by soaking into the ground, and decrease the pressure on municipal potable-water processors. When you think about it, it's really unnecessary to wash in, flush toilets or water plants with treated, potable water.

A non-potable rainwater-catchment system is fairly straightforward: Water falls from the sky onto a roof or other surface and flows via a series of gutters and pipes into a storage unit, where it stays until you open a valve on the storage unit and drain it. The only complications are debris and algae.

Leaves, twigs, bird droppings and the like are also going to wash off a roof, and you don't want them clogging your system. The best way to avoid debris is to, first of all, not set up your system under a tree and secondly build a "roof washer" feature into your design. This diverts the first ten or so gallons of water, so that most of whatever washed off the roof doesn't go into your storage.

If you never cleaned out your cistern it would eventually grow algae, so you must periodically empty and sterilize it with bleach. The tank must have an overflow mechanism and a cover to keep out impurities and minimize evaporation. If you intend to irrigate, keep in mind that the cistern must be lower than the collection plane but higher than the area you want to water (unless you want to incorporate a pump).

Water collected in a cistern can be made potable, but in addition to everything else it must be treated for bacteria and filtered. There are companies that offer such systems.

Insulation

People have gotten creative with insulation in the past couple of years, using everything from wool scraps from a local mill to shredded blue jeans. As someone who sat on a bale of fiberglass insulation as a five-year-old wearing shorts and sandals, I salute them. Typical applications include:

- **Blanket/Batt:** These are formed to fit between joists but must be hand-cut anywhere there is an unusual space. Any un-insulated space creates a virtual wind tunnel of cold air, so you have to be thorough.
- **Spray:** Spray insulation can fill in nooks and crannies that would be hard to get with rolls of batt insulation. Some are foams, which harden, and some are cellulose bits, which remain loose. This method is preferred in retrofits and upgrades, as it can be blown into existing walls through small holes.
- **Board:** These are rigid sheets of foam with varying R-values. They are useful against exterior walls and under floors.

Don't just insulate your attic and walls. If you can, dig away from your foundation and attach "blue board" insulation. This may require some excavation and re-planting of vegetation around the house. Some people put "quilts" over their windows during the winter, or use the disposable plastic film you can get in hardware stores. I am not usually a name-brand stickler, but if you use the plastic film buy the 3M kind, not the store brand. It's worth the extra money in its superior sticking to the window, becoming perfectly clear upon heating, and coming off in the spring without taking your sill paint with it.

When choosing your insulation, keep in mind the depth of the space for it—compressed insulation loses its R-value.

Insulated concrete forms (ICFs) are gaining attention as a foundation material for new builds and additions. Styrofoam replaces the traditional wood forms used to hold the concrete into a wall before it hardens, and is then left in place, as it becomes a part of the wall itself. These walls are better insulated than a traditional concrete wall. You have to be *really* sure of where the floor joists, etc., are going, as they need to be added at the time of the pour.

Clothesline

Hanging the laundry is one of those ridiculously simple economies that used to be ubiquitous and has now virtually disappeared from the United States. No one questions buying an enormous machine and paying for gas or electricity to cook plastic sheets laced with toxic chemicals into their clothing, when there is fresh air right outside! While the invention of the washing machine saved people hours of hard labor in front of a steaming washtub, a dryer saves virtually no time or effort at all.

Which isn't to say that I don't own one. An outdoor clothesline is only practical for part of the year, and I still use the dryer to dry socks, towels and jeans. My Carhartts are stiff and uncomfortable enough without allowing them to harden into cardboard. And while I enjoy the time I spend pinning larger items to a line, I'm not about to hang dozens of socks individually.

There are a number of forms a clothesline can take: one is shaped like an umbrella or spider web, depending on how you look at it, mounted on a center pole. There is the dual T-pole configuration, with lines extending between them. We inherited with our house what I consider a superior product: a set of pulleys on which is laced a single loop. One loop was attached to a post next to my deck, the other out in the yard. I brought a basket out, plopped it on a bench and never had to move—I just hung something and then pushed it away. And nothing was on top of something else.

On a windy day, thin things, like sheets, and any type of "performance outdoor" clothing (made of high-tech polyester) can dry in twenty minutes. If it is hot as well, you can almost watch the water evaporate. And the smell! No chemist can replicate the fragrance of freshly dried clothes on a line. Especially if it rains a little while they're out there. It's simply…fresh.

When hanging, make sure to jam the clothespin all the way down, or else the edges of things that you carefully separated will slide together, and you'll come out to find the shirts and pillowcases have dried into smashed-up wads. No one said I wanted to revive ironing.

I've heard people talk about drying their laundry in freezing weather, which has made no sense to me—how would the water evaporate if it's frozen? But it does evaporate (think of neglected ice cubes in your freezer shrinking over time). My grandma says that her mother would hang things outside for a while and then finish them off in the house. I doubt I will ever try this, but Grandma swears that freeze-dried sheets smell even better than rain-dried sheets.

For delicates, woolens and inclement weather (if your household is small), I recommend one of those wooden rack-type dryers. They can fold up out of the way if needed, but unfolded really don't take up much room and can hold quite a bit… not everything but certainly all the wool and high-tech sweaters, shirts and socks. Another option is to string lines across a little-used room.

The best money I've ever spent on a clothes-dryer was actually for a washing machine—a fancy pants front-loading washing machine that spun like a jet engine so the clothes came out half-dry. Not to mention that it used way less water and soap than a conventional top-loader.

Chapter 9
Outbuildings

Any outbuildings that are already in existence can stay where they are. If you add a building, you'll need to check into the permitting process. Where we lived, buildings were all supposed to be forty-three feet or more from each other, I think for fire-abatement concerns, and one hundred feet from any property line, and not an additional living quarters. Once a permit is issued, you have to maintain progress on your project—if the permit lapses it becomes null and void, or costs you extra fees.

But ask around: the enforcement of permitting may be somewhat lax in your area. Our county was notorious for it, to the point that we saw people building new homes just a few feet from creeks, and no one who could do anything about it seemed to care.

I'm not advocating that you break laws, of course. It's sort of a "when in Rome" principle. A friend was remodeling her home and—having previously remodeled homes in the city, where the permitting was fastidious and unforgiving—called the inspector at every juncture so he could approve her work. He came over a few times and, once he saw that she knew what she was doing, said, "Look, just call me when all the wiring is in, okay?"

No inspections may be necessary at all; outbuildings are generally not adherent to the same Uniform Building Code as domiciles. If you have a good building site and are on a budget or just don't want the hassle, there are many pre-fabricated options:

- **Yurt:** This is a temporary or semi-permanent structure, native to Mongolia, that has a round, lightweight frame and canvas walls. More stable versions of the design, using wood and other sturdy materials, are also built. There are many manufacturers of yurt kits in the United States.
- **Pre-Fabricated Kits:** Creating low-cost, portable, sustainable modular housing units is a hot international topic. Dozens of architects and designers are throwing amazing designs into the world—the only limits are budget and imagination.
- **Metal Shed:** Standard American fare—the ten-by-ten metal shed with an access door on the front. Larger sizes are available. Some come in very small pieces, which can be extremely frustrating to assemble.

- **Greenhouse:** This can be a lean-to or self-standing building that has glass or plastic walls that let maximum sunlight in, and keep heat and moisture in, to nurture plants. If it is attached to the south side of an existing building, make sure that building is equipped with a heavy-duty vapor barrier. Either way, it should also have a few temperature-controlled vents and a floor that can deal with dirt and spilled water—either a dirt floor, or a brick or tiled floor that rests on gravel and/or has a French drain.
- **Pole Barn:** These are also kits of nearly every size and description; anything from a freestanding carport to a fancy horse arena can be a pole barn. They consist of a roof supported by posts; the exterior and interior walls and finished floor are optional. You may need to hire a crane to get the posts set and the beams placed. Pole barn kits can include many, many accessories—cupolas, sunroof panels, wainscoting, barn doors, sliding doors, garage-type doors, "man" doors. They are generally roofed and sided with galvanized sheet metal, but other options exist.

Whatever building you end up with, make sure that you give it a solid foundation on a graded, level building site. Find out what precautions you need to make regarding the soil type. Does the ground freeze solid during the winter? Is it excessively rocky? Is it swampy? These conditions will affect what kind of foundation you'll lay.

Other considerations include running plumbing to the building (at least a clean-up sink), and electricity—do you need 110 current or 220 (if you'll use large-load appliances or tools)? Those in Northern climes should be sure the roof is rated to handle the area's average snow load. Will you insulate? Unadulterated pole barns are frigid in cold weather and stifling in hot weather; insulation can help.

Section Three
Animals

Animals

Having animals on a farm is a given. But before you start buying two of everything, make sure you're ready for the responsibility. Animals limit your time away from home and, once you graduate from pets to livestock, pretty much eliminate your ability to travel. It's the special (or expensive) housesitter who can take on the chores and feeding schedules of a farm.

As you consider bringing animals (or anything else, for that matter) to your farm, think it through. Don't just plan how you'll "use" an animal now—think about how you will fix it when it's broken, and how you will dispose of it at the end of its life. Additionally, animals are living creatures; you need to have a plan for them and be able to implement that plan. Look beyond the romance of acquisition.

Consider the following for every animal you own:

- **Raising**
- **Feeding and watering**
- **Housing and fencing**
- **Maintenance and grooming**
- **Protection from predators**
- **Troubleshooting and treating disease and injury**
- **Harvesting product/s**
- **Managing waste**
- **Slaughtering/euthanizing**

Because livestock is a centuries-old topic, this section does not go into fine detail for every animal. You will need to supplement the information here with other sources. This means more books, the Internet and—most importantly—talking to other people. I advise finding people who have the animals you think you want to have, and asking them lots of questions while they show you how their operations work. You can also hire out some tasks at first, so you can see them done; the first time I dressed a bird I had three books open on the counter and still felt unsure of what I was doing. Farm duties are so foreign to urban life that you are much better off to watch someone, who knows what they're doing, do it.

There is plenty of information about raising animals—remember that most of it is about raising animals *for profit*. I never fooled myself into believing that we were saving any money by raising ten chickens and eating their eggs. When one of my chickens went broody (stopped laying in order to sit on the nest), I let her. During the winter, when chickens naturally stop laying unless you create artificial daylight by using light bulbs, I stopped eating eggs. Or—*shudder*—I bought some at the grocery store. Our chickens were much more akin to pets than to livestock; a real farmer would have rolled her eyes at the lack of cost-effectiveness, but we were okay with that.

Very few farm animals live long enough to experience a natural death. If you expect to keep animals, you pretty much have to be resigned to deal with death. Moreover, causing death. A friend of mine had very old chickens, and one day she noticed that one of them was dragging something behind her as she walked. The hen's uterus had prolapsed. She already had one foot in the grave; cutting her throat was a merciful act. City folks leave it up to the vet to put an animal down. In the country, the vet is not always available; it may not be practical or possible to transport an animal that's in pain; most people would not take a chicken to the veterinarian's office to be euthanized.

I ended up finishing off some of the sparrows that my cat had tortured and then left for dead after he tired of the game. I tried not to interfere too much with the so-called Circle of Life, but sometimes those poor, mangled souls deserved to find their eternal reward a little sooner than scheduled.

And, as you'll find in the Food Section, you might even resign yourself to murder in order to defend your crops.

One other thing: You might occasionally come across some livestock in a field that *look* dead but are just relaxing. Though horses and other animals are always shown standing in photographs and movies, they sometimes do lie on the ground. Horses even roll around on their backs, just like dogs, simply because it feels good.

Chapter 10
Pets

What constitutes a "pet" on a farm basically comes down to whether you plan to work with it, eat it or just have it around. A lot of ranchers keep a bunch of cow dogs as well as some kind of terrier or lab—the working dogs are never allowed in the house but the pet dog is.

I have met rural kids who've kept as pets traditional livestock, as well as what would normally be considered a wild animal: wolf-dog hybrids, crows, skunks, antelope and deer. Country kids sometimes acquire a wild pet when an adult shoots its mother; this is how a girl I know acquired and raised a baby badger, of all things. (It is, incidentally, illegal in many states to raise a wild animal without a permit.) Or, they get the runt of the litter, as has been immortalized in the children's book *Charlotte's Web.*

Exception: Every horse owner has a pet except someone who rides to manage a cattle herd, or to compete in dressage or rodeo events. You could argue that a horse-breeding operation would fit under this category. Regardless, pet horses and working horses receive basically the same care.

No matter how much you love animals, you have to agree that veterinary care for cats and dogs has gotten a little out of control in the urban United States. Health insurance, acupuncture, surgery, tooth-brushing, naturopathic vets…pet care has become big business. If those things seem normal to you, it may be a bit of a shock to bring your pet to the country. Mike was once visiting a cattle operation; he and the rancher came across one of his dogs, which had gotten hung up in some barbed wire and had a long, nasty laceration on his back. The farmer stapled up the dog's skin and threw him in the back of the pickup; he got the rest of the day off. Problem solved.

None of this is to say that country people don't love their animals. On the contrary. But, they have a different kind of love for them, less of a "this is one of my children" kind of love, and more of a loyalty and deep respect for the work that they do together, tempered by the understanding that animals are not people—they don't experience pain the same way people do, and aren't afraid of death in the same way that we are.

Cat

If you have a cat that spends any time outside, the best advice is "don't get attached." While cats are predators that eat mice, rats, gophers, rabbits (especially babies), lizards, snakes and birds, they are also prey. Coyotes, mountain lions and owls will happily scoop up your kitty for a meal. A bigger, tougher, feral cat might challenge your cat for its territory. One friend had rats in her barn so big they ate kittens, and even killed one of her cats! And many cats end up as road kill.

While your cat is capable of feeding itself, putting out some kibble will ensure that it considers your farm home base. If the cat is not allowed in the house, put the food in a sheltered place inaccessible by other beasts, especially raccoons. We mounted a series of small platforms inside and outside our barn, which gave the cat a way to get in a high window and have a place to stay out of the elements.

Cats rarely have ticks on them because they can reach nearly every part of their body to bite them off. If your cat does get one (usually on her head), and she will let you, pick it off the same as you would on a dog. There are tick repellant chemicals for cats, but I didn't use them because ticks were not a big problem for our cat, and because cats are better at being able to lick hard-to-reach spots; I didn't want him eating the chemicals.

Cats are generally more self-reliant than dogs, but they are more likely to be eaten and more likely to simply disappear for days at a time.

Dog

First things first: People in the country do not go chasing after their dogs with plastic bags in their hands, waiting to "clean up" after them. If your dog does his business, it is usually left there unless it's on a walkway. Country dogs generally have the sense to poop in a field or other out-of-the-way place.

If for some reason you have a small dog in the country, see the part in the Cats section about predators (read: Keep them in at night).

Country dogs ride in the backs of pick-up trucks. A friend told me that she was leaving the grocery store one day, and as she was about to get into her pickup a young man (clearly a tourist) ran up to her and scolded her for endangering her dog, which was wagging its tail in the bed of the pickup. She managed to remain civil, but was irate.

"Who does he think he is?!" she sputtered to me on the phone.

Don't let this be you. I know it's not "safe" to have one's dog in the back of a pickup. That isn't the issue. You don't have to transport your dog that way, but don't tell other people what to do.

Protective Dog

Dogs aren't socialized the same way in the country as they are in the city; a dog typically has one family to which it is loyal, and little additional socializing. People rarely bring their dogs to other people's homes, as it will often result in a fight. Or, the dog will be in the back of the pickup and it will stay there during the visit. If you bring your dog to someone else's house, do not let it out of your vehicle until you've asked permission, so they can secure the chicken coop, turn on the electric fences, and whatever other dog-proofing they need to do.

The dog's job is to watch the property; it is to some degree the transference of human values to think that a dog doesn't enjoy this role or is bored. While many people bring their dogs hiking or cross-country skiing, others don't because it's a sensitive area or a sensitive time of year for wildlife, or because the people want to increase their chances of viewing wildlife, which is unlikely when a dog is part of the hiking party.

Most country dogs are not fenced or tethered, and will race up to their property line if you're walking by. This can sometimes be dangerous if you're jogging or riding a bicycle, as a dog might interpret this as running away, in which case its natural reaction is to stop you, and its only means of doing that is to use its mouth.

If you're accosted by a dog, stop and face it. If you have a bicycle, dismount on the side opposite the dog. Put your hand out, palm up, at his nose level so he can sniff you. Depending on how he reacts (growling, tail wagging, tail tucked under legs) you can consider trying to pet him. True working farm dogs should not be petted in this situation; just calmly go on your way. Walk slightly sideways so you're not turning your back on the dog but also not challenging it. If the dog seems menacing or persistent, yelling "No!" or "Go home!" is usually effective. Pointing in the air may also be a familiar command (pointing toward home).

When a dog is in the back of a pickup, it becomes the dog's "property," meaning it will defend it in a similar manner as it would its land. Do not approach a dog that is in a parked pickup, no matter how friendly it looks. As soon as you extend your hand toward it, you are compromising its perimeter—its demeanor may change abruptly.

The dog might even leap out of the truck bed, especially if the gate is down, to defend its property. If that happens, do the same as when a dog accosts you on a country road. Back away slowly.

Wandering Dog

As you meet your neighbors, you'll also meet their dogs. If you notice a dog on your property that isn't yours and recognize it, try the following:

- Go outside and yell "Go home!" at the dog. Most dogs are just on a walkabout and will return on their own.
- Phone the owners and let them know, so they can come and get it.
- Go out and call the dog, secure it if that is safe to do and then phone the owners.
- Pretend you didn't see it and go on with your day.

I say that last thing because if you do decide to engage with the situation, you could waste an hour of your time. When I was working at home during the day, I'd sometimes give myself a hall pass, reasoning, "If I were in an office in town, I wouldn't even know this was happening." Do not go out and give the dog food or otherwise reward it for coming over, especially if it had to cross a road or otherwise endanger itself to visit you.

If you have livestock and find a strange dog on your land, you have a legitimate complaint. Dogs that harass livestock on others' land may be shot. You probably don't want to take such drastic action, but it's fair to talk to the dog's owner and let him/her know that you can't have that kind of thing happening on a regular basis.

Conversely, don't let your dog wander around. If you live near temptations like a roadway (road kill is hard for any self-respecting dog to resist, which might result in your dog becoming road kill as well) or open water, or if your dog just wants to check things out, you must create a physical barrier like a fence, kennel or tether. There is a product called an "invisible fence" that keeps animals in by means of a rather convincing electrical shock administered via a special collar. The boundary is determined by burying transponders at the edges of your property. All but the most determined (or stupid) dogs can be contained with this device. Keep in mind that an invisible fence keeps your dog in but does nothing to keep other animals out.

Country Dog Fun

In the city, dogs can get in plenty of trouble—eating garbage, rolling in poop, digging holes, chasing cats and getting into fights with raccoons or other dogs. In the country, there is even more fun to be had!

Skunk

If your dog gets into an altercation with a skunk, the most common ways to try and neutralize the smell are tomato juice and peppermint soap. There are also commercially produced shampoos and lots of country recipes that people swear by. But really, nothing helps except time. If your dog was hit point-blank, he may vomit and be temporarily blinded, so you may need to rinse out his eyes and give him lots of water to drink. Make a nice bed for him—outside.

Porcupine

This is a real bummer. If your dog frightens a porcupine, either you or a veterinarian are going to have to pull the quills out. If there are just a few of them in the dog's leg or something, you can try to get them out yourself with a pair of pliers.

If it's anything other than that, I recommend going straight to the vet, especially if there are quills in the dog's mouth. Porcupine quills are rigid, but dog saliva breaks them down, so the longer you wait, the more the quills become slimy goo-sticks that are difficult to get a hold of. And a baby porcupine's quills are flexible and only an inch long, making them difficult to extract intact.

A veterinarian will give your dog a general anesthesia, and possibly a sedative, to minimize the trauma of having the quills ripped out. She will give you prescriptions of antibiotics and possibly anti-swelling medication; when the dog revives the affected area will swell up and be extremely sore.

If a few of the barbs break off and remain in the dog, just keep an eye on them; they will fester and eventually work themselves out, like a sliver.

There are two types of dogs: One learns from the experience and never goes near a porcupine again, and one develops a vendetta. I spoke with a veterinarian who had seen the same pair of boxers six times in a two-year period. They simply could not concede defeat. One got a quill through its ankle, which permanently lamed him, but it only fueled his mania to get that damned porcupine.

Fights

Some dogs will fight with just about anything, and they don't always win. Badgers and raccoons have sharp claws and teeth, and wild animals rarely back down. If you witness a fight, your inclination might be to try to break it up with your arms or legs. Don't. Keep your body away from the fight, or you may end up more injured than your dog. If you have access to a water hose, try to break up the fight that way, or throw something at them, or make a loud noise.

Lots of dogs get into a fight because they think (wrongly or rightly) they're protecting you. One friend lost a dog to a rattlesnake this way...but wasn't bitten herself.

If your dog gets shredded in a fight, there are two considerations: repairing the damage and fighting infection. The most thorough way to treat your dog is to take him in to the vet, but if you can't for whatever reason, try home treatment. Most country vets will offer telephone consultation, but that only works during the day unless they have an after-hours service. Some vets sell "over-the-counter" medicines, including antibiotics, and bandaging.

Carcasses

One autumn, our dog kept disappearing after sundown and returning about an hour later. We didn't even realize it at first, but after a couple of nights of letting her outside and then having to call for her rather than her simply reappearing on the back deck, we knew something was up.

We also noticed that when she finally came to our call, she looked really happy, like she'd gotten away with something. After she returned, she would collapse on her side on the living room rug, bloated, panting and emitting the worst gas I've ever known—and she was not normally prone to such disgraces. Something *was* up.

"I wonder if there's a carcass in the far field," said Mike. I looked at the dog. *Pant, pant, floof.* Hm.

The next day, we went out and sure enough, a deer had been hit on the highway and stumbled to its death in an adjoining field. Its abdomen was wide open. It had been there a while.

Our dog was nine at that point and had learned some things, one of which was that if she rubbed her face in a carcass, which she found exquisite debauchery, we would notice it right away and ruin everything by bathing her with peppermint-smelling soap. So, being a smart dog, she rubbed the rotting flesh of this particular deer on her interior instead of her exterior.

In the country, your dog is going to get into things. Try to keep her out of the rat poison and the chicken coop.

Ticks

Ticks love hairy mammals; they crawl up between the hairs and suck away unnoticed. Except for the species that carries Lyme Disease, ticks are more of an aesthetic affront than a threat. But it is an affront—ticks release an anti-coagulant to expedite the drinking of enough blood to make their bodies expand exponentially. It's gross to be petting an animal and run your fingers over a rubbery appendage that doesn't belong there. An engorged tick is repulsive yet comical—it's like a giant gray Tic Tac with tiny black legs sticking out of one end. It can hardly walk, and if you throw it into the toilet at this stage it sinks straight to the bottom.

I have heard numerous strategies to remove a feeding tick over the years, many of which involve matches, which I do not endorse. The main idea is to get the head to come out, because if it stays embedded it usually gets infected. However, I've yet to discover a way to approach a cat with a hot match. Sometimes I've found a tick, and if I moved I would lose the tick's location under all the hair, so I just grab it as close to the skin as possible and rip it off with a little snap of the wrist. I have left many a tick head in my animals and all that happens is there is an inflamed lump for a week or so; no permanent damage that I can tell.

I also own a tick-extracting implement, which again is worthless on a cat but works well on a dog that is trained to sit still when you want her to. It's a simple metal wafer that has two prongs on one end; the prongs are wider at the end and narrow toward the base, so you slide it on either side of the tick's head and it leverages the thing right out. I think I got it at a hardware store for a couple bucks. I've also heard of one called a "Tick Twister."

It's impossible to crush a tick between your fingers; their little exoskeletons work! Mike had a technique whereby he plucked off the tick's tiny head between the tip of his forefinger and his thumbnail. I dropped them in the toilet and covered them with a couple squares of toilet paper—they often float on the surface, and I wanted to make sure they didn't somehow swim to shore (flushing seemed to me a waste of water). Another friend crushes them with the edge of a glass against the countertop. There is some debate about what to do with a deer tick because of Lyme Disease—some argue that these methods could release the toxin. Their advice: Entrap them in tape and throw them away.

When I lived in Portland, I never would have dreamed of putting one of those expensive, toxic insecticides on my dog. We took her to a naturopathic veterinarian, for crying out loud. But, I had never picked ten ticks off my dog in one sitting. Or eighteen ticks. Or twenty-three. Seven were in her ears. Need I add that if there are a dozen ticks on your dog, a few will find their way onto you as well. Especially if she sleeps on your bed…

Friends who live in New York, where Lyme Disease is rampant, got their dog vaccinated for the disease, figuring it couldn't hurt.

Mowing paths through your fields will help immensely. Bonus: Mowing also keeps seeds from your dog's pelt. Our first year on the farm, we had tarweed and numerous grass species. The dog ran through the field; the tarweed made her coat sticky and then the seeds stuck to it. She came back looking like some second-grader's handicraft.

We mowed paths, rather than the entire field, in order to maintain habitat for small animals like snakes, rabbits, lizards, quail and other birds. To mow the entire field would simply create millions of four-inch spikes, which cut the dog's paws and aren't comfortable to lie down in—it's no urban soccer field of soft, green grass.

Chapter 11
Livestock

The information I give about livestock is intended for small herds raised for personal use, or just a little extra to trade or sell. Large-scale operations are another matter that requires much study—in fact, many young ranchers and farmers go to college after a lifetime of observing their parents and grandparents. Just as I emphasize organic gardening in this book, so I support "organic" farming and ranching.

The main factors that set apart organic farming and ranching are:

- Animals graze on organically grown pastures and feeds.
- Animals are not given antibiotics on a regular basis.
- Animals are not kept indoors or in confined conditions. (If they are in a barn, they have adequate room and are not kept there at all times.)
- Animals are not physically altered. (This includes tail docking of sheep, beak clipping of chickens and de-horning of cattle, but does not include castration—see "Males" below.)
- Animals are slaughtered on an individual basis.

It is possible to administer the occasional non-organic antibiotics from time to time and maintain an organic operation. The afflicted animal is tagged and sequestered from the rest of the flock. There is a waiting period before it can be reintroduced.

Organically raised or not, I recommend exhaustive research about any animal you plan to raise. This is not like a sweater, which you can return to the store if it "doesn't work out." That said, most animals are not around very long on a farm, so be acquainted with how to slaughter and dispose of an animal when the time comes. Most likely you'll hire it done, at least the first few times.

I also support raising heritage breeds, which are breeds of livestock that can be traced back centuries, mostly to Europe. Because these breeds did not become the selected breeds for the Unites States' mass-production ranching machine, they are dying out. Some of the breeds are smaller than standard breeds, making them more manageable—a good choice for the beginning farmer.

Just like wild animals, each farm animal has evolved to increase its chances of survival. Farm animals are complicated, however, by having been coaxed in certain directions by humans. The result is that they have evolved to survive and to do things that benefit humans, such as grow quickly or lay an egg every day. In order to understand each animal, it's worthwhile to consider its ancestors and its evolution. For example, grazing animals' basic intelligence is being alert for predators. They have rectangular pupils that increase their peripheral depth perception; their bodies are built to accommodate sudden evasive movement, especially movement toward them. Knowing this can give you compassion for a horse that spooks—you'll understand it has a heightened sense of danger and work with that animal to feel more confident with his surroundings.

General Maintenance

For any animal you keep you should own or have unlimited access to a means of transporting it, whether to a veterinarian or a slaughterhouse. This means a kennel for smaller animals and a trailer for bigger ones. I have heard of quite a few people who use minivans to haul medium-sized animals like sheep and donkeys. I don't recommend this, but it is easier and cheaper than using a trailer. For safety's sake, install some kind of barrier to keep the animals from interfering with the driver, and some kind of liner to facilitate clean-up. Some people hire themselves out as animal "taxis."

Hoofed animals require foot care. One of the saddest things I've ever seen was a neglected old goat whose hooves were so overgrown that they curled around themselves in three directions like fancy elf slippers. The poor creature could hardly walk. Horses, alpacas and llamas are curried (brushed). The udders of milked cows and goats are rubbed down to protect them from cracking and becoming infected.

In order to perform these tasks, you need to train your animals to hold still. The best way to train any animal is by rewarding good behavior and correcting, but not punishing, bad behavior. Beating an animal simply makes it afraid of you—the goal is to make it want to do your bidding. Treats grease the skids.

Check your fields for potentially poisonous plants, like water hemlock and noxious plants, or hazardous ones like cheatgrass (See "Noxious Plants" in the Land Section). The original owner of our house planted rhododendrons all around it. A subsequent owner had goats. The goats nibbled on the rhodies and died. When we bought the house, there were no rhododendrons.

Fencing

Note: Fencing is considered in more detail in the Land Section.

Fencing serves two purposes: to keep animals in a certain area, and to keep predators out of a certain area. Animals are motivated by few things, two of which are eating and mating. If they see greener grass, either literally or figuratively, on the other side of the fence, they will do anything in their power to get to it.

Different species (and individuals) have different levels of determination in this regard. Horses and llamas will generally respect a regular old four-foot fence. Sheep will, too, provided their pasture is sufficient. Cattle need a little more encouragement, in the form of an additional strand of electrical or barbed wire. Even then, you may have an animal that ignores the jolts or pricks, and presses on your fence until she pushes it over. Sheep will sometimes require wire as well, though that may be ineffective because a sheep can't get zapped through its wool; it only works if the sheep touches it with its nose. Pigs can be kept in a pretty rickety pen if the perimeter is lined with a strand of electrical wire about six inches from the ground.

Goats are a whole 'nother story: They are curious, first and foremost, and playful, and willful. This makes them master escape artists. They can jump over or crawl under nearly anything. A sturdy four-foot fence, fortified at the bottom, is fine so long as there is nothing inside the goat pen that's close enough to use as a launching pad. Because they will.

Personality

If you've observed over time any kind of animal, even a turtle, you will notice that it has unique characteristics. The more evolved the creature, the more complex its "personality." Farm animals are no different—years of intensive breeding haven't eliminated this fact. Even cloned animals have different characteristics.

As the steward of these animals, you will start to pick up on your animals' idiosyncrasies. And their voices. All horses whinny, but each has its own sound. I could even tell the difference between my chickens' eggs. I had chickens that laid in two colors, granted, but even so: Sylvia's were more round than Francesca's; Baby Chicken's were darker brown with spots; Natasha's were a mint green while Josefina's were khaki.

Training

All sentient beings have wills, and even the "dumbest" farm animal is no exception. So, you have to train them to do what you want them to do and to ignore, at least momentarily, what they want to do. The most successful means of training animals is bribing them with treats. Pigs love marshmallows, licorice and other sweets; chickens wheat and corn; horses apples, sugar cubes and carrots. All grazers love alfalfa.

The basic things to teach an animal are to go somewhere (a stall, a stanchion, a trailer) on command and to let you touch it. I trained my chickens to come when I shook a glass jar that had "scratch" (cracked corn and wheat berries) in it. The scratch jingled merrily against the tin lid of the jar and those ladies came running, sometimes even wiping out around a corner they were in such a hurry. This training came in handy if Mike and I were leaving in the afternoon and wouldn't return until after dark; that way I didn't have to fumble around in the dark to latch the gate when I returned. The chickens enjoyed roaming but were definitely more vulnerable then; a few times I hastily gathered them into their pen because the neighbors' semi-feral dogs had decided to come over for a visit.

The most training is done with a horse, which is taught to be ridden, sometimes to pull a cart, and to allow important maintenance to be done on them, such as having its feet cleaned.

Handling/Safety

Any farm animal needs to be handled regularly so it is used to human interaction. There is more about the specifics of each species further on in this section; the main thing about being around animals is confidence. That doesn't mean racing toward an animal—that will spook it. But don't be spooked yourself. This may take time—many farm animals are bigger than you, which can be a little intimidating.

If you are at someone else's farm, do not enter a pen with animals unless you've gotten some input from, or are accompanied by, the animals' owners. Before you get your own animals, particularly a horse, meet some horses and their owners and ask lots of questions.

Approach an animal quietly and gently, but firmly. Always approach the front of the animal; to approach from behind may result in being kicked. It's okay, advisable even, to talk to it. Even if it doesn't know what you're saying, it can read your temperament and emotional state from your voice. You can blow softly into a horse's nostrils so she can get your scent (other animals don't appreciate this). Pet her neck; once she's used to you, you can scratch her ears, pet her nose, etc.

Keep in mind that being conscientious does not guarantee that the animal won't, as my friend Nancy puts it, "knock the stuffins out of you anyway." Animals can be gentle and animals can be brats. Some are even assholes. They have good moods and bad moods. As you get to know your animals you'll know what behaviors to expect from each. (And, if an animal is acting strangely, there's usually a reason, such as illness or a predator nearby.)

If you're performing maintenance on an animal or saddling it, move smoothly but confidently, always being alert for kicking, pulling or other resistance that might endanger either of you. Start your hand on its neck or back and run it down below, rather than reaching straight for its belly. Keep a hand on the animal so it knows you're down there, and keep a hand on her rump if you must pass behind her. Avoid caging yourself between the animal and a wall, fence or gate. When cinching a saddle or pack, be sure you're not pulling the creature's hair or pinching its skin.

When leading an animal on a rope, hold the rope near your hips rather than your shoulder. Never wrap the rope around your hand; fold in four-inch lengths, flat, and hold it that way. Animals can spook and yank at any time; don't put yourself in a position to be injured. If an animal has really lost it, let go of the rope entirely and get out of the way. No need to lose an appendage or be dragged around the corral.

Feeding

To some degree, domesticated animals can feed themselves, like wild animals do. However, the growth and nutritional demands that we put on some of them—for example, steers would not weigh a half-ton in sixteen months under normal circumstances—require more and better food than can be found on the ground. The supplemental nutrition requirements of each animal are listed further in this section, in addition to other information and anecdotes about them.

During the summer, grazers can fend for themselves in a pasture. How much land your animals need depends on where you live and what grows there. The animals need to be rotated around to different parts of the pasture (use cross-fencing to create a series of mini-pastures within your land) or they will deplete the whole thing. Pasture rotation gives a piece of land a chance to grow in again.

During the winter, feeding is a different story. Since the pasture grass is dead and/or buried under snow, you need to provide hay that was cut during the summer and baled to keep it dry. This hay can consist of a number of types of grasses, usually native grasses, timothy or fescue. Grasses are cut in late spring, and then in a second or—if it's a good year—third cutting, and baled by a fascinating machine. The cut grass lies in windrows to dry. Then, a baler follows a row, scooping up the hay and pounding it into a couple of different shapes (small rectangle, giant rectangle or giant cylinder), winding it in baling "wire" (plastic string these days), and spitting out perfect bales. They are collected onto a truck that follows the baler. Sheep and llamas eat about five pounds of hay per day; horses eat twenty; cows even more.

People who didn't grow their own hay, or enough of it, buy more during the summer, usually all at once to save on delivery charges. This might mean that five tons of hay arrives at your farm. The ideal storage for hay is covered and ventilated. The hay needs to be clean and dry; some animals are pickier than others (cows, less; goats, more). If the hay becomes moldy, it can actually kill your livestock.

Incidentally: There are two uses for the many grasses that people grow—to eat and to use as bedding. "Hay" is a cutting that includes the nutritious seed heads. "Straw" is just the stalks. The blonde-colored bricks that decorated the set of Hee Haw and line the Halloween pumpkin display in front of the grocery store are straw bales.

For a treat, people offer grazers alfalfa, which is rich in protein but must be introduced gradually and given sparingly to avoid various problems, including:

- **Bloat:** This occurs when foam builds up in a ruminant's stomach, distending it. It's merely uncomfortable for most animals, but can kill sheep.
- **Foundering:** This affects a horse's feet; one friend likens it to gout, but worse. There are different theories about why it happens, including a change in feed and eating a lot of rich food. The horse's circulation in its feet changes, making them hot, which results in the walls of its hooves peeling off. To treat this condition, people limit the horse's diet to simple hay and sometimes have it shod with special shoes, but sometimes the damage is irreparable.
- **Colic:** This can be deadly. Again, the exact cause is debated but it is generally attributed to stress, dehydration or rich food. The animal's intestines twist on themselves, causing a lot of pain and making it impossible to digest food. My friends' Great Dane suffered from this once, resulting in a $2,000 emergency surgery. I know of a horse that had surgery for colic, and the vet unloaded fifteen pounds of sand from his gut.

A vet I talked to compared eating too much alfalfa to downing a giant platter of fettuccine alfredo—rich and heavy food.

In the Midwest, "silage" is chopped-up feed corn, grass or other green fodder that is fed to ruminants. It is stored in airtight conditions without having first been dried. The traditional storage for silage is a silo; it is loaded into the top in the summer and pulled out as needed from the bottom in the winter. Becoming more popular are giant extrusions ("caterpillars") wrapped in white plastic.

Another incidental: Grazers have compensated for their lack of opposable thumbs by developing prehensile lips. With them, they can pick the most succulent leaves and grass blades. Sheep and other grazers even have a split front lip, for more control. They can be fascinating, and sort of creepy, to watch.

Animals need fresh water as much as they need food. The main challenge with this is to keep it liquid during the winter. If their water is near a barn or other source of electricity, you can drop a waterproof heating element into the tank. Otherwise, you are toting buckets of hot water to your animals, or driving a big tank into your field on the back of a truck.

Some animals, such as horses, also need mineral supplements. This may be as simple as putting out a "salt" lick, which is a big, white or red mineral block. Different animals have different mineral requirements on different types of terrain; nutrition and mineral balance are crucial to promoting healthy immune systems.

Check with a local animal owner or vet to be sure you're giving your animals what they need to thrive.

Vaccinations and Parasites

Vaccinating pets and livestock is common in mainstream America, just as it's common to vaccinate children. There are people who choose to not vaccinate. I have never received a flu shot and don't intend to. Mike and I also never got a rabies shot for our dog, to the chagrin of our country vet. This decision was based on the advice of our naturopathic city vet, who argued that there were few, if any, rabies cases in our region, and that introducing that antibody to the dog did more harm than good. I never vaccinated my chickens, and they were bright-eyed and healthy.

However, it's possible that my chickens, dog and I were benefitting from what is called "herd immunity." Because most of the population is immunized, we got lucky.

Vaccinations have become a way of life for most farmers because of the size of the herds they deal with, and because the animals are transported to slaughter. Industrial ranching creates unnatural stress on the animals, leading to a greater susceptibility to pathogens that cause disease. Industrial herds are also fed growth enhancers and, in some cases, food their bodies are not made to process (i.e. the successfully marketed "corn-finished beef"—corn actually makes cows sick). If you have a small herd of unstressed, free-range animals that are intended solely for personal use, vaccines and medication-laced feed may be unnecessary.

This is one of those things you'll have to research yourself in order to decide. Different animals require different medications; talk to the person from whom you acquire the animal, as well as your vet, neighbors and people at the feed store. But, never withhold medical attention for a sick animal.

Treating for parasites is a different matter. All animals get parasites of one kind or another. External parasites, like flies and ticks, are generally ignored. Internal parasites, like worms, require medicine because can they divert enough nutrition from the animal's digestive system to cause malnourishment or other problems. As one veterinarian put it, "Would you rather feed the animal or its parasites?" There are "natural" formulas made of non-synthetic ingredients.

Manure Management

Possibly the biggest—and certainly the most tedious—issue regarding livestock is dealing with the…byproduct. All that grass and feed has to go somewhere and, since livestock are confined in one way or another, there are only so many places for it to go. Because most farm animals are not particular about when or where they defecate, it is your job to keep their living quarters clean. Excess feces and the attendant flies that thrive in such conditions can bring a host of problems. So, it's up to you to remove it. This is called "mucking."

Where do you take it? Most people compost it—once manure is aged it is spectacular compost. But, it must age—otherwise the acids in it will maim or kill whatever young plant you're trying to nurture. Compost manure, including the straw or woodchips it's mixed with, in a pile somewhere on your land that's not too close to your house, and make sure you turn the pile periodically to keep the composting action active. While one mucks out one's barn by hand, a manure pile is turned with a tractor.

Do not ignore this facet of your responsibilities as a livestock owner! Unmanaged manure can quickly become a smelly, disgusting health hazard, not only for your animals but for yourself. Raw manure attracts any number of pests, can cause foot infections in your animals and can contaminate bodies of water.

General Rules of Cleanliness:

- Clean feed buckets and watering troughs regularly. With horses, assign a specific feed bucket to each horse.
- "Muck out" stalls and other bed-down places regularly (weekly to daily, depending on type of animal and amount of time in the stall) and replace with fresh straw or woodchips.
- Disinfect used or borrowed equipment with bleach water (one-to-nine concentration) before use, and in between uses on different animals.

Males

I will address a couple of specific species below, but generally speaking—and this is not just my college Women's Studies classes talking—male animals are nearly more trouble than they're worth. Testosterone is a hormone to take seriously on a farm. It makes animals competitive, aggressive toward others (including you), and borderline-abusive in their quest to mate. And it makes them fight each other—sometimes to the death.

One way that males demonstrate their dominance is to exude musk, an earthy odor that can be overwhelming—which is, of course, the idea. Un-castrated males, particularly of the goat or sheep persuasion, can be positively rank.

Because of this, most four-legged breeding males are housed separately from the females and, sometimes, from each other. I know a woman who keeps her female llamas on a completely different ranch, four miles away.

The other upshot of this reality is that most male animals are castrated when they're young. Only the finest specimens are kept "intact." Now you know where the colloquial term "stud" comes from. The studs are sort of like queen bees; they are treated especially well but can live somewhat lonely lives. They are hired out to waiting females, either in the flesh or via semen samples for artificial insemination. Other than that, they just hang out (so to speak).

Gender Names

Just like the proverbial hundred words for snow, there is a bit of jargon to describe not only the species of animal, but also its gender and reproductive status.

	Chicken	Sheep	Pig, Hog
Baby	Chick	Lamb	Piglet
Adolescent	Pullet (female) Cockerel (male)	Yearling	Shoat Gilt (female)
Mature Female	Hen	Ewe, Dam	Sow
Mature Male	Rooster, Cock	Ram, Buck	Boar
Castrated Male	Capon	Wether	Barrow
Meat	Chicken	Lamb (immature) Mutton (mature)	Pork

	Goat	Horse	Cattle
Baby	Kid	Foal	Calf
Adolescent	n/a	Filly (female) Colt (male) Yearling	Heifer (female, including unbred adult), Yearling
Mature Female	Doe, Nanny	Mare, Dam	Cow (bred adult)
Mature Male	Buck, Billy	Stallion	Bull
Castrated Male	Wether	Gelding	Steer, Bullock
Meat	Goat	Horse	Veal (immature) Beef (mature)

Specific Species

Birds

My city friends were always intrigued by our chickens and asked me lots of questions: Does it hurt when they lay an egg? Are the Araucanas' eggs green all the way through? Do ducks lay eggs? How long do chickens live?

I could answer all but the last question (Yes! No! How else would one get a baby duck?). I think the life expectancy of a chicken is around ten years, but I could never find out definitively, because no one keeps a chicken around long enough to find out.

All fowl on a farm are messy and rather loud, but relatively easy to care for. Because our chicken coop included a completely enclosed house with an attached yard, we did not worry if we left the chickens for a few days to go to the coast or something—we just filled their food and water hoppers before we left.

While adult birds are also bought and traded, most fowl are usually acquired as fertilized eggs, which you incubate until they hatch, or as days-old, fuzzy babies. They grow out of the tiny peeper stage after a week or two and have a rather awkward adolescence, with the shafts of adult feathers sticking out unattractively (and, it looks to me, uncomfortably). They need extra warmth, usually provided by a heat lamp, until they have grown all of their feathers, which takes about six weeks. They reach maturity after five to six months.

If a chick/gosling/duckling is unable to break free of its shell alone, the prevailing wisdom is not to help it—it probably has some physical defect that will hinder it from leading a normal life. A friend of mine couldn't resist the urge to "help" a couple of her chicks, which ended up having leg deformities. However, her flock self-regulated—by cannibalizing the poor things soon after they hatched.

Avoid slick surfaces in fowl housing to avoid leg injuries. Also avoid old wood floors (unless you've sanded them) with exposed nails, broken glass or anything on which a bird can get a sliver or other foot injury—these don't heal very quickly. Wood shavings are better for bedding than straw because the shavings absorb moisture.

If you want to be able to handle your birds when they're grown, you need to pick them up and pet them gently from Day One. Even then, some will never take to it. I fed my chicks from my hand, but eventually had to stop because they had grown enough to peck harder, and it hurt! It never occurred to me to put a glove on…

Chicken

Chickens are the most ubiquitous domestic animal in the entire world. Evolved from Asian jungle fowl, chickens live on every continent except Antarctica. Chickens have been in our culture long enough to spawn a lot of chicken-related language. Consider:

- Cooped up
- Hen-pecked
- Pecking order
- Be chicken or chicken out (afraid)
- Cocky
- Ruffled feathers
- Chickens come home to roost (you get what you had coming)
- Broody
- Feathers are flying (big fight)
- Running around like a chicken with its head cut off
- Tough old bird
- Chicken scratch (messy writing)
- Spring chicken
- Crestfallen
- Madder than a wet hen
- Which came first, the chicken or the egg?

And, of course, there was Herbert Hoover's famous presidential campaign promise of "a chicken in every pot."

My favorite chicken characteristic (besides laying eggs, of course) is that their feet naturally close tightly, which enables them to roost on a branch. When they wake, they hold their feet open to walk on them. They are not particularly intelligent, and prone to beating up on each other. Though I've seen devout chicken-lovers, I found my chickens interesting and fun, but not sentimental in the least—therefore it was hard to develop a deep emotional attachment to them. They did come running when they heard my voice, but I think that had more to do with "Food!" than "Friend!"

In the residential areas of many cities, it has become modish to own the limit of chickens, usually three. Roosters are not allowed because they are loud (they crow any time of the day or night, contrary to popular belief) and aggressive. Hens may not be as loud, but they certainly can make a racket—cackling when an egg is laid, fighting over food or who knows what. One of my hens, Kiki, had a Moment nearly every afternoon. No one knew why; she would simply be walking around, and then stop and begin to cluck really loud, as though she just laid the biggest egg on the planet. Ironically, she had stopped laying after her first winter. The first time she did this, I ran out to find her because I thought she was being eaten by a coyote or something. Nope, just having a Moment.

When you're buying baby chicks, usually from a feed store or a mail order (yes, they actually ship baby chicks in cardboard boxes), make sure you're buying the kind you want. Selective breeding has created two separate-but-equal types of chickens: the genes of "layers" create a less meaty chicken in lieu of developing a daily egg-laying routine; the genes of "fryers" focus on growing big muscles. Fryers are butchered at six to ten weeks of age. Yes, I said "weeks."

In Hot Weather

A chicken has a pretty simple temperature-regulation system—its comb and wattles. When it really gets hot, the comb craps out, and the poor girl starts to pant and hold her wings out to the side. If that doesn't cut it, chickens can overheat and keel over (that's how I lost Yolanda, as far as I can tell).

One way to stave off overheating is to mist the chickens with a spray bottle of water. You'd think they'd run to it like inner-city kids around a fire hydrant. No. Unfortunately, their little pea-brains find the mist dangerous somehow, and they run away. So, you have to balance the benefit of being misted (if you're a good shot and can get a chicken while she's running) with the additional stress of being pursued and/or cornered by the hissing water-demon. You can try dropping some grain and then misting them as they eat. The best time to do it is after they've roosted—though of course it's dark by then and probably cooled off.

In Cold Weather

Chickens are cold-tolerant, though mine wouldn't walk on snow. While roosting, their bodies cover their naked feet, and during the day they just don't seem to mind. There is a slight chance their combs will freeze, but we had cold snaps in the single-digits with no losses. The main thing is keeping their water liquid. If you have an open trough you can drop a line of heating tape into it (this requires an electrical power source). I had a closed, vacuum fountain system, and for the first couple of winters tried to find the perfect solution—or at least an alternative to trading warm water for ice twice a day. I first hit on a plant-germination pad, which was the right idea but not quite warm enough. Then, one day while trolling the aisles at the feed store I noticed a plastic pad that goes under a dog bed. It was watertight, made for outdoor use…we had a winner! I got the size for small dogs and put it under my waterer, and it worked perfectly—the water was still plenty cold and sometimes developed a thin skin of ice, but never froze solid.

Housing

There are dozens of chicken-coop plans online; books about chicken coops; even chicken coop tours. My chickens were pretty spoiled: Mike and I converted two milking stalls into their house. There was a hole in an outside wall that led to a ten-by twenty-foot, covered outdoor pen. Beyond that, we often opened the gate and let them wander around the yard.

Rooster

First things first: as a chicken rancher, you do not need a rooster in order for the hens to lay eggs. Hens lay eggs nearly daily for most of the year, in accordance with the length of the day (i.e. waxing in spring and waning in winter). The only thing a rooster can do that is useful to humans is to fertilize the eggs if you'd like to have chicks. Fertilized eggs have no more nutrients than unfertilized eggs.

Notice that I wrote the only "useful" thing. Just about everything else a rooster does is completely obnoxious. They crow—not just in the morning but any old time. Sometimes all night. And it's not necessarily a quaint "cock-a-doodle-doo;" it might sound more like someone is strangling the poor creature, which you will be inclined to do before long.

There's a reason words like "bantam" and "cocky" have the meanings they do—roosters are chock-full of testosterone. A rooster's idea of foreplay is dancing around in a circle with one wing dragging on the ground. That's not so bad—so why are the ladies running away? Because then the rooster chases down a female and jumps on her, pushes her into the dirt, pins her head down with his beak (usually pulling a couple of feathers for effect), tries to keep his balance for a few seconds, and then hops off.

Their other charming quality which, to be fair, is understandable and rather noble, is to protect the eggs. Guess who wants to come in and take the eggs? You. They may attack with both their beaks and with their spurs, sharp protrusions that grow on their legs. I know people who have had their clothes torn by an attacking rooster. One friend enters her chicken yard with a large walking stick to keep her rooster—a bantam no less—off of her. Never let a rooster near a small child.

The first batch of chicks I bought had two males, which I butchered after they started demonstrating their skills at about five months. A few years later, well-meaning friends brought us two chicks as a gift (Note: LIVE ANIMALS ARE NEVER A GOOD GIFT), and of course one grew into a male. I tried to give Mr. Man a chance. *Maybe I overreacted last time,* I thought. *Maybe he won't be so bad since he started out so much younger than the hens.* When he started crowing, it was entertaining—sort of like a teenage boy whose voice is changing and cracks at inopportune moments. He had amazingly beautiful feathers—males grow more showy feathers around their necks and big tail feathers that arc up over their rumps. He grew tall and proud. He was afraid of me and of the hens on the high end of the pecking order. *See, I told myself, this will all work out.*

And then Mr. Man got randy. I started noticing feathers in the yard (no one was molting). I started noticing that the chickens were hiding in the hen house during the day instead of being in the yard. And then Mr. Man started mounting chickens, even upper-caste ladies, right in front of me. I tried to convince myself that I was projecting my human ideas of healthy sexual relations on the chickens, because what was going on in the henhouse sure looked like rape. I tried to be open-minded. *Maybe the hens like the sense that someone is in charge*, I thought.

The day that I made up my mind, I was mulching garden beds. I heard a commotion. I had coaxed the lowest-rung chickens out of the henhouse to forage (they'd been hiding there all day), and now, they were all yelling and clucking. I looked up to see Mr. Man in hot pursuit of Billy Sue. Those chickens can run fast when they want to! He chased her in circles, unrelenting, until she ran under the deck and started beating herself against a window in the basement wall in an attempt to get away from him. Billy Sue did not look like she was in *any* way complicit in the proceedings. Mr. Man ended up in the freezer.

I have read heart-warming accounts of roosters standing guard over "their" hens; protecting them from predators and pointing out food to them. Maybe after puberty, which Mr. Man did not survive.

I've considered the argument that what is going on in there is "natural." But when it comes down to it, almost nothing a chicken is or does is "natural." Humans have made chickens (and to a lesser extent other domesticated farm animals) what they are, over centuries of selective breeding. Do you know of any other bird that lays an egg each day?

Duck

"Runner" ducks are really adorable, so earnest and walking upright together in a line, chattering softly to each other. They've been bred to be neither inclined, nor particularly able, to fly, so they're more like penguins than true ducks. They are descended from mallards.

Cooks and especially bakers prefer duck eggs to chicken eggs. They're slightly bigger; they have a richer flavor and the extra protein they contain makes baking a breeze. Some people who are allergic to chicken eggs aren't affected by duck eggs. One reason they are not the standard egg in grocery stores is that their shells are more porous, so they don't keep as long. Because of this, it's not recommended that you wash a soiled duck egg; rather, wipe it with a dry cloth.

Runner ducks are similar to chickens in some ways but very different in others. Ducks like to roam around the yard like chickens, and need extra grit and calcium like chickens. But, they don't naturally roost at night like chickens; you'll have to round them up and put them to bed or risk losing them to predators. They don't like an at-will feeding system; they prefer to be fed at a certain time each day. This severely limits your traveling unless you have a trusted duck-sitter. They don't scratch like chickens, so they can be let into the garden once the plants are big enough to not be fazed by a couple of duck-nibbles. Unless you feed them kitchen scraps from a young age, they're not too keen on eating them.

In fact, they're generally suspicious of change—one friend inadvertently freaked out her ducks when she went out to feed them in a new red raincoat.

Ducks need fresh water to drink but not to swim in (ducklings can even drown in their drinking water). However, the adults do *like* to swim. If you provide swimming water, keep it clean—the ducks will defecate in it.

Muscovy (sometimes called Barbary) ducks are a little bigger, and a lot uglier, than runner ducks. Their grunts are a bit more gruff and guttural, and their heads are covered in bulbous red caruncles, like a turkey. These ducks will roost in trees. Their meat is said to be more like beef, richer in flavor, than runner ducks. They are not available via mail order; you'll have to find a local breeder or hatch out your own eggs.

There are feral flocks of Muscovy ducks, especially in the Southern United States, which is addressed in the Wildlife Chapter, below.

Goose

These birds are best known for their temperament, which can be not-so-nice. Certain breeds are testy and will hiss and even bite, though it doesn't really hurt so much as pinch. They are effective guard animals, creating quite a commotion when someone arrives at your house. They're also smart and playful, especially if you work with them as goslings. People who own geese swear that they can be like having a dog.

Geese love to eat grass, so they're good at keeping the lawn or orchard mowed. If there is a particular broadleaf weed you want them to control, give it to them cut as youngsters so they get a taste for it.

Some geese lay eggs year-round and some only once per year, in which case they intend to raise a brood.

Guinea Fowl

Guinea fowl are known for two things: eating ticks and honking really, really loudly. How loud? "Deafeningly," says my friend Eileen. "When they sound the alarm, look out." Better than a watchdog, she says. The trouble is, they're rather nervous birds and lots of things can set them off.

If you decide to weather their squawking, barking calls and constant "buckwheat" murmuring, you will be rewarded with diligent insect-eaters. And, neat ones—they won't dig up your garden beds the way a chicken will. Keep them in an enclosed coop for at least six weeks so they can bond with the coop and consider it home—otherwise they will hearken back to their African origins and roost in the trees.

Guinea fowl are bossy like geese—they'll even herd your dogs and chase your cats. This makes them less likely to be predated than more docile breeds. They look a little like buzzards, with bare, white heads, and taste like pheasant.

Guinea hens can be housed with chickens. They prefer higher roosts and game bird feed (more protein content), but can manage with chicken feed. They need to be able to roam around and forage on at least an eighth of an acre. The flock works out a route, which they follow every day. They can fly—not just the flying leaps that chickens and turkeys make, but real flight, which is why you want to be sure they've bonded with your coop before you let them out.

Guinea eggs are smaller than regulation chicken eggs—similar to bantam eggs. They prefer to nest in the grass, which makes it tricky to find the eggs and makes the hen vulnerable to predation. Some people try to put up a small fence around a hen that is broody, but you run the risk of scaring her from the nest and causing her to abandon it. Baby guinea fowl are called "keets." It is difficult for a guinea hen to successfully raise keets without your help—the babies tend to get hung up in dewy grass and die.

Turkey

Turkeys can basically be kept like chickens, but with everything a little bigger. They should be allowed to roam around. They will make their own nests in secret places, meaning that if you were hoping to eat some of the eggs (which taste like chicken eggs but are about three times as large), you will need to find the nests. Their egg-shells are tougher than chickens'.

Turkeys are fun and relatively easy to keep, especially if you're into the heritage breeds, such as red Bourbons and Narragansetts. Modern grocery store-bound turkeys are a triumph or a travesty, depending on your view. These birds have been bred to emphasize a large breast, since that's what American eaters want. The breeders have been so successful that today's turkeys have to be artificially inseminated, and can hardly breathe or walk.

If you're picking up a turkey, hold its wings against its body as you would a chicken, but turn the body around to it can't try to peck at your face.

Camelids
Alpaca

Alpaca wool is one of the most durable, soft and warm substances on the planet. The alpaca and its larger relative, the llama, are pack animals that come from the high desert steppes of the Andes Mountains in South America. Alpacas are less prone to spitting and kicking than llamas.

Question: Does soft wool and a decent personality make a breeding alpaca worth $30,000? The alpaca business is one of the strangest pyramid-scheme-esque institutions in farming. Alpaca breeders can bring in tens of thousands of dollars for one animal—if they can find a buyer. And they do. The alpaca business is less about animal husbandry and more about buyer husbandry.

I'm not saying alpaca ranchers are bad people—in fact, other types of farmers might learn from them. Alpaca breeders have figured out how to make the ranching lifestyle sexy, when it's really the same shit-encrusted drudgery as owning any other type of livestock. In a country in which most family farmers are selling out because none of their children wants to take over the farm, alpaca ranchers make their money from recruiting new, non-family alpaca ranchers.

Llama

Llamas are best used as pack animals. They can be slaughtered for meat, but this is rare. Their wool is serviceable, mostly felted. Llamas respect the most rudimentary fence and make excellent guard animals for a herd of goats or sheep. They are less fond of horses but will live with them. Any combination is okay, except a solitary llama.

Mostly, llamas carry gear. They wear special saddles that support two panniers. They are sure-footed and stable hikers (though they must be trained to walk through water) that can weasel their way through tight spots. A llama is less likely to spook than a horse, and if startled will simply jump a little, rather than take off running. Or, freeze. A llama that doesn't like where you're leading it will simply stand in one place, set its feet and refuse to budge. It might even hum at you to voice its unease. You can give its rope a firm tug, rather than pulling outright, and coax it along—if it's regular Tug-of-War, the llama will win.

Llamas are known for having a less agreeable disposition than alpacas; mainly they will spit at another llama if it's too close. That said, llamas can and will kick in any direction. Llama safety includes never putting your face lower than the llama's back and never reaching over the llama's head when it's down; it can raise its head quickly and break your nose. You can pet a llama on the neck but not the face. They're not particularly emotionally attached to humans; one llama keeper I met likened it to a human-cat relationship—interest, on its terms.

Like any animal, a llama must be trained to accept being felt by human hands, including under the beltline. It must also present its feet and mouth for inspection and maintenance. When approaching one, speak to it so it knows you're coming; put your hand on its back or side, and work your hand down with a series of pats so it knows you're reaching underneath. Llamas have a soft pad on the bottom of their foot from which a small nail protrudes. Llama teeth never stop growing, and so older animals need their teeth shaved down occasionally. They only have teeth on the lower mandible.

Llamas are ruminants with three stomachs; they can burp up smelly mouthfuls of half-digested grass at any time. They enjoy a diet of grass hay, with small alfalfa pellets as treats. They have prehensile lips that are best able to eat from a slightly cupped hand, if you're feeding one. Their manure is easy to manage—they defecate medium-sized pellets onto a community pile, which should be composted before use.

If you raise an "exotic" animal like a llama, be sure there is a veterinarian within driving distance that specializes in the breed. Otherwise, you get the regular vet improvising with diagnoses and filing your llama's teeth with his horse file, which is too big for a llama's mouth and has less-than-perfect results.

Bovines
Bison

Bison (buffalo are native to Asia and Africa) are massive creatures that are surprisingly agile for their size—bulls can jump six feet and run thirty-five miles per hour. They also have unpredictable temperaments. So, prison-grade fence is of utmost importance—a loose bison is dangerous to anyone near it. Their meat is lean, and there is a lot of it; a large bison can yield 450 pounds.

To start a bison operation, estimate the same number of bison per acre as cattle in your area. Bison like to wallow in dirt, especially when shedding their winter coats, and will likely create one somewhere in their pasture. There is little threat of predation, as they can run just about anything off, including wolves.

Bison are not domesticated animals; the reason they've been adapted successfully to farms is because they are grazers. This means some benefits: they calve on their own and require little if no Western medicine. However, they may not be kept with other farm animals. If you feel compelled to go into the bison business, please do a *lot* more research.

Cattle

American cattle have been bred over the centuries for their brawn, not their brains, and it shows. To look a cow in the eye is to see a sentient being, yes, but not much beyond that. There are no big thoughts going on in there. There *are* intelligent cattle breeds—which is why I support raising heritage breeds—but Angus, Holsteins, Jerseys, etc. have had the smart bred out of them. They've also had the multi-purpose bred out. Back in the day, heritage cows could provide meat, milk *and* brawn, in the form of pulling plows and oxcarts. Farmers have learned the same lesson as doctors—it has paid to specialize. Nowadays, there are beef cattle and there are dairy cattle, which are different animals, insofar as that is possible, with different needs.

For beef cattle, it's all about putting on the pounds as quickly as possible. And then, about eighteen months later, it's curtains. There are different breeds for different climates: for example, there are few, of any, Angus cattle roaming the scrub desert of the Southwest. Instead, you'll find Zebu cattle, including the Brahman strain that people associate with India. Also, the stocking rate varies drastically; whereas most cattle ranchers talk about how many head per acre, a veterinarian told me her family in New Mexico stocks just four to five cows per *section* (a section measures 640 acres—that's one square mile). There's just not much food or water. What's more, the region is much better suited for sheep. So, why do people raise five steers where they could have a herd of sheep? Americans buy beef far more than lamb.

Dairy cattle are subjected to a lifetime of pregnancy or twice-daily milking, which, in this day and age, usually means having the milk mechanically extracted. It's practical for a small farm to milk one or two cows by hand. Even cows don't produce milk out of nowhere—they have to carry a calf to term. That calf is separated from its mother, after as little as one day, and bottle-fed. A dairy cow produces milk for forty to sixty days; then, she's impregnated again. She produces milk for nearly a year, until the last few weeks of her new pregnancy.

Cows eat pasture grass and hay, just like horses. Dairy cows are given more alfalfa hay because of its protein content, and grain concentrates. Because of the high-stress situation of either a beef cow or a dairy cow, lots of things can go wrong. The predominant illnesses:

- **Hypocalcaemia:** Commonly known as "milk fever," this affliction is caused by a cow's loss of calcium in her blood because it's all gone to her colostrum (first milk) in preparation of giving birth. This can lead to death.
- **Infertility:** The inability to become pregnant can be caused by a number of things, including foot problems!
- **Mastitis:** Same as with humans—inflamed, painful teats. Milk from an infected cow will have globs of pus in it, which is just one reason milk is filtered before human consumption.

"Polled" cattle are naturally horn-less, and valued because they can't hurt each other and can't resist your bidding as easily.

Cows are pretty tough but do need at least a three-sided, covered shelter; calves need a draft-free stall. Because cows push on things, whatever is used as a shelter must be extremely sturdy.

Hand-feeding a cow is a lot different from hand-feeding a horse. While a horse can grab an apple neatly with its lips, to feed a cow you have to shove the whole thing in—all the way in. The cow may try to help by slinging out its rough tongue, which succeeds only in covering the back of your hand in slime. If you don't get the apple perfectly in the center, it will pop out the side and you have to start over. They're a lot more successful with things like corn stalks.

A calf that has been orphaned or rejected by its mother is called a "bummer" (other names include "leppy" and "dogie"). It will need to be fed every two hours with a bottle. Goat's milk can be used, as well as milk from other cows. If it never got to nurse with its mother, it will need colostrum—the first milk a mammal produces, which is rich in nutrients and antibodies—as well. Once a calf has been introduced to bottle-feeding, watch out—it will butt into you, which is its instinct.

Equines

The way an equine is valued comes down to its conformation, or how its body parts come together, and its temperament. The perfect beast has strong legs and a strong back that is relatively straight. Horses in particular are known for "spooking," that is, being frightened by sudden movement, which might cause it to buck or bolt. That sudden movement might be a wolf, or it might be an errant plastic shopping bag. Seek an even-tempered animal, especially if it's intended for a child.

All equines have similar nutrition and vaccination needs. They are happy eating grass in a pasture during the spring and summer; they must be fed dried grass in the winter. Treats include store-bought alfalfa nuggets and the classic staples: apples, sugar cubes and carrots. You can cut them into pieces, which you hold on your palm (held completely flat) in front of the horse's nose. Or, hold the whole carrot or apple, and the horse will snap off a bite of it. Horses have semi-prehensile lips to grab with, and may also use their teeth a bit, which is why you keep your fingers out of the way.

Equines need foot care. They are susceptible to foundering, which is caused by eating too much rich food, usually spring grass or alfalfa. They need their hooves trimmed, which most horse owners learn to do themselves (which also involves training the horse to let you do). The purpose of shoeing an animal is to protect its hooves and avoid injury. You will need to hire a farrier to put shoes on your horse if it's going to be on a road or hard trail. It's a little like for humans: You could walk on most rough terrain barefoot, but you have more confidence if you're wearing shoes.

Equines require de-worming a few times per year (particularly after a killing frost in northern climes) due to the botfly. This fly lays its eggs on a horse's legs, which make her itch, which incites the animal to groom her legs and eat the eggs.

Or, you scrape the eggs off while brushing her and they land in the grass, which she eats. Either way, she ends up with larvae in her digestive system. The larvae compete for nutrients and can cause ulcers.

Get to know a few horse people, and take riding lessons, before you acquire a horse. And be sure you can commit to the responsibility—horses need to learn a job (trail riding, roping, herding) and then perform that job often.

Donkey

The donkey (or "ass") is a short, stocky horse relative known for its comical braying and stubborn disposition. They have tall, narrow torsos that are more difficult to saddle and ride, but it can be done. They tend to be less interested in obeying a human than a horse, which is why they have a reputation for stubbornness. But some of that reputation is just their being more laid back than a horse, which makes them a nice starter animal for a child (unless it's an intact male). They're smart and curious, too.

Donkeys can be used as guard animals for cattle or goats—they will run a coyote off a pasture. Because of this, donkeys and the coyote's cousin, the dog, generally don't mix. I also know a guy whose German shepherd killed one of his donkeys. No one was around to see what exactly happened. Best to keep the dogs out of the pasture.

Donkeys have the same nutritional needs as a horse, just a smaller appetite. They can also share the bad habit of cribbing (described in "Horse")—our lean-to posts were all gnawed to bits by a previous owner's donkeys. The worst thing for a donkey is to become overweight.

Donkeys are sometimes used in a unique-to-the-country fundraising event called "Donkey Basketball." Local celebrities are invited to play a game of basketball—on donkeys—in the school gym. In this case, the donkeys are shod with rubber shoes to protect the gym floor and prevent slippage of the animals. This is as comical as it sounds.

Horse

Horses used to be non-optional farm animals—they provided transportation and muscle for farm machinery (which is why an engine's capacity is measured in "horsepower"). In some cases they are eaten, but horsemeat has never really made it on the American market. They live up to thirty years.

Horses are one of the most personable farm animals. They get to know you, and care if you come to visit. Most rural children grow up with access to a horse; when acquiring one, temperament is the key factor.

If you live in the western United States, you may hear of wild mustang auctions. The U.S. Bureau of Land Management controls wild horse populations—when there are too many horses (which becomes a greater problem every year as more and more formerly wild land is "developed" into residential housing), the BLM removes some animals and sells them to the public. Those that aren't sold are killed (called "destroyed" or "recycled," depending on whom you're talking to).

This may seem like a cheap, environmentally responsible way of acquiring a horse. The trouble is that you are acquiring a wild animal. "Breaking" (taming and training) a horse is a big job best left to a professional. So, if you can't afford to hire someone to break your wild horse, you're better off buying a domesticated one. There's more about training a horse below.

As with dogs, some people are obsessed with a horse's lineage and some couldn't care less about it. Unless you value papers to prove your horse's bloodline, I recommend focusing on the animal's personality, physical health and characteristics. Whatever you do, make sure you're not taking someone else's problem off their hands.

If you're just looking for what a friend calls "pasture ornaments"—that is, animals on your land that you're not going to give a job, consider adopting elderly horses from working farms. You may have a little more veterinarian expense, but you'll be giving some good horses a nice retirement home.

Shelter and Maintenance

A horse doesn't need any kind of shelter. In the wild, a horse is lucky if it finds a tree to stand under during a storm. However, most people provide at least a lean-to roof—to keep the hay dry and clean if nothing else. Horses grow a thick coat for the winter that keeps them warm. Then, they hunker down and wait it out.

Some people buy waterproof "jackets" or "blankets" for their horses; mostly these are show horses, and the owners don't want them to mess up their pretty summer coat with a shaggy winter one. If you use one, you have to commit to keeping it on, because the horse won't have grown a winter coat. Blankets are also good to have around in case the horse is injured—one might keep it from going into shock. And if the horse is going into a drafty trailer wet.

Blanket or no blanket, horses need access to thawed water in all weather.

Because of their popularity and showmanship, there is no end to the number of products and implements that you can purchase to use on your horse—shampoos; brushes, curry combs, and clippers; conditioners and moisturizers for its coat. Detanglers for its mane and tail. Trimmers, picks and polish for its hooves. Whiteners. Sunscreen. Vacuums. Really, all you need is a hoof pick, brush, and a curry comb to get the dirt out of its coat, on a daily basis if possible. In the winter, brushing the mud from the horse's coat fluffs up its hair and keeps it warmer.

Training

Unlike most farm animals, a horse can be trained to do many things, from simple jobs like letting you hold one feet so it can be cleaned or shoed, to complex things like pulling a wagon as part of a team, getting into and out of a horse trailer, or jumping over a fence without pitching you off his back. The first thing a horse needs to learn is to respect you. I recommend hiring a professional horse-trainer to help you work with your first horse—as you become more familiar and more confident with horses, and have the inclination, you may be able to train subsequent ones yourself.

A common training practice is the round pen. The rider stands in the middle of a pasture with a fourteen-foot rope and a training stick, and puts the horse through its paces: running, stopping, turning etc. This reinforces in the horse that the rider is its leader and that it should wait to receive orders from her before doing anything (rather than making its own decisions). An interesting quirk with horse training is that, because a horse's left and right brains work independently of each other, both sides must be trained. To put it another way, if you always approach your horse from the right side and then one day approach it from the left, it won't recognize you.

One of the first things horses are trained to do is not startle, which is a natural instinct. Horses jump at simple noises and quick movements, and if they're really freaked out can run for miles before they calm down. Horse training needs to be constantly reinforced, or they forget it.

Horses have nearly 360-degree vision, except for directly in front of and in back of them, which is why you don't walk up to a horse from behind and then give it a friendly slap on its rump; you will find yourself flying backwards across the corral. Horses like goats and cattle, but don't like pigs. Some horsewomen told me horses don't like llamas; they've been on a trail and encountered llamas, and it made their horses nervous. On the other hand, our neighbors boarded a couple of horses and a llama. So, it might depend on whether the horse has seen a llama before.

Horses have a number of "bad" habits; here are a few:

- **Cribbing:** This looks like the horse is eating wood. Actually, it's hooking its front teeth on the post or fence and pulling back, which forces air down its throat in such a way that it gets a little high. In addition to destroying fences and posts, it can cause infection in the horse. Horses crib when they're bored.

- **Weaving:** A horse develops this habit in a stall, weaving his head back and forth incessantly, like a human who doesn't realize she's bobbing her knee up and down, or twiddling with her pen.
- **Kicking and Striking:** Horses can kick with all four legs; "striking" refers specifically to a horse kicking straight forward and then scraping his hoof down your front. Any horse kick can severely injure a human.
- **Head Tossing:** Some horses naturally throw their heads in the air, but it could be a sign of mouth pain, allergies or excess energy derived from feeding grain. Or sensitivity to strong sunlight. Or ear mites. Or annoyance with being trained.
- **Breaking Away:** This can be extremely dangerous—a horse that panics and bolts can run off a cliff, into traffic or a barbed wire fence, etc.
- **Bucking:** This is big in rodeos but not good in daily practice. A horse tries to get you off his back by kicking his front and back legs alternately.

Mule

Mules are a cross-breed of a female horse and a male donkey. As are all hybrids, the mule is sterile and is usually taller than its parents. There is also, parenthetically, an animal called a hinny, which is a cross between a male horse and a female donkey.

Male mules and hinnies are neutered because, while they're shooting blanks, they still have hormone surges. Mules are smarter than horses; you can train a mule and then not ride him for a while, and he will remember the training. They also have more stamina than a horse (even a draft horse!), and can jump higher. They are sometimes considered stubborn, but this is more due to an avoidance of danger. Mules can be used in any situation in which you'd use a horse.

Mules are more "needle-shy" than horses, and more accurate kickers—a dangerous combination. Many mule owners take their mules in to the veterinarian to get their shots.

Pony and Miniature Horse

A "pony" can technically be just a petite horse, but there are specific breeds of pony as well. They were originally used to pull carts, and were especially useful in the mining industry. Contrary to popular belief, this is not a good animal for a child. Ponies are known to have bad dispositions, what a vet I talked to considered "little man syndrome." A couple of horsewomen I know consider the Welsh the best option.

Like a donkey, a pony is "thrifty," meaning it doesn't eat a lot. They are comfortable to ride but difficult to stay on, because they have round bellies that don't offer much to hold onto.

Miniature horses are regular horse breeds that have been selectively bred over centuries to be small. Newborns can fit on your lap! They are mainly a novelty animal, used for carts in parades and the like. They should be kept in at night to avoid predation.

Honeybee

Setting up a couple of beehives for household use can not only generate beeswax and honey but also ensure that your fruit trees, vegetables and flowers will receive the attention they need.

There are two ways to get bees: buy them or find a migrant swarm and incorporate it into your hive. Many communities have "bee-alert" lists—when someone calls 911 because a swarm is occupying one of their trees, a beekeeper is called to fetch it. A swarm occurs when a queen abandons an existing nest, usually because it has become overpopulated. Her worker bees swarm around her, anxiously awaiting her decision of where the new nest will be. Bees in this state are so absorbed with following the queen that they are quite docile. This is what's happening when you see someone wearing bees like a beard—he tied a queen around his neck and the colony swarmed around her. If you ever have the chance to see a beekeeper pick up a swarming colony, do—it's fascinating stuff.

A colony is really one entity comprised of thousands of little units. The queen mates and lays eggs; the worker bees do everything else, nursing and feeding the queen and the larvae, collecting nectar and pollen, and building wax cells; and the drones fly around in hopes they'll find a queen to mate with.

Commercially made beehive boxes (called "supers") are simple and well designed, so there is really no reason to build one unless you really want to. For the most part, bees are self-sufficient; your main concern is keeping the hive clean and disease-free. The perfect spot for a hive is near an orchard or garden, and away from your house. Specifically, the fifteen-foot "runway" toward and away from the entrance to the hive must be kept clear. If you block this runway your bees might feel under attack, and if this is the case they will counter-attack. Once a single bee sends out the distress signal, all the bees attack. Beekeepers are calm individuals, even when stung, because they could initiate their own demise if they freaked out.

By way of self-defense, most beekeepers use smoke when they are messing with the hive. Smoke disorients and calms the bees, making stings less likely. The traditional bee smoker looks sort of like a fancy coffee press, with a small bellows, in which a variety of materials (including pine needles, burlap, rotting wood) are burned slowly. Some beekeepers prefer to spray diluted liquid smoke in a mister bottle, called a chemical smoker.

All beekeepers use a veil to protect their faces; some also wear a full beekeeping suit or a specialized jacket; most just wear a set of coveralls and tuck their pants into their boots. Oh, and don't forget thick leather gloves.

Word to those in rattler country: snakes like to hide under rocks, logs and—supers! So when you're accessing or moving your hives, proceed with caution.

Colony Collapse Disorder has caused a lot of disagreement within the beekeeping community. Some blame it on a lack of genetic diversity and reliance on antibiotics (a recurring controversy in farming and ranching); some on the introduction of new pests from other parts of the world. At this point, raising the healthiest bees you know how is the best you can do to avoid it.

Harvesting wax and honey requires good timing and the right tools—I recommend joining a beekeeping group and going out with a neighboring beekeeper to see how it's done.

Goat

Goats are raised for their milk (and cheese), skin, hair and meat. Both the milk and meat carry a musky flavor, though I've been told that fresh goat milk, especially from the Nubian breed, doesn't. Many people who are allergic to or intolerant of cow's milk can consume goat's milk with no consequence. Goat's milk can also be fed to orphaned or abandoned animal babies.

Goats are smart and can be trained to come when called by name. They do not like to be rained on—most other animals are tolerant—so they need a simple shelter of some kind. They need hoof trimming on a regular basis. Goats are happier if there are at least two of them.

Goats are similar to sheep but much more curious and strident. If a goat is not happy, you will know it. Obstacles are something to be outwitted or obliterated. A goat can be trained from a young age not to butt by not engaging it if it butts you—to push back is to challenge it.

Because goats have so much personality, people who like goats *love* goats. I know of a couple who used a human nursing bladder with their baby Nubian. Yes, they both nursed their goat.

Goats are known for eating tin cans, which is not entirely accurate. However, they will eat many grasses and weeds that grazers can't or won't eat. In the Pacific Northwest, they are known for controlling stands of invasive Himalayan blackberry. People actually rent out their goats to homeowners who need weed control. But, you have to tether them to the briar patch—they are browsers and if there's sweet, succulent grass nearby, they'll choose it.

Oh, and did I mention the necessity of good fencing? "Four-legged devils," one friend calls them.

Pig

Pigs are smart. I'm not sure what good this does them since their lives are pretty monotonous. They're not animals I'd really want to get in the pen and hang out with, but I know people who loves pigs. They eat pellet feed and any household scraps you can get your hands on, but they also eat meat. Any meat. They'd eat a downed pig, or baby pigs, and if they got a chance they'd eat you. Wear boots, pants and keep your hands up high. They always appear hungry, rooting in the mud and nibbling on wooden fence slats if they can reach them, but just need to be fed in the morning and evening. Do not feed them meat; even though they like it, it makes them ornery. And there are the Mad Cow-type of considerations when feeding a species to itself.

Pigs have extremely tough skin with sparse, wiry hairs and do not require a lot of grooming maintenance or hoof care. However, they can sunburn if they have light skin. If in a really wet environment all the time, they may need hoof trimming.

Pigs are playful and will nudge and chase each other around their pen. They can be let out to roam but it can be hard to get them back in—train them with marshmallows, pieces of licorice or other sweets. It's also hard to control where they will wallow if they're loose, so you might end up with dug-out spots where you don't want them. If you plan to show your pigs, you'll need to train them to get in a scale and a trailer. They dislike being confined, so this takes some effort.

Pigs don't enjoy extreme cold but can fend for themselves, provided they have shelter from inclement weather. They'll appreciate a windbreak and a dry shed with hay in it. Pigs roll in the mud in the summer to cool themselves; they lack the ability to perspire through their skin. Despite this, they are clean animals. They can be trained to use a litter box in a house (hence the popularity of pet pot-bellied pigs a few years back). They tend to create a "latrine," or one spot in their yard in which they defecate. Keep it cleaned up to avoid unpleasant odors.

Pot-bellied pigs are, judging by the number of animals housed in nonprofit "rescue" facilities, not a good long-term pet. If you insist on having a pig, make sure the zoning in your area allows it. Even a "mini" pig is at least sixteen inches tall and a hundred pounds. Be extra, extra sure you are not getting a pot-belly/regular pig hybrid, or you will have a much bigger animal on your hands than you wanted. Always spay or neuter a pet pig.

Rabbit

It's common practice to keep rabbits in a wire cage for their manure, which is like gold in the garden. The pellets drop through the mesh of the cage, where you collect them and include them in your compost, or just drop them directly into the garden. I personally don't find that particularly humane; I think all domestic animals should be able to stretch their legs and be true to their nature. But it is *really* rich manure...

You may also let rabbits roam around in a fenced area, or train them to walk with you in a harness. To cool rabbits in hot weather, get your hands wet and then run them across the rabbits' ears. Even though they live in a cage, make sure it is protected from dogs and coyotes, which will eat rabbits' feet off if they can get a hold of them. My friend Shari has hers inside her fortified chicken yard.

Sheep

Sheep can provide a number of products: meat, milk (and cheese), wool as well as keeping grass down by grazing. Their bleating sounds like people pretending to sound like sheep bleating—hilarious. They are not the brightest animals (one friend calls them "unbearably stupid") and prefer to be given direction. They frighten easily: While dogs that herd cattle actually bite the cows' ankles to get their attention, sheepherding dogs simply get in a sheep's way and scare it into compliance. Sheep can actually be frightened to death; they often faint during shearing.

Sheep are sheared in the spring, which gives them a chance to grow a new coat in time for the following winter (though their wool would keep them cool in summer as well). Unless the sheep were "coated" (literally dressed in jackets to keep their wool clean), raw wool is filthy—full of ticks, grass and debris. But the finished product is worth the trouble. You might be able to sell the raw wool to someone who spins, or you can learn to spin and dye yourself, and create a value-added product! (See the Making a Living Chapter.) Some breeds shed their winter coats and don't require shearing at all. Some sheep produce so much wool—twenty pounds per year!—that they're shorn more often.

"Polled" sheep breeds are naturally horn-less, which ranchers prefer because they can't hurt each other or the rancher. Sheep are flock animals; you can't have just one. If you have sheep in your orchard to keep the grass down, be sure you select a breed that doesn't girdle the trees as well.

How fast a sheep's hooves grow depends on whether it's on a rocky hill or a nice, grassy paddock. White-faced sheep's feet grow faster than black-faced sheep's feet (say *that* ten times!).

Chapter 12
Wildlife

There are many lines to draw when considering animal life. Is a deer a beautiful example of nature? A pest? Dinner? It can be any of these things, depending on whether it's simply meandering through your yard, munching on your new dogwood trees, or minding its own business in the forest and you have a hunting permit. In this section, I write about wild animals except in the context of when they're directly assaulting one's garden—those critters ("vermin") are included in the Garden Chapter of the Food Section—and hunting, which is included in the Wildcrafting Chapter.

Invasive species are a little easier to identify. A little. Wild horses are, technically, invasive—Spanish conquistadores introduced them to North America in the 16th century. There was a three-toed horse relative native to this continent before the most recent Ice Age, but it was not the horse we know and ride. However, if you ask a wild mustang activist you'll get a very different—and not untrue—answer: mustangs are losing their habitat to housing developments and ranching interests. Five hundred years of residence has to count for something.

At a trailhead in the Wallowa Mountains, a city friend with whom I was hiking mentioned nervousness about the possibility of coming across a wild animal: mountain lions, bears, etc. were active in the mid-summer snowmelt. I began to list the different strategies one takes if that happens. My intention to empower Laura with knowledge, thereby easing her fears, had the opposite effect—she spent most of our hike peering nervously into the forest and marching around every blind turn in the trail, singing and clapping loudly in order to scare off any bears. (I had said, "The last thing you want to do is surprise them.") Laura hardly enjoyed the scenery, or noticed flowers and interesting rocks on the trail, because she was so preoccupied with our impending attack.

When I lived in the country, I met a "tracker." This is someone who goes out in the wild, far out, and looks for animals. She had some great stories, but a lot of them were about the tracks she saw, not the animals. Even a tracker has a hard time finding wildlife, because animals are generally aware of us long before we're aware of them, and they want nothing to do with us. So, don't worry too much about having a scary wildlife encounter; they are rare.

If you happen across an injured wild animal, your inclination may be to "help it." Unless you're carrying a weapon or a portable cage, the best thing you can do is keep walking. Nature takes care of its sick and injured. The last thing you want to do is wrap it in your sweatshirt, carry it to your car and try to drive into town to see the vet. This is extremely dangerous—you don't know why the animal was lying there, and you don't know when it will revive. What if you're driving down the road, and it suddenly flies into a panic inside the car with you? Or attacks you because it's afraid? Bad idea.

Along the same lines, if you come across a tiny fawn curled up under a fern or in a field, leave it alone. Nursing does temporarily abandon fawns to look for food, and to avoid advertising the fawn's whereabouts to area predators. The fawn is fine or, if not, will provide some other creature a meal. If your children bring home a fawn, take it back to the place they found it—the mother will look for it for a day or two before she gives up.

If you hire a professional animal trapper to remove an animal from your property with the understanding that it's a relocation, make sure she actually releases the animal, rather than killing it. Ask where she releases her animals. But also think about the idea of trap-and-release. Why make the animal someone else's problem? What makes you think the animal won't return? Why not try to co-exist? Why not euthanize it? Some animals mate for life. Just food for thought.

There are many more critters in the United States than I can describe in this book. I list the ones that have the most significant human interaction, and talk about them in those terms.

The Most Dangerous Wild Animal

Where we lived, people are more afraid of mountain lions (also called "cougars") than they are of deer—and yet, *exponentially* more people are injured in deer-car collisions. I found a report that a professor named Paul Beier wrote in 1991, in which he searched various records to quantify the threat of cougar attacks. He found that from January 1890 through December 1990—one hundred years—there have been nine fatal cougar attacks and forty-four nonfatal attacks in the United States, resulting in ten human deaths and forty-eight nonfatal injuries (some attacks involved more than one person). Most of these took place during the last two decades of the study (1970 to 1990) because humans keep encroaching on mountain lion habitat with their dream homes. It's safe to assume these numbers have risen since 1990. Let's say they've doubled—so, eighteen fatal attacks from 1990 to 2010.

Meanwhile, the Insurance Institute for Highway Safety estimates there are 1.5 *million* deer-vehicle collisions annually in the United States, causing more than 150 fatalities and $1.1 billion in property damage. Every year. That would add up to roughly 1,500 deer-related fatalities in the same time period.

But truth has never stood in the way of perception. The county in which Mike and I resided even paid a few in-town trappers a bounty for mountain lions, and if a lion was considered a renegade (usually because it had eaten a couple of housecats), it was unceremoniously hunted and killed. These hunts inevitably made it onto the front page of the newspaper, perpetuating fear of the animal. While potentially dangerous, mountain lions are generally secretive and keep out of sight of humans. Smart creatures.

Shortly after moving to our farm, Mike and a neighbor, Jim, met over the fence in the woods. When Mike casually mentioned cougars, Jim said that he drove his school-age daughter to the bus shelter at the top of the driveway, rather than let her walk the few hundred yards, so that she wasn't eaten by one. When Mike questioned the necessity of this precaution, Jim emphasized his point with tales of sightings throughout our area.

"A cougar ate one of Pete's donkeys a couple of years ago," Jim said. "Dragged it right over his fence."

As the Ocean of Evidence washed over Mike, Jim left him with some parting advice: "I wouldn't turn my back to the woods if I were you."

A few years later, my sister and her spouse were out for a visit. At breakfast, we sat at the table that overlooks our south field and our neighbor's property. As Les went to the bathroom and I grabbed the last piece of bacon, Linda looked up, squinted and asked, "Is that a mountain lion?"

Doubtful, Mike and I turned to look. On the far end of our neighbor's property there was indeed a large, buff-colored feline walking on some rocks. I got up and ran for the binoculars; we took turns to gape, astonished, at the thing. It was hard to tell its true size because of the distance, but it was certainly bigger than a housecat.

We wanted to go outside for a closer look but were reticent to startle it or, worse, provoke an attack. Les—who, not insignificantly, grew up in Wyoming— returned and asked what was going on.

"Come on," we said, "there's a cougar outside!"

Mike, Linda and I crawled across the driveway on all fours to try not to attract attention. I wondered if I should run back into the house and warn the neighbors, but I was torn because I didn't want Jim to shoot it. We stalked through the tall grasses and peered over them to the scene below. The animal was walking toward us.

"That's a big cat," said Les. I turned and noticed that he was not crouched in the brush like the rest of us.

"I know!" I said. "Get down, so it doesn't see you."

"No," said Les. "It's a big cat."

The three ex-suburbanites sheepishly stood up and realized he was right—though it was probably a twenty-five-pound cat, it was a cat. *Felix domesticus.*

Insects and Arachnids

There are lots of beneficial insects—butterflies pollinate flowers (it's not just the bees doing all the work) and simply delight with their beauty. Lacewing and hoverfly larvae eat pest insects. Ladybugs eat aphids. Parasitic wasps lay eggs in pest pupae. Beetles scavenge dung and carcasses like tiny vultures.

Spiders are unequivocally beneficial—even the poisonous ones make themselves useful by eating insects. For the most part, Mike and I let the few spiders we had in the house be, sometimes capturing a big one under a drinking glass, sliding a piece of stiff paper under it, and then releasing the spider outside. (This was fun because you could safely examine the spider before letting it go.) Unless my grandmother was coming to visit. Then, I apologized to the spiders as I unceremoniously sucked them out of their corners with the vacuum.

I do not recommend chemical intervention except in extreme cases, but balance that prejudice with the fact that a lot of sprays—for example, copper sulfate for peach trees—are natural chemical compounds. I did break down after a few years and spray rotenone on some things, especially aphids (see the Garden Chapter). Read the instructions carefully; there is a period of time after you spray produce that you cannot eat it. Always keep all of your bottles and sprayers labeled so you know exactly what's in them.

There are a few ways to encourage beneficial insects to live in your garden—growing specific plants, like cosmos or alyssum, for example. Mason bees are attracted to small, deep holes. You can make or buy a mason bee house, and even some mason bee larvae to get a colony started. You can buy other insects as well, such as ladybugs, parasitic wasps and nematodes. The trouble is, there's no way to make them stay at your farm. And, while this practice is approved by a number of organic farming organizations, I worry about releasing any creature into a new area. This strategy has gone wrong so many other times before (read: invasive species).

Pests that affect the garden are listed in the Food Section.

Carpenter Ants

A previous owner of our house made a path from the front door around to the back deck using ten-inch-thick log rounds. This seemed like a good idea—there was plenty of wood around, after all! But when we were selling the house, the buyer's inspector dug one up and pointed out the reason you don't use log rounds as stepping stones—each had been turned into a carpenter ant nest.

Carpenter ants don't actually eat the wood; they clear it out in order to build a nest. So, in our case, it was good that they were in the rounds instead of the house itself. On the other hand, they were only a few feet away from the house and might have decided to migrate at any time.

Chiggers

This is a microscopic mite that causes severe itching by biting you in thin skinned areas—often Where It Counts, if you get my drift, dissolving a few layers of skin cells with an enzyme, and sucking up the slurry. The best defense is to wear socks and loose pants when hiking in chigger territory, which is any shady spot with greenery in the Southeast and Central United States.

Bites can be treated with Benadryl, calamine lotion and oatmeal baths. The main thing is not to scratch, which can cause a secondary infection. The itching will abate after a week or so. There is an old belief that chiggers burrow under the skin, and that you can suffocate them by covering the "hole" with nail polish. This is not based in fact, and yet I have friends who swear by it. So, if slathering nail polish on your chigger bites makes them feel better, by all means, slather away.

Cockroaches

One of my favorite public relations stories ever is how Florida tried to dress up their cockroach problem by changing the insects' name to "palmetto bug." I guess turning on the kitchen light at midnight and seeing fifteen "palmetto bugs" skitter across the walls isn't as disturbing. They are also called "water bugs."

Cockroaches live throughout the Southern United States as well as in urban regions in the North (which is a testament to their tenacity, as they're not evolved to deal with cold). Besides being creepy, they carry disease by walking around in the filth of your pipes, etc., and then traipsing along your countertops.

The best ways to deter cockroaches is to seal up places under sinks and such that could provide an entrance to your house; keep your kitchen meticulously clean *and dry*; remove piles of debris outside the house that could harbor the bugs, which like to hide during the day.

Fire Ants

I'll never forget the time I was standing in the grass near Lake Ponchartrain, Louisiana, minding my own business, when I felt a pinch on the top of my foot.

"Ouch, what was that?" I said. In the time that it took to utter this phrase, dozens of fire ants had crawled up over my sandals, up both my legs and launched their attack. I must have been standing on or near their hill. It was like being stung by tiny bees, over and over. Mike couldn't help but laugh at my crazy dance, shrieking and leaning over to whisk them off while jumping up and down.

It feels like fire for two reasons: First, there are dozens of them; second, they are not only biting you with their mandibles but stinging you with their abdomens. Over and over. So your brain gets bombarded with individual pain messages and turns them into one large burning sensation.

If the bites raise into red bumps with white pustules— go to a doctor immediately—you are allergic. If you have an epinephrine auto-injector, use it. Don't break the pustules—this can cause a secondary infection. Treat non-allergic cases with Benadryl and calamine lotion.

Mosquitoes

Just when we get malaria and yellow fever under control...

In the last few years, mosquitoes have returned from simply being annoying to once again being dangerous to humans and horses, as West Nile virus has become more pervasive in the United States. Keep their numbers down by eliminating stagnant pools of water in clogged gutters, under leaking hoses, on exposed tarps and the like. Ponds with larvae-eating frogs and fish are okay, as is moving water.

A mosquito has a long, pointy proboscis, which she drives into your flesh in hopes of hitting a blood vessel, from which she drinks. It's an enzyme that she injects into your blood to thin it that causes the itchy, inflamed lump. Bites can be treated with Benadryl, calamine lotion and oatmeal baths. The main thing is not to scratch, which can cause a secondary infection. The itching and swelling will abate after a week or so.

Scorpions

Different types of this arthropod can live nearly anywhere on the planet; in the United States, they are most prevalent in the Southwest. Only one, the bark scorpion, is life-threatening to humans, and even then being stung doesn't guarantee a problem because a scorpion can control how much poison it injects. You might be stung but not receive any neurotoxin at all. Most scorpions deliver a sting, not unlike a bee's, with a barb on its curved tail.

It's perfectly reasonable to, if you find a scorpion in your house, capture it in a glass and put it outside. You'll probably get into more trouble trying to kill it. If you're lucky, someday you might see a female carrying her young on her back (hopefully not in your house), like an opossum.

The best way to dissuade scorpions from hanging around your house is to eliminate big rocks, lawn furniture and other items under which they can hide. I've also heard that they dislike lavender, so you might plant a hedge of it around your house or patio. A friend saw lavender in window boxes at a bed-and-breakfast in Europe for that reason.

Subterranean Termites

While termites are found in every state except Alaska, they are most active in warmer climates. They can do tremendous damage to wood, which is fine in the forest and not so good in people's homes. They look a little like white ants but have fatter abdomens, and live in similar colony structures.

Termites eat wood for sustenance; they build mounds to live in. They avoid open air, tunneling through wood and even building little tubes for themselves in places they can't tunnel (such as the concrete foundation of your home).

Watch for infestation anywhere there is a wood-to-ground connection on your house (even a trellis), and for tunnels elsewhere.

Ticks

Any time you walk through a field or in the woods, but especially in spring, you should check yourself for ticks afterward. The way a tick eats is by drinking blood; the way it finds blood is by crawling to the top of something, generally a blade of grass, and waiting for a mammal to walk by. This is called "questing." When one does, be it a deer, a dog or you, it jumps.

Mike was once on the side of a road in rural Oregon, trying to get a good angle to photograph a barn in the sunset. Upon returning to his hotel, he undressed for a shower. Clustered on the inside collar of his shirt were twenty wood ticks. In the shower he picked off twenty more.

While this sort of story is of course offered to induce shivers of dread, wood ticks really aren't that bad once you get used to them. They don't move very fast, and they take their time before latching on. It's rare that you wouldn't notice a tick crawling on you, long before it's attached. They tend to crawl up and to look for a warm, dark place—your crotch, armpit or head—so you usually feel it crawling. The main thing is not to panic. The first year we lived on the farm, Mike or I would completely lose it when we felt a tick—it's hard to resist the GET IT OFF! dance. But we quickly realized that if you freak out and start whisking at it, you'll just knock into some dark corner whence it will crawl up to the top of something and quest again.

If the tick is on your lower leg, simply pull up your pant leg and grab it. If it's on your thigh, put your hand on top of it so it can't go any further, carefully peel down your pants and grab it. No big deal. Right?

After a while, even you will become accustomed to ticks. A friend of mine was ready to pack up her kids and dog after a week, and leave her husband to his new farm, because they had ticks everywhere—in bed, in the laundry and of course on themselves. But they're just a part of country living.

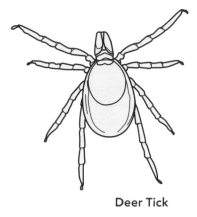

Deer Tick

Your livestock will have ticks. Your cats' and dogs' ticks, and how to dispatch them, are addressed in the Pets Chapter.

Deer ticks are another matter. These are the ones that can carry Lyme disease. They are tiny; the size of a poppy seed, so it's nearly impossible to see them. One telltale sign that you've been bitten by a deer tick is a ring of scaly, red irritation around the bite. I can't get into the politics of treating Lyme disease in this book, but do your research if you feel you have it. Some people think that you just pop a few antibiotics to treat it; others feel Lyme disease might be behind serious afflictions, such as chronic fatigue, Alzheimer's and multiple sclerosis.

Wasps

The day we moved to our house we threw a barbeque for the friends who had helped us to load a moving van, drive seventy miles and then unload it. Everyone piled food on their plates and found a seat on the deck or picnic table. Within seconds, every plate was covered with yellow jackets.

Miraculously, no one was stung. It was early August; yellow jackets don't get cranky until late summer, when things get dry. Most of the time you can just wave them away.

The other hazard with yellow jackets is they build their homes underground; the entrance is usually between some rocks or pieces of wood. I once was walking on an old fallen log in our woodlot, and went crashing through the top. Mike was a few steps behind me and yelled, "Run!" Without even looking back I knew I had blundered into a nest. We ran as fast as we could. I was lucky—only stung twice.

We learned that yellow jackets are called *meat bees* where we lived, because instead of sucking nectar, they scavenge carcasses (including fried chicken). The guy at the feed store showed us a plastic trap to hang near our house. A packet of pheromone-laced liquid is emptied into a cotton ball in the base of the trap, which lures them in. It doesn't attract other wasps or bees, just yellow jackets.

"If you do it in the spring," he advised, "you might get the queen."

Every spring thereafter, we hoped that we would.

Wasps generally get a bad rap—they mostly keep to themselves. Yellow jackets are a kind of a wasp, which is why people are generally fearful of all wasps, which isn't fair. Wasps eat and otherwise jeopardize the lives of pest bugs. They build beautiful nests.

Paper wasps, mud daubers, umbrella wasps: these are all names for *Sphecidae*, *Polistinae* or *Crabronidae*, those with the sleek, thin-waisted build that fighter-jet and motorcycle designers seem to emulate. These wasps build nests under eaves, in attics and just about anywhere they can get out of the rain. Unless you are directly menacing their pupae, they want nothing to do with you.

One June, Mike and I noticed that we had a steady stream of wasps coming and going near one of our exterior doors. They had found a way in between the main house structure and an addition, and were building a colony. We weren't too concerned since they weren't aggressive and, we figured, they would die once the temperature dropped below freezing, and then we could cap the hole and that would be the end of it.

Over the next few weeks we began to hear a clicking noise inside the wall in the kitchen: the wasps seemed to be flourishing. We started to get a little more nervous. Paper wasps chew wood, we thought—what if they're eating the rafters to bits? And, we thought, if they're so close to the warm kitchen maybe they wouldn't freeze after all…

By late August, the noise was getting louder. The crescendo came when I was awoken from sleep at three a.m. by a crunching, clicking sound, in my bed in the next room over. The following morning, I called an exterminator.

"Oh sure, I can take care of that," said John the Exterminator. When he learned where we lived, he said, "I have to go to my kid's high school open house; I'll come by on my way home." (You think *that* would ever happen in the city?)

Sure enough, at 7:15 John was stepping into his beekeeper's helmet and unwinding his pressure hose, which shoots a fatal distillation of a chrysanthemum flower, called pyrethrin. He found the "runway" and listened to the noise inside the house. "Yep," he said with a nod. "That's a pretty good one."

Without further ado, I sequestered myself in the house, behind a door that had a window so I could watch, and John started squirting poison up into the nest.

The clicking noise doubled in intensity. A buzzing sound was added. John was certainly getting their attention. I felt guilty about enjoying the death throes of who knows how many sentient beings, just trying to make it in this cruel world. The sound was awesome in the true sense of the word—the wasps sounded like they were boiling.

"Is it quieting down?" mouthed John from inside his mask. I shook my head. He stepped away from the battle zone, then slipped into the house using another door and came over to listen himself. Looking up at the ceiling, he said, "Do you see that?"

I looked up. All I could see on the white ceiling was a rough oval shape about five inches across, a slightly puffed area, as if the wallboard had a small amount of water damage. John raised his hand and gently poked the oval with his finger. It rippled like tissue paper.

"The only thing left there is the paint," John said. "You had two, maybe three days before they would have come through there."

The gravity of this sunk into me—we were leaving the next day for a weekend getaway. We would have returned to a house filled…with…wasps. I paced the floor to work off the adrenaline.

John chuckled and gingerly stuck a long, tubular nozzle onto a spray can of pyrethrin. He carefully poked the nozzle through the paint skin, and gave a good long spray. The clicking-buzzing noise stopped instantly. "That should do it," he said, slapping a piece of duct tape over the hole.

My hand shook as I wrote his check. Wasps…throughout…the…house. I had never been so happy to pay someone $95 for twenty minutes of work.

Fish, Reptiles and Amphibians

Let me begin this section by saying that, if you own an animal that you purchased at a pet store, mail order or other source, and you tire of taking care of said animal, it is illegal and irresponsible to release this animal into the wild. Pet stores and other sellers favor species that are hardy so they can withstand the rigors of captivity. When those species are released into a foreign habitat, they have no natural predators and tend to take over, decimating the native populations that have no defense against them.

The triumph of non-native species is a major problem in the United States. This section deals with just a few species, but there are plants, mollusks, mammals and other life forms creating headaches all over the country. Some listed here are native, some invaders, some native in some regions but have moved into others.

Alligator

One of the favorite genres of live television drama is to follow around a Department of Natural Resources employee as he deals with wild populations of reptiles in the Southeastern United States. As with horses in Nevada and grizzly bears in Montana, as humans encroach on alligators' native habitat there are more alligator-human encounters. They frequently show up on patios and in swimming pools.

If you see baby alligators, get away from them—mama alligators protect their babies as ferociously as mama bears, for as long as two years. Other than that, most alligator attacks are defensive, not offensive. An alligator will hiss if a defensive strike is imminent.

Boa Constrictor and Burmese Python

While alligators are native to Florida, boas and pythons are thriving as invasive species. These former captives have reproduced (people don't tend to bother spaying or neutering their pet snakes!), creating a thriving population of feral killer snakes slithering around Florida and other states.

Constrictors are unceremoniously hunted in the South. If you are so inclined, you can be trained to capture these snakes, but the best bet is to phone the police when one is spotted. Pythons don't attack humans (though they could, so don't provoke them) but eat endangered, native species of wood rats and muskrats in Florida. Some have been known to eat deer and alligators.

Catfish

There are many different invasive catfish species in the United States. Introduced by anglers, catfish are voracious eaters, making them a particularly challenging invasive species—in addition to out-eating the native species, they eat the native species.

Catfish are on the rise in the southern and Midwestern states, to the point there are "Catfish Days" celebrations in Illinois, Wisconsin, South Dakota, North Dakota and Minnesota. A friend said they're starting to cause fatalities by jumping up in the air and then hitting people in speedboats—no one wants a catfish in the face at 60 miles per hour.

In Florida, a particular breed of catfish known as "walking catfish," is especially notorious because of its ability to skim across bogs and even dry land after a good rain. They breathe air and are covered in a mucous that protects their skin. Walking fish. Great.

Frog

Bullfrogs are big—measuring as much as eight inches in length and weighing one pound! Because bullfrogs' legs can be eaten, humans have encouraged their thriving. However, they have extended far beyond their original, native range in the central and eastern United States, and are now considered an invasive species—they can take over a pond in just one season. They eat smaller, native frog species and just about anything else they can get their mouths around. We're not talking flies here—bullfrogs have been found with mice, bats, turtles and small birds in their stomachs.

Even smaller bullfrogs. They are cannibals, but that doesn't seem to put much of a dent in their overall population.

Iguana, Lizard and Gecko

These critters are alarming more than dangerous to come across, if they catch you off guard. I find them adorable, especially the little ones. They are quick but you can catch one if you move slowly toward it and then strike quickly.

I had to do this once in my house. About to leave on a camping trip, I came out of the bathroom, and there was an alligator lizard! It had walked in our back door, which was wide open. I stood there for a minute, assessing the situation. I didn't want to leave him in the house all weekend; he'd probably starve. I moved slowly toward him with a hand towel, and then dropped on him fast. Got him! I fished him out of the towel and released him outside. Pretty painless.

On a hike in the woods, my friend Sarah once came upon a lizard that had gotten its entire head stuck in an acorn shell. She chased it down and caught it, walked it home (note: she did not put it in her car with her), and cut the acorn off with cuticle scissors. Now, that's one lucky lizard.

Iguanas are yet another invasive species let loose into the wilds of Florida by irresponsible pet owners. They are often spotted lying about, like snakes, on sidewalks and streets—they're cold-blooded and trying to raise their body temperatures. In severely cold weather, they "freeze" solid, falling out of trees and hibernating until the temperature rises.

Iguanas are native to Mexico, Central America and South America, where certain species are raised like chickens for food. Some are dryland species and some, like the ones that live on the Galapagos Islands, can swim.

Some people wrap the bottoms of their trees in sheet metal to dissuade iguanas from descending into their yards. If trapped, iguanas must be turned over to the proper authorities to be euthanized—they can't be relocated, because they are non-native.

The biggest lizards in the United States are the Gila monsters of the Southwest. These slow-moving, massive creatures can measure two feet in length! They are poisonous, though not deadly to humans. But you wouldn't want to be bitten by one, as they tend to not let go. They typically hunt at night and avoid open spaces.

Snakes

Most snakes are beneficial, eating the rodents you don't want near your house anyway, but a few notable exceptions exist. One is the brown tree snake, which is decimating the songbirds of Hawai`i, as well as lizard and bat species there.

Garter snakes are harmless and rather fun to catch, to be honest. But watch out. If a garter snake feels threatened—and who wouldn't feel threatened by being picked up—it can shake and emit a foul-smelling musk that will get all over your hands. I once "saved" a garter snake that was stuck between a road and a wall too smooth to climb by picking it up and putting it in the grass above the wall. And then had to go into my business meeting and ask directly for the restroom, reeking of snake-panic.

Snakes (or any wild creature, for that matter) want as little to do with you as you them. They usually attack in self-defense, thinking they have no other choice. If you live in an area with rattlesnakes, cottonmouths or other poisonous snakes, the key is to not surprise one. Snakes sense vibrations above all other senses, so make some. If you're entering a shed or dark room, kick the wall or stomp your feet before entering so the snake knows something is coming. Don't reach onto a high shelf or into a tree that a snake could access, without looking first or tapping with a long stick. Don't start taking apart an old rock wall until you've knocked a sledgehammer into the rocks a couple of times. Rustle around a blackberry patch before you start picking.

If you do come upon a snake, you have three choices:

- **Get out of its way**
- **Relocate it**
- **Kill it**

If you're hiking and can just move past the snake, do it slowly. Most snakes must coil to strike, so if it's not coiled up you're in less imminent danger.

If you want to relocate the snake, calmly put a metal rake, face up near its head. The snake will wrap itself around the rake. You can then calmly turn the rake over and dump the snake into a cooler, bucket or something that has a cover and take it to wherever you want to release it.

If you choose to kill the snake, a shovel or hoe is the best tool. Chop its head off. Don't miss. As with anything that is killed, the snake's reflexes will be active for some time after the animal is dead. Severed snake heads have been known to bite! So be careful.

If you are bitten, move slowly toward help. If it's not dead (so you can bring it with you for identification purposes), try to remember what kind of snake it was, or what it looked like. Try to stay calm; the faster your heart beats, the faster the venom gets into your bloodstream. Do not apply a tourniquet á la John Wayne movies, or try to suck the poison out.

Turtle and Tortoise

There are two kinds of people in this world: those who will run over a turtle in the road for fun, and those inclined to stop their car, go back and carry the turtle to safety. There are two kinds of turtles in this world: box turtles (tortoises) live on the land and aquatic turtles (tarrapins) live in water. Box turtles tend to have taller shells, and eyes closer to the sides of their heads. Aquatic turtles' eyes are closer to the tops of their heads so they can hide underwater and still look around.

All turtles can live for decades. I have friends who own a box turtle and, because it will likely live longer than they, have written its care into their will. If you find a turtle, it's okay to examine it, but put it back where you found it. And then wash your hands! Turtles carry *salmonellosis* bacteria.

Snapping turtles have sharp beaks and extremely strong jaws. You can usually tell them because they have excessively spiked shells, compared to regular turtles. If you are relocating a snapping turtle, pick it up from the back of its shell. It can crane its head pretty far backwards, so watch it. Another strategy is to place a stick in front of its mouth, perpendicularly, so that it latches on to the stick and can't bite you (make sure the stick is thicker than a pencil or the turtle will simply snap it in half).

Pet-store turtles have been released where they shouldn't, and threaten the native populations. One example is the red-eared slider, which is native in the Mississippi River Valley of the central United States but is threatening native species in states like Pennsylvania, not to mention all over the world.

Mammals

Wild mammals are one or more of three things: predator, prey or scavenger. I talk about some animals in a specific context elsewhere in the book, such as skunks, which are mentioned in terms of their appetite for fresh chicken and their occasional run-ins with your dog.

You will never see most of nature's wild creatures, especially during the day. They are secretive and usually aware of you long before you would have noticed them. If the wind is blowing away from you, and you've managed to not make a sound for a while, you'll sometimes surprise one. And sometimes, they simply appear where you'd least expect it. Once, I looked out the kitchen window in the afternoon and saw a big coyote nonchalantly trotting across our field.

There's nothing as alarming and annoying as being awoken from sleep to the banging of trash-can lids as a raccoon or a bear gets into your garbage or petfood. Or to go to the kitchen in the morning wanting nothing more than to make some coffee and cook a nice breakfast, only to find mouse poop all over your counter.

Humans make all kinds of yummy food, and scavengers want to share it. Can you blame them? Your only recourse is to make it impossible to access, and they'll go looking elsewhere. Keep your garbage in a critter-proof can and, even better, in a shed or other building that has a closed door. If not, use a bungee cord or other device to hold lids on cans. Ditto animal feed. Plastic garbage cans are not sufficient for feed, as rodents can chew through them.

Encounters with wild animals can be thrilling and scary. Sometimes spiritual. Some animals are tamer than others—while most creatures will run away from you on sight, a raccoon may stand its ground, and even growl at you, if you challenge it. Especially if it's sitting on your deck, eating your cat's food. Rule of thumb: If you are in its territory, leave it alone. If it's in yours, run it off. Brooms come in handy for this sort of thing. Or rifles, depending on your tolerance for critters and for violence.

Badger

Badgers are complete bad-asses but pretty much keep to themselves; you are unlikely to just happen across one. I include them because they dig holes in fields, which are a boon for burrowing owls and coyotes, but dangerous to a galloping horse, which can break a leg in a badger hole. For this reason, some ranchers shoot badgers on sight.

Bat

These little guys get a bad rap, which is unfair because they pose no threat to anything but insects. While there are larger bat species in the world that feed on fruit and animal blood, the species that live in the United States use echolocation, or sonar, to capture mosquitoes, moths and many other types of insects (read: agricultural pests). A bat is not pretty or graceful, but it gets the job done—consuming thousands of insects per night.

A fungal infection called white-nose syndrome is doing great damage to bat colonies in the Northeastern United States, and is spreading westward. Bats are also thought to be more adversely affected by wind turbines than birds. So, put up some bat houses in your area! They need all the help we can give them. But—not too close to the house, as there can be an odor issue. Bat poop ("guano") is a great fertilizer, with high levels of nitrogen and phosphorus. However, it's too acidic to put directly on a plant and must be composted first.

While bats do fly erratically, and very near your head if they're flying low and you're standing still, they will not get entangled in your hair. If you find a bat in your house, open all the doors and windows so it can find its way out again. Turning lights off or on is irrelevant as it uses sonar to navigate. If it gives up and lands somewhere, treat it like you would a bird: catch it in gloved hands or a small towel (still with gloves) and bring it outside. Very few bats carry rabies, but if it came in contact with someone in the house you might have it tested just to be sure. There's no need to go after it with a tennis racket—it's not attacking you, it's just lost. Plus, if you do want to test it for rabies, the head must be intact.

That said, you do not want a colony living in your attic; if you have one, contact a pest-control professional.

Bear

There are two kinds of bears in the United States—grizzly bears (also known as brown bears and Kodiak bears) and black bears. Either bear can range in color from brown to black—even white! Generally, bears are shy and will run when they smell/hear/see (in that order) you. Most attacks involving humans occur when someone has snuck up on a bear at close range that has food or offspring nearby.

Grizzlies are bigger and have a hump over their front shoulders; most of them are in Alaska and northwestern Montana. They are solitary except to congregate at the mouths of rivers in the Pacific Northwest to feast on salmon. They are more carnivores than herbivores.

Black bears are sort of like big dogs. They are more herbivores than carnivores and are more likely to dig through your garbage than go after your livestock. And these are your honey-mongers. They are widespread throughout the mountainous and/or forested parts of the United States. Unlike grizzlies, black bears don't truly hibernate, they just hang out (sometimes called "Seasonal Lethargy"…I think I do that in the winter, too).

Beaver

The North American beaver is the largest rodent on the continent (the porcupine is second); adults can reach one hundred pounds! They live anywhere there is aquatic habitat. They are excellent swimmers and engineers, known for building dams and underwater lodges. Beaver activity benefits numerous bird and fish species and regulates surface water and ground water. But, in the process they can decimate tree stands and alter waterways, creating flooding in people's yards and fields. They are, therefore, controversial.

If you live on a waterway that is affected by a beaver dam, contact your local U.S. Fish and Wildlife office.

Coyote and Wolf

I was once sitting on a giant rock under a full moon in Joshua Tree State Park. Everything was glowing in an ethereal blue light, bright enough that I could write in my journal without a flashlight. The rock was as big as a car, lifting me several feet off the ground. From this vantage point, writing in my journal, I noticed a dark shape coast fluidly around my rock and off toward some brush. I felt it as much as saw it. Even though I had never encountered one before, I knew it was a coyote.

It's not happenstance that the coyote plays a big role in Native American mythology across the Northern Hemisphere. Coyote is known as a trickster, one of the many anthropomorphized creatures of the world who stole fire from the gods and gave it to humans. He is not seen as a hero but as a flawed troublemaker.

If nothing else about Coyote translates to modern-day mainstream culture, his anti-hero status certainly does. Coyotes are generally considered a menace. They feed on small mammals in the wild but are known to take lambs, calves and even sheep from pastures. In places where the rural-urban boundary is rapidly growing, coyotes eat garbage and household pets.

The call of a pack of coyotes is otherworldly. They mostly converse during the spring and fall, a haunting, high-pitched whine-turned-scream chorus that can raise bumps on your skin. I have always found it charming, but then, I knew my chickens were safe in their bunker. (Although, the morning after being awoken by coyotes in the middle of the night, I always approached the chicken house with a bit of trepidation, hoping the coyotes hadn't figured a way in.)

The existence of wolves is an extremely controversial issue. Why wolves and not coyotes? Because, while ranchers and government workers kill tens of thousands of coyotes every year, wolves have spent the last few decades on the Endangered Species list. In the 1900s, they were reintroduced in Arizona (tenuously successful), Idaho and Yellowstone National Park (successful; even moving into Oregon), and North Carolina and Great Smoky Mountains National Park (failure), places that had successfully eradicated them. This is a triumph for wolves and for the humans who love them; it's a travesty and a farce to many others, mostly ranchers.

Wolves prey on deer, elk, moose, caribou, and smaller animals like beavers. If coyotes are in the same territory, wolves will also kill (but not eat) coyotes. They occasionally hunt livestock.

You'll find that born-and-raised country folk will not hesitate for one second before raising a gun whenever they see a coyote or a wolf. It's an innate reaction, and a straightforward argument. When they see a coyote, they see mangled fawns and mauled calves. I read once about a rancher who went out at two in the morning to check her herd and found a mama cow that had given birth. It took a minute, in the darkness and driving snow, to realize that the calf was half-eaten, as was the back end of the cow, which paced nervously in circles, not sure of what to.

If a rancher has to choose between a coyote or wolf in her field, or $2,000 worth of beef in a steer, she'll shoot that critter without hesitation.

Javelina, or Peccary

This American native (and by that I mean native to the Americas, not just the United States) is often confused for a wild hog, which originated in Eurasia. In the U.S., javelinas are found in southwestern Texas, Arizona and New Mexico. Smaller than hogs, javelinas are omnivores that live in packs. In some neighborhoods, you'll see them rooting through garbage. Like wild hogs, javelinas are hunted for sport and meat.

Mouse and Rat

Most country homes have mice. Our house was remarkably sound around the foundation (mice can squeeze through all but the tiniest gaps), and the only time we had one was because our cat had brought a live one in and then lost track of it under the couch. The best defense against an infestation is to not have anything for it to eat—keep grains stored in jars (this also thwarts moths), or in drawers or on inaccessible shelves (though they are remarkably adept at jumping and getting almost anywhere). Clean up your kitchen thoroughly every evening. It only takes a few toast crumbs on the floor to keep a mouse going. And there are, of course, traps.

If you're from the city, you're familiar with rats. I was once visiting a farm and the farmer was showing me her henhouse, and noticed that a narrow corn-feeding chute was empty. She spotted the reason and sighed, grabbing a rat's tail from the top of the feeder and ripping it out. It had gorged itself, gotten stuck and suffocated.

The same strategies for mice work for rats. Keep food inaccessible (including birdfeeders and pet food). Set traps. Have cats or rat-killing dogs (terriers were specially bred for this job).

Porcupine

The North American porcupine is a nocturnal, slow-moving rodent that pretty much keeps to itself, eating twigs and roots, and sleeping in trees. Its main impingement on humans is gnawing on plywood, garden-tool handles and other items in search of salt.

It is unfair to refer to the damage done by porcupine quills as an "attack"— while the porcupine might raise its quills and swing its tail, it cannot throw or shoot its quills; they lodge in another animal when it comes into contact with the porcupine. That is self-defense.

Here's a good one: Porcupines have antibiotics in their skin. Why? Because in their quest for the most succulent leaves and branch-ends, they often fall out of trees and stick themselves with their own quills!

Raccoon

The raccoon is a true omnivore, and a successful animal that has adapted to nearly every environment in the United States, so long as there are things to climb (it prefers to nest in oak trees). Its predominant sense is touch.

Raccoons are not shy of humans; on the contrary, many will come right up to your patio. A friend had one actually coming into the house; it had figured out how to reach around the edge of the cat door and pry it open. She had been wondering why her cat was making such a mess around its food bowl...

Do not feed raccoons. They are not pets, and don't need encouragement. If you have raccoons in your attic, it's most likely a female looking for a place to nurse her babies. If you have dogs, don't send them out after raccoons at night, because a raccoon will not back down, especially if it's a mother. Our friends' cat got into a fight with a raccoon and ended up at the emergency vet with forty puncture wounds.

Razorback, or Wild Hog

Wild, or feral, hogs are thought to have been released by Christopher Columbus—he thought it could provide future excursions a food source. Others followed suit, and wild hogs now live nearly everywhere in the world, including the United States (excepting Alaska but including the Hawaiian Islands). They are considered a pest animal, and hunted for sport and for meat. Their wallowing and foraging habits tear up farm fields and pastures, undermine roadbeds and embankments, and stimulate the growth of invasive weed species in forests.

Squirrels, Chipmunks, Ground Squirrels

Rats don't get much respect. How do I know this? Because anytime people want to denigrate another animal, they liken it to a rat. Hence "tree rat" for squirrel.

Squirrels, like raccoons and pigeons, have adapted so successfully to urban life that they've achieved pest status. They're no less successful, and no better respected, in the country. When I went to southeastern Oregon on a writer's residency, one of the first things to greet me as I drove into Hines was a fifteen-foot-tall metal sculpture of a ground squirrel ("sage rat"). The business was an outfitter—apparently, wealthy West Coast CEOs come to Harney County in the spring to blow off some steam by going into the desert and blasting a few dozen ground squirrels with rifles. So long as they leave enough for the raptors and coyotes, I guess.

There should be a book of homespun designs for squirrel-proofing a bird-feeder. My mother could contribute about ten designs herself. The place it's hung, the way it's hung, the material with which is covered and hung—so many strategies, so few successes. Squirrels are hungry little Houdinis—they can jump ten feet. They can weasel between wires. They can hang upside-down by their back feet. Whatever it takes.

Mike and I rather liked the squirrels in the woods by our house. They were a smaller species, called Douglas squirrel. They would make a great racket when we went down the woods, alerting their friends of our presence. But they never tried to get into our house or anything.

If you feed squirrels on a platform right outside your dining-room window because "they're cute," and are subsequently dismayed that they've moved into your attic, I have no sympathy.

Birds

One of my favorite things to do in the winter is sit near a picture window and watch birds on a feeder. We had many visitors during our time on the farm—the regulars: golden-crowned and other sparrows; juncos; finches; chickadees. The ones that were usually, but not always, there: varied thrush; nuthatch; spotted towhee. The rare treats: Bohemian waxwing; evening grosbeak; Western tanager.

There are differing schools of thought regarding feeding birds. Some people feed them all year; some only during the winter. The main thing about feeding them is this: If you feed birds so well that they decide not to fly south, then you'd better keep it up. If you go on vacation in January and stop feeding them, they may starve. My way was to not feed them unless snow had completely covered the ground. This didn't happen until late fall, so any bird that wanted to migrate had done so. Once the snow melted, I figured there was plenty of food in the field and woods for them. I only put out songbird food—the jays could fend for themselves. Though sunflower seeds would have attracted grosbeaks.

Make sure you're feeding wild birds seed that is part of their natural diet—thistle, sunflower, etc. Do not feed them the ends of your bread loaves—that is made of processed flour that they are not evolved to digest well.

Hummingbirds drink nectar, and people replicate nectar by feeding them sugar-water. All hummingbird feeders are red because the birds are most attracted to that color (which you'll notice if you ever go out in your garden wearing a red shirt). Do not put red food color in the sugar-water; it's a chemical they don't need in their systems. Again, if you start feeding them in the fall, you must feed them all winter.

Set up your feeders so that you can see the birds but, ideally, they cannot see you. If they're too close to the house, movement inside the house will scare them off. Put the feeder near a bush or tree so that the birds have a safe place to monitor the feeder before flying to it—sitting on a feeder exposes them to predators. More than once did I see a sharp-shinned hawk whiz through the yard and pluck a poor songbird from the air. And, of course, our cat was always nearby, scheming.

European Starling

I include this bird mostly because of its fantastic "introduction" story. In the late nineteenth century the American Acclimatization Society, a group that wanted to help New York immigrants from Europe feel more at home, released all of the birds mentioned in Shakespeare's works into Central Park, including the house sparrow, nightingale and lark. Starlings (from *Henry IV, Part I*) took this invitation and ran with it, chasing native songbirds away from their nests and eating their food, and marauding crops, from sea to shining sea. Even up to Alaska.

Flicker

Part of the woodpecker family, flickers either delight or terrorize, depending on how you feel about them vis-à-vis your house. Not because they're hungry—flickers are ground feeders, mostly feasting on ants. They nest in a cavity, which is drilled out of wood. This might be the wood of a dead tree, or the wood that is your siding or soffit.

To find a good nest site, flickers tap here and there. If a place sounds hollow enough, the flicker will excavate. That is how people get four-inch holes in their houses. Many a quiet Saturday morning, lounging in bed, was interrupted by the ratta-tat-tat of a flicker testing the siding at the top of our house. We'd have to jump up and pound on our wall or, if that failed to impress, run outside and chase it off the house.

Another way flickers use your house is as a giant resonator, especially during spring mating season. They communicate with each other with a shrill cry, as well as with tapping noises that they make with their bills—the louder the better. And, what could be louder than your chimney pipe?

Hawk

Hawks, eagles, harriers, kites, vultures, ospreys and falcons are all raptors, birds that hunt on the wing. Most hunt live prey, while vultures (and sometimes kites) eat carrion. Owls are also raptors, but they get their own segment, below. Some specialize in hunting, like ospreys, which prefer fish, and some specialize in stealing from hunters, like eagles. They won't make a significant impact on you or your land unless you start losing chickens, rabbits or ducks. Keep the animals in a place that has at least partial overhead shelter, and this shouldn't be a major problem.

Muscovy Duck

Mucovies are native in just a couple of counties in southern Texas; elsewhere in the United States they're an invasive species. In Florida in particular, muskovies are considered a scourge because they challenge suburban communities' standards of appearance by soiling driveways, lawns and patios with their feces, and nesting in bushes and eaves. They are considered disease-carriers, though no health agency has found them to be a health risk to humans except as a newly hatched chick, which can carry salmonella.

The main deterrent to these ducks is to not feed them. You can also purchase fox or mongoose urine and spread that around your yard. If a duck nests in your yard, you can remove the eggs or shake them to kill the contents. Once the duck abandons the nest (she will figure out that her fetuses are dead after a few days), be sure to compost or dispose of the eggs, which will become rotten and smell.

Before you write off the Muscovy duck as a pest, remember that it eats many other pests, including mosquito larvae, roaches, small rodents and snakes.

Owl

You will probably have owls all around you in the country, but you may never know it, save for the late-night hooting of great horned owls in late winter, when they mate. These nocturnal hunters rely on stealth to capture small mammals and birds. Their downy feathers make them silent in flight, and their ears are slightly cockeyed so that they can triangulate the location of a sound (the "facial disk" helps direct sounds to their ears). Because their eyes are fixed in place, an owl has to turn its entire head to see! It can also turn its head upside-down.

Owls generally eat their prey whole and then regurgitate the bones later in a compact pellet. Where I lived, there was a thriving business based on collecting these pellets and them selling them to schools, where they're used in science classes (it's fun to take a pellet apart and try to reassemble the tiny skeletons!). "Independent contractors" would develop collection routes, getting permission from farmers to regularly harvest owl pellets from barns and woodlots. Sort of the Klickitat County version of Avon.

Because owls provide natural rodent control, many people encourage them to take up residence on their property by posting nesting boxes (owls do not construct nests but seek out hollow trees and other cavities).

Quail

I love quail. I love their little headdresses. I love the way they move in a group, some going ahead, the most following and then the stragglers scurrying to not be left behind, running, running, then Away! They all fly to a nearby bush or tree. They talk to each other a lot, mostly worrying I suppose. They're easily startled; being constantly on the run seems to be their only defense.

Quail, also called partridges, are native in some areas and naturalized in many others. They attract raptors because they're so plentiful and easy to catch. If you see a covey of quail, look up—there will be a male stationed on a fencepost or other high spot as the guard. You'll hear him calling to the others, giving the all-clear or sounding an alert.

For a while, one group of quail chose our hawthorn tree to be their roost site. It was fun to watch them fly up and arrange themselves for the night.

(Wild) Turkey

I remember seeing a bottle of Wild Turkey as a child and not comprehending the bird depicted on the label. That isn't a turkey, I thought—turkeys are those nearly round things we associate with Thanksgiving, not the lithe creature on the bottle. It turns out that the fluffed out turkey is the equivalent of the NBC-type of peacock. Both of these images are of males during mating season—tails fully extended in order to intimidate other cocks and attract a hen. Most of the time, both turkeys and peacocks look relatively unspectacular. (And while we're clearing up misconceptions, the latter animal is a "peafowl," which male is called a peacock and which female is called a peahen.)

Once the chicks have hatched, mama turkeys group together in twos and threes and take their charges (up to two dozen!) on a circuit that, if you're lucky, includes your property. They move so gracefully and regally as to appear to be floating through the grass. They are aware of everything around them, clucking out observations to each other and answering, "Right here," to the chicks' frightened cries of "Where are you?" (They aren't tall enough yet to see above the grass.)

Wild turkeys are smarter than domestic turkeys, but that isn't saying much. They will fly into your fenced garden, and then forget how they got in and not be able to get out. After watching them race around the perimeter of the garden a few times, you may need to go out there and flush them—once they see you coming they'll finally remember their wings and fly away in a panic.

Section Four
Food

Food

When I first started gardening in Portland, my sister-in-law was in her early twenties, in the process of feeling out the world, her place in it, and her opinions about it. She grew up in a suburban household in which nutrition was a factor in meal-planning but "local" and "organic" had not come to the fore. When I mentioned that I was growing organically, she asked what that meant. I told her that I wasn't adding fertilizers or chemicals.

"Then won't the plants die?" she asked.

"No, I use compost, which can be even better than fertilizer."

"What's compost?"

I told her and she recoiled. "You mean you're eating food that's grown in *poop*?"

I tried to explain that while compost had started out as poop, it had "aged" and now was just rich dirt. She would have none of it. It was years before she would even try organic food because she was grossed out by it.

It's interesting to study the history of agriculture, particularly over the past century. In the 1800s, farming in the United States was typically a family affair. The first large-scale farming operations were successful in the South with the use of slave labor. The North's smaller farms raised food for personal use (food as well as grain for livestock) and for a local market. The dust storms and erosion that plagued the central United States during the 1930s was on everyone's minds as farmers and scientists worked to establish new strategies for growing the nation's food.

As the reputation of chemists and other scientists grew during the 20th century, so did their influence into spheres outside of warfare. Fertilizers were discovered to improve yields, and pesticides, herbicides and insecticides killed unwanted interlopers. Improved preserving and transportation methods made it possible to export food products to other parts of the world. Side effects to the environment and to animals and humans were not yet on the radar: As far as science was concerned, a Golden Age arrived.

As the modern "locavore" movement gains momentum the idea of conquering nature with science is falling out of favor, to the chagrin of postindustrial giants like Monsanto and Cargill. These kings of grain and soybeans will probably never be completely deposed, but they are being challenged by people who prefer to work within the limitations of what nature can provide, rather than overwhelming those limitations with chemicals which ultimate impact has never been fully measured and may affect the earth for decades.

Chapter 13
Buying

Animal Products

While I have never been a vegetarian, I like vegetarian food and avoid mass-market meat. The way the animals live, what they are fed, how they are slaughtered, and how the workers who were involved were treated all factor into the equation for me.

There are two ways to support humane meat: own livestock yourself or buy into someone else's. Most people who bother to raise animals raise more than enough for themselves; they usually just give or sell it to family and friends. So, ask around until you find someone who has extra animals to sell.

You generally put in your order in the spring, when the farmer is buying/birthing babies, and pick up your meat once the animal matures (this varies; you will be notified). Chickens and turkeys are sold eviscerated but whole unless you make a special request. Larger animals can be halved or even quartered, and come in wrapped packages with different cuts. A whole steer can be 800 (!) pounds of meat cut into various steaks, ribs, burger and sometimes sausage. If you decide to order beef, start with a quarter-cow at the most—it is a lot of meat, and even if the per-pound price is low it's still a major investment. And make sure you have a freezer big enough to hold it.

Eggs

Chicken and duck eggs are sold year-round, sometimes at the feed store, sometimes at a local grocery, sometimes at the library, sometimes via a CSA (which stands for "community-supported agriculture" and means you buy a share of the farm's produce for a season; see below). Or, you might befriend someone who sells them.

Three things about store-bought eggs:

1) Farm fresh eggs are infinitely better. The yolks are firm and orange in color. There have been studies that indicate they're healthier than caged chickens that are given the cheapest feed—usually including remnants from other processing plants. My reaction to that: Do you need a study to prove that? Look at the eggs!

2) There is absolutely no difference between white- and brown-shelled eggs—farmers charge more for brown eggs because consumers think they're somehow more "natural." It's just a different breed of chicken.

3) I roll my eyes whenever I see someone in line with a carton of "vegetarian-fed" eggs. Chickens are *not* vegetarians. If you put a plate of broccoli and a plate of slugs down in front of chickens, guess which disappears first?

There is one thing that store-bought eggs have over fresh eggs—they make better hard-boiled eggs. But this is because they're already a couple of weeks old when they hit the grocer's cooler, and the albumen has evaporated enough to make an air-space inside the egg. If you kept fresh eggs around long enough—go ahead and try; I dare you!—they would work as well. If you hard-boil a fresh egg, it's delicious, just difficult to peel.

You will have a better outcome with cracking eggs with tough shells, like turkey and quail, if you crack the egg as per usual and then carefully run a paring knife through the membrane.

Refrigeration: If you have fresh eggs that have never been refrigerated, you don't need to refrigerate them. However, refrigeration does make them last longer, and once they've been refrigerated they should stay refrigerated until use. If you wash your eggs, wash them in hot water and then refrigerate them. Or, you can wash them directly before use. You run a slight risk of salmonella from a dirty shell, but cooking the egg kills the bacterium. Eggs can last for many weeks. Store them with the wider part up; this centers the yolk in the albumen. However, a country egg probably won't last long enough to matter!

Milk

When milk is harvested from dairy cows, what comes out is a far cry from what pours from our familiar cartons and plastic jugs. Real milk has cream, whey and other components that are separated off. For most of post-hunter/gatherer human life, milk was harvested from cows and consumed raw. In the late 1800s, pasteurization was used to sterilize the milk but, as those who use acidophilus know, when you kill all the bacteria you kill both the bad and the good. Homogenization followed to bring us consistent, white milk from which cream doesn't separate.

Raw milk became a dirty, coarse thing of the past until—you guessed it— the 1960s back-to-the-land movement. Since then, its value as a cure for digestive problems and an immunity booster have been an underground hippie/whole foods junkie secret. People who swear by raw milk, which is illegal to sell in many states, accuse the Food and Drug Administration of kowtowing to the dairy lobby. The FDA cites E-coli, brucellosis and salmonella outbreaks that can be traced to whole milk.

In no state is it illegal to use raw milk from your own cow in any way you want (personal use). In the states that it is illegal to sell, there are loopholes for raw milk sold for pets, or you can buy into a cow so it technically belongs to you (at least in part). If you drink home-produced whole milk, be sure to maintain a spotlessly clean operation—E-coli and salmonella contamination occurs when cows' udders have feces on them when they are milked, which is not uncommon. There is a vaccine for dairy cows called Bangs, which protects against brucellosis. It must be administered within the first year to be effective.

Take advantage of a modern convenience—the food processor—and churn your own butter! Or, learn how to make cheese. There is a bit of investment in equipment, but people go gaga over fresh cheese.

Goat milk is also popular, and its popularity is growing. Goat's milk doesn't affect people with lactose issues, and it can be made into kefir, cheese and other "dairy" products.

CSA

CSA stands for Community-Supported Agriculture, and has come to mean a farm that sells subscriptions. These farms may have only a handful of subscriptions, or hundreds; it just depends on how much food they intend to grow. Some have animal products as well as produce. Some CSAs welcome visitors only on special days, and some expect subscribers to come and help on a regular basis. Most grow organically.

Subscribers absorb some of the risk of farming—you pay for your subscription up front; if there is a bumper crop, you reap the benefits. If there was a less-than-expected crop, you share in the starve.

Your share is usually delivered, if not to your house then to a centrally located pick-up spot. If you are a two-person family and don't need oodles of produce, you might consider splitting a share with someone. Ask the farmer for a "menu" of what they plant. Getting a CSA box can be like your birthday: Ooo, look; raspberries! And it can also be slightly depressing if all you get is bok choi and turnips.

Big-Box Stores

Ironically, many ruralites are as far removed from locavore culture as anyone else. They plan trips to the nearest city that has a Costco or other big-box discount grocery and stock up on the same cartons of cereal, bales of toilet paper, and plastic-encased roasted whole chickens as their suburban and urban counterparts.

It's a good policy to have a lot of back stock—you just won't get into town all that often, and it's better to have two extra tubes of toothpaste in storage than to run out. Even if town isn't all that far away, what if you wake up to two feet of snow, or your car won't start?

Chapter 14
Domestic Animals

Anyone who tries to tell you that evolution is not real needs to study selective breeding. Over centuries, humans have accelerated natural selection by exploiting favorable characteristics in animals and minimizing unfavorable ones to serve our dietary needs. Which is how you get Angus cows, brawny creatures that are dumb as posts. Or fryer chickens, which are grown for their meat, and layer chickens, which are grown for their egg-laying. Or turkeys with breasts so large they can hardly walk.

This legacy of domestication is tricky. Domesticated animal breeds are dependent on us for life, yet most die at our hands. Vegetarians are able to avoid the issue by virtue of non-participation, but the fact remains that if the entire planet decided to stop eating meat and turn the domestic animals loose, most of them wouldn't go anywhere. Not that sheep or cows have this sort of complex thought process, but: If you had to choose between being shot in the head one day, and running in terror from a coyote or a cougar, being caught, having your stomach eaten from your body while you were still alive and then slowly dying while your blood drained into a field, which would you pick? Domestic animals are hard-wired, because of us, to rely on us for food and protection from animal predators. It's a predicament.

Which is where terms like "free-range" and "naturally nested" come in. Compassionate carnivores do not endorse the corn-glutted meat factories set up in the Midwestern states, but do like to eat animal protein. Their compromise is to pay twice or three times the market value of mass-produced meat in order to support a small-scale operation that treats animals with respect and dignity, and butchers them humanely.

There is more than one way to skin a cat, and to kill a chicken. Old-world farmer ladies would march into the hen house, grab a chicken by its head and unceremoniously whip it around in a circle, snapping its neck. There is the familiar hatchet-and-chopping-block. Cattle, goats and hogs are shot. If you butcher a rabbit, which provides a white meat that can be made into delicious sausage, prepare yourself mentally for the task; rabbits often scream when they're killed. They are usually hit sharply on the back of the head with a mallet or club.

Hiring a Butcher

So. After you've bought another farmer's meat and fallen in love with the flavor of respectfully raised and slaughtered animals, but before you get into butchering yourself, there is some middle ground, namely a professional butcher. There are two ways to put the responsibility of killing your livestock on someone else's shoulders— take your livestock to a slaughterhouse or hire an on-site butcher to come to your farm. Either way, you want to ask around for the person's reputation for quick dispatch and sanitary processing practices.

The advantage of using a slaughterhouse is the no-mess factor of it—you drop off your animal and come back a few days later to pick up a parcel of wrapped cuts, labeled and ready for your freezer. The advantage of bringing in the mobile slaughter truck is you don't have to transport your animal.

Most animals that are raised for slaughter have pretty short lives, the shortest being fryer chickens—killed at ten weeks of age! Farmers and ranchers try to balance raising the biggest animal possible without compromising its tenderness. One autumn evening, we were planning to butcher a rooster and ended up taking a three-and-a-half-year-old hen as well, because she hadn't laid an egg since she was a pullet and while we were making a mess we might as well get it over with. The four-month-old rooster was svelte but delicious, baked in the oven with vegetables. The hen, on the other hand, was so old and tough that even being cooked in a soup for hours did nothing to tenderize her. She made flavorful stock, but we had to eat around the rubbery nuggets of meat.

Butchering

Once you decide to cross the line into killing and "dressing" (a euphemism for removing the organs and cutting the carcass into pieces) livestock yourself, I recommend starting with chickens. They're small and relatively easy to manage.

If you're growing chickens for meat with the intention of butchering a lot of them at once, you'll probably want to skip the chopping block and invest in a killing cone and a sharp knife. This handy device serves the dual purpose of holding the chicken still and holding it upside-down, which facilitates the bleeding-out. If you will only occasionally be killing a chicken to cull non-layers or take care of errant roosters in your flock, you can either cut the corner from an old pillowcase and shove the chicken into it, or simply hold it with your (gloved) hands while someone else kills it.

It's less mess later if you keep a doomed chicken from eating for at least a few hours before slaughter, so nothing is in the upper portion of its intestinal tract. Chickens are easier to manage if you pull them at night from the roost; they are very docile when they're sleeping. Even if you choose to butcher during the day, turning a chicken upside-down calms it; make sure you keep the wings from flapping.

I have participated in both knife and hatchet butchering, and think either is efficient. Whichever means you employ, make sure that:

- You have a sharp implement.
- You have a bucket for blood drainage.
- You have a clean bucket for the carcasses.
- You take aim and give it your all—no one wants a half-killed animal.

Using a hatchet is fairly straightforward—stretch the neck out a bit and chop through the center of it. If you use a knife on an upside-down chicken, stick the blade in its throat so that the blade is facing toward the ground, between the neck bone and the cluster of trachea, esophagus and major blood vessels; turn the blade toward this cluster and push the knife through all of it.

Brace yourself; the chicken will flop around a bit. It's nothing more than a burst of synapses firing after the spinal cord is cut, but it can be a bit freaky. If you cut a chicken's head off and put it on the ground it might run, but I don't recommend this because it will get dirty and will splatter blood all over. The severed head's eyes might blink and the mouth move; the wings will definitely flap if they're not restrained; it might make some honking sounds through its severed windpipe. And then it will stop.

Taking a life is a significant thing. Give yourself a little time, maybe not right afterwards, but later in the day maybe, to grieve. This may sound silly, but unless you've grown up killing animals, it can be a little traumatic. You'll get used to it.

Butchering Ages (in months)

189

Dressing

Again, I'm using a chicken as an example because it's small and easy to work with. There are plenty of step-by-step instructions for dressing an animal in books and on the Internet; I'm providing an overview. The best way to learn this process is to watch someone else do it.

So, you've got your carcass—now what? It should be hanging by its feet—the blood needs to drain from the body. Larger animals stay hanging to be processed but chickens can be handled. After it's bled out, the main things are speed and cleanliness. The sooner you get that meat into the refrigerator the better.

I recommend having an outdoor work area—it's easier to clean up and keeps your house from smelling like guts (an absolutely disgusting aroma). If you plan to keep the chicken in its skin, you need to pluck it. This is accomplished by dunking the chicken in very hot water, swirling it around for a few minutes to get the water up into the feathers. This relaxes the muscles that control the feathers; they should rip out easily. The tricky part is the pinfeathers, little spines that stick out from the skin. You can remove them with a pliers or wax (tedious), or burn them off with a torch (smells bad). If you plan to do this a lot, invest in a rubber-fingered chicken-plucker. Really! It's a machine that rubs your chicken with dozens of rubber appendages, wearing off the pinfeathers in a few seconds. Or, you can buy the plans to build one.

Next, you have to remove the internal organs. If you have a cat or dog, they are probably at your feet by this point, hoping for a treat. The heart and liver are good treats; gizzard and intestines are not. The trick with removing the organs is that the intestine is full of feces. Feces and edible meat do not mix. If you pierce or otherwise break the intestines, you will taint the meat and the whole project will be a loss. So, concentrate.

The intestinal tract is a grand tube that begins with the mouth and ends with the anus. If you control the two ends and keep the rest of the tube intact, it's a closed system. You've already severed the throat; now you need to free the south end. You do this by cutting oh-so-carefully around the anus, disconnecting that tissue from the rest of the body. To make a little more room for the impending entrails exodus, you can cut up toward the thighs as well. Then you reach carefully around the anus and up into the body cavity and try to coax the whole kit and caboodle out the back door. I did this once with a quail, and it was like a gut explosion—How did all that fit in that little quail body? Once the organs are out, get them off the table and into a bucket or other disposal unit. You can pick the edible organs out if you're so inclined.

It might seem to make more sense to pull the guts from the much larger hole at the neck, but doing so would run the risk of releasing fecal matter from the anus on its way through the body cavity.

Get that chicken into ice water as soon as possible to cool the meat, and refrigerate afterwards until the rigor mortis has eased. We didn't know this when we dressed our chickens, and couldn't figure out how to get the legs tucked back into the body! Because they died hanging upside-down, they barely fit in the freezer, and we had to cut the legs off to fit them in a baking dish.

Chapter 15
Gardening

Planting something in the ground and watching it grow can be a heady experience. Looking out the window and seeing a plum tree, so full of fruit that it's bent over, can make a person weep. To think, you can eat as many of those plums as you want! They're yours! For every food-related plant you grow, you need to know the following:

- How to grow it from seed (unless you plan to always buy starts from another farmer or a plant nursery)
- Where and under what conditions to plant it
- How to nurture it during its growing cycle
- How to combat the pests that attack it
- When and how to harvest it
- How to process and store the harvest

You also need to keep a clean operation, which means completely removing the residue of annuals in the fall and pruning perennials in the spring.

Design

In order to harvest, you must first cultivate. Before you can cultivate, you must lay the groundwork for a successful garden. And that means a plan. How much food do you want to grow? Is one tomato plant enough (No.)? Are ten too many? Don't plant a quarter-acre of garlic unless you know how you're going to handle it.

Our garden was round-ish in shape and one hundred feet across. If I can dredge up my old geometry smarts, I believe that makes 7,854 square feet. Bigger than our house lot in Portland; a pretty big garden for two people. We tilled the back half (furthest from the house) with a tractor and planted it with the things that take a lot of space: corn, potatoes, squash and melons. The front half consisted of intensive-gardening beds that were hand-tilled (and minimally at that), slathered in compost and planted with everything else. The design was inspired by the tenets of permaculture.

Just as you consider a building site as the ideal place for a home, you should look around your land and figure out the best place for your garden. Things to consider:

- Is there enough water available for irrigation?
- Is the plot south-facing? Is there full sunlight, or do mature trees block it?
- Which garden-eating critters are in your area?
- Is there an area that collects water or cold air?
- Is it close to your house?
- Is it exposed to wind?
- Do you want a garden big enough to eat from just during the summer, or do you want to preserve food for winter as well?

The best garden plot is level or terraced, and south-facing with some but not too much wind. If there are above-ground critters that love produce as much as you, the garden will need to be fenced, or you'll need to plant extra to accommodate losing some plants. You need access to water.

Terrain is a major factor as well. Think of air as an ocean and you will be able to visualize how cold air sinks down slopes and settles in the hollows. If your garden happens to be in a hollow, your frost dates are going to be accelerated—even when compared with your house. I could look out my kitchen window in the fall or spring, and see by the pattern of frost on the ground where the cold sinks were.

Ditto drainage. We planted our orchard where we wanted it to be aesthetically, rather than where we knew the ground drained better. Not a good idea. While the trees will likely survive, we had to fight for them the first couple of years because they were all swamped during spring thaw. Fruit trees do not like to have "wet feet," and the poor little feet of these young bucks were soaked. Mike dug channels away from their trunks that let at least some water drain off.

Don't bother to plant a crop unless you have a plan for bringing it water. There are a few, but very few, plants that don't need extra water, and even most of those need it when they are young. And, this may be a drought year, you never know. The simplest irrigation system consists of you and a hose or watering can; the most complex involves digging trenches and laying pipes that feed into small drip-irrigators that are carefully hand-placed at the roots of each plant in the ground. In between are the ditch-diversions, rainwater-catchment systems, soaker hoses, and sprinklers of all shapes and sizes, from the one in the side yard that your kids jump through to the industrial units that stretch a half-mile across a field. Some are less efficient than others; some cost a lot at the beginning and pay for themselves in water-savings.

There are many ways to minimize water waste-by-evaporation:

- Limit your irrigation to early morning and early evening, or overnight

- Use a timer
- Use drip irrigation

If you've got a fancy timer, with daily start and stop settings, then you don't have to think about watering at all—it just happens. If it's more of an egg timer on the bib of your hose, at least you won't overwater if you forget you turned it on three hours before. Drip irrigation is the most efficient and beneficial—it eliminates over-spray and also minimizes disease by keeping the plants' leaves dry.

It galls me to think about gardening in terms of science (for me, it's all touchy-feely, plus I'm a bit of a hack), but it surely can be approached that way. Those of you who share a scientific approach to raising crops will want to have your soil tested for its Ph balance. Ph measures whether a soil is acidic, neutral or alkaline; with that knowledge you can add various components—lime, blood meal—to amend the soil as per your plants' preference. There are simple little tests you can purchase from gardening centers, or you can contact the local extension agency, which is an office that is usually affiliated with a college, whose employees specialize in local agriculture. This office can be a fantastic resource, though we found our agent difficult to get a hold of and, once we did, she was more oriented toward commercial farms and not our little home garden. Retail nurseries are also a resource.

Aligning all of these factors is a lot to ask. There will be compromises; just pick the best spot you have and try to accommodate for the other factors. For example, if it's really windy you'll need to use soaker hoses and extra water to minimize evaporation.

Give your plants the best chance to thrive by putting them in well-prepared soil. And that starts with compost.

Compost

As an avid composter, it pains me to visit someone who doesn't compost. All this great material going to waste in a garbage can or down the sink! So much garbage in landfills or wastewater-treatment facilities that doesn't need to be there!

Composting is fairly straightforward. If things didn't rot and "ashes to ashes and dust to dust" and so on, the planet would be covered in a thick, stinking layer of dead animals and plants. So, you're just harnessing a natural process.

The key to successful backyard composting is mixing wet and dry materials. If the pile is all kitchen scraps, it will be too wet and will simply rot (and smell very, very bad). If it's all dead leaves, it will be too dry and essentially do nothing.

For two people, a commercially made compost storage unit works very well. Ours was about four feet tall, a bit of a rounded cone shape, with a top that came off (for loading) and a trap door that slid off at the bottom (for harvesting). Since the kitchen scraps, etc. were fully enclosed, raccoons and other pests couldn't get to them. For this reason, we included meat scraps, fish bones, etc., though most compost literature will tell you not to. I made sure that meat scraps were small and well covered, and not sitting on top where flies could lay eggs in them.

We emptied the unit in the fall, spreading the compost on the garden beds nearby, and filled it the rest of the year. Composting action happens much faster in the summer than in the winter, so it always worked out. If there were a few pieces of unfinished kitchen scraps (usually grapefruit rinds, and avocado skins and pits), they either disintegrated in the garden beds over the winter or, if they were still there in the spring, I just chucked them back into the composter.

People who have bigger families and more kitchen scraps, or want to incorporate horse manure or the like are better off with a big pile. Build a corral for the compost, a box maybe six feet cubed. If you're really smart it will open at the front and be wide enough that you can get your tractor's bucket in there. Make it close enough to your kitchen that you aren't carrying a full container half a mile, but far enough away that if it does smell (ours did for a day or two after it had been newly filled) you won't get it in the house. You might factor in the direction of prevailing winds.

Every composting person has a recipe for the perfect mix. Adapt it for the materials that you generate. Here's what worked well for us: We scavenged six three-gallon ice cream buckets (with lids) from the local café. We had a small bucket on the kitchen counter for little bits and teabags, and one of the three-gallon buckets under the sink; we emptied the little bucket into the big bucket. I lined the bottom of the big bucket with a full sheet of newspaper—that made cleaning it out later a *lot* easier. I also crumpled a sheet of newspaper on the top when it was full, snapped the lid on and carried it down to the composter, where it sat and waited until the rest of the buckets were full. If you use a bigger bucket than this, make sure it has a handle—three gallons of kitchen scraps and coffee grounds is pretty heavy.

Once all six buckets were full—a day I dreaded—I went down to the composter with some gloves on. If there was material in it already, I stirred it up with an aerator tool. The aerator is a long stick with two or three flanges at the bottom. You stick it straight into the pile; when you pull it out, the flanges open. This mixes the materials and creates a pathway for oxygen, which accelerates the composting process. Many people also use a digging fork or a pitchfork for this job, which is why this is sometimes called "turning" the pile.

I dropped in a dry layer first: either dry maple leaves that I stored in a barrel next to the composter from the fall or chicken dung-encrusted newspaper. You probably won't have the latter as an option: The reason I had these sheets of newspaper is that we had converted the chicken house from two milking stalls; therefore, there were places for the chickens to roost that I really wished they wouldn't because their droppings fell into their nesting boxes (which weren't boxes but dividers in what had been the cows' hay trough). Long story short, I laid down newspaper in a couple of spots so I could keep them clean more easily, and then collected them in yet-another-bucket. I tore these sheets into strips and laid them into the composter. It was a fluffy layer that compressed when I dumped the kitchen scraps onto it; maybe six to eight inches deep. You could also use straw bedding from your animal stalls, or bring in a load of manure from another farm. Or, get inventive and make a deal with the local café for their coffee grounds. I wouldn't use sticks because they take a bit too long to decompose.

Then came the fun part. I peeled the lid off of three of the buckets and dumped them in. If you have a weak stomach, don't look and don't breathe. Another dry layer, three more buckets. I topped it off with a dry layer. I cleaned the buckets and rejoiced that I wouldn't have to do it again for another four to six weeks. After a couple of days, and every week or so, I ran the aerator through everything to mix the top and bottom piles a little. In the summer, if it looked a little dry, I ran the hose into it for a minute or two. When compost is really happening, the interior of the pile is too hot to touch. It's fun to turn the pile in the middle of winter and see steam come out!

When a pile stalls, it's called "anaerobic." This can be benign and just be stagnant, or be nasty and smell bad and have maggots crawling around in it. If it's just sitting there, it's probably just too dry; turn the pile and add some water. If it's fetid, add lots of dry material and turn it often until it mellows out.

Some of our houseguests were freaked out by the compost. They were intimidated by the fact that we had six different places for recycling, two compost buckets, a bowl for eggshells and a bowl for chicken treats. Some were afraid to get it wrong, and some thought this kind of micro-management was a spectacular waste of time. These were all understandable reactions, but our intention was to be as waste-free as possible, and to use everything to its greatest purpose. To the bitter end.

Basically, anything that is organic (meaning "of the earth," not "grown without pesticides") can go in the compost. Everything decomposes, though you want to keep things with a ridiculous half-life—like plastic, rocks and steel—out of there. This means:

- **Any peel, core, root, seed or stem of fruit or vegetable matter, raw or cooked**
- **Any grain or its byproduct** (bread, pie crust, stale crackers or tortilla chips)
- **Teabags and coffee grounds with filters**
- **Tissue paper**
- **Hair and fingernail trimmings**

- **100-percent cotton tampons** (I didn't! But one could.)
- **Grass trimmings** (this is considered wet material)
- **Eggshells**
- **Spoiled milk and juice**
- **Salad dressing**

We even put cheese, shrimp tails and fat trimmings in, though compost gurus frown upon including animal products. I only did it because the pieces were small and we had a fully enclosed composter, so the scavengers (raccoons, skunks) attracted to those products wouldn't be able to dig into the pile to retrieve them.

You can put paper in, but remember that it's a dry material, and tear it into strips or, ideally, shred it to create more surface area. Keep in mind that if it's paper that has been bleached white or was printed with toxic, colored ink, you probably want to keep it out. Ditto a paper towel that was used with a toxic cleaning product (though, you're not using those, are you??).

If you have chickens or pigs, a lot of kitchen scraps can go to them. Chickens can also be fed crushed eggshells to augment the oyster shell you buy at the feed store.

I have tried to compost those "compostable" cornstarch-based containers. I'm sure they actually do break down in an industrial, temperature-controlled composter, but not in a backyard pile. I can't tell you how many times I had to pry a muck-encrusted, weakened-but-still-intact cornstarch container from my aerator tool.

Do not combine your garden waste with your kitchen compost. This may seem like a good idea, but those dead tomato vines, sunflower stalks and brassica remains may carry diseases that could contaminate future plants. I had a separate pile for those materials; the pile decomposed and shrunk over the summer, and then I piled more stuff on it in the fall. It never moved, and I never pulled compost from it. If you're really desperate and want to make a huge mess, you could sterilize the compost from that pile, in small batches, in your oven.

Compost Tea

This is extremely rich fertilizer; great for the garden. It is nearly as simple it sounds; you put a few handfuls of compost in a five-gallon bucket of water. The additional factors are oxygen and food, in the form of sugar and citric acid, or molasses, and an electric aerator. Why? What you are farming here are microorganisms that will benefit your garden plants. The idea is to get more nutritional bang for your compost buck.

There are numerous step-by-step instructions for brewing compost tea on the Internet; the main pitfall to avoid is overcooking the tea, which leads the concoction to become anaerobic (read: stinky and gross; in which case, dump on the compost pile and start over). If you are using a public water source, let the water sit for at least a day in a separate container, or run your air pump through it for at least an hour, so the chlorine that was added by your municipality evaporates out.

Original compost tea recipes were developed before an aerator was in existence; those recipes call for seven to ten days, as opposed to today's two or three. Be sure to stir it frequently, and pour it on your garden right away.

Worm Bin

A confession—I have never successfully kept red worms. Worm ranching, or vermicomposting, takes a special box and special monitoring, and I would simply release them in my compost pile. They would thrive for a while, and then run out of food and move on (or, die out; I was never sure). The remaining ones would end up in my garden beds when I took the compost out in the fall. I would still find them here and there, but not the writhing mass they were when I first got them.

If you are good at it, you have the special box. You have moist newspaper in there and you have a pile of kitchen scraps on one end of the box. You put the red worms in the box and they go to town on the kitchen scraps. Once they have pretty much devoured that pile, you put a new pile in the other end. The worms migrate over to the new pile and eat it. And so on. Sometimes you need to add new newspaper. When they are all busy on one side of the box, you can dig their feces (called "castings") from the previous side. It is extremely rich compost material; people buy it from gardening suppliers for $3 per pound. People also sell fancier versions of a worm box that can exceed $100.

Hand Tools

Everyone I know has bought a bunch of tools and then gravitated toward two or three. A guy at the feed store once sold me on a short-handled adze—"It's the only thing I ever use!" he said. While I liked it, it just wasn't my tool. I prefer the digging fork. After I used a regular hardware-store model to death (its wooden shaft snapped in half while I was hand-cultivating a hardened plot in spring), I invested in a fancy, solid metal one with a round, ergonomically designed handle. Once you find "your" tool, buy the best model that you can afford, and then take good care of it. You'll maximize efficiency and minimize wear-and-tear on your body.

Common tools:

- **Adze:** Short-or long-handled; head has two cutting blades that are different widths. Used to cut a furrow, uproot weeds and dig small holes. Similar to a pickaxe.
- **Cultivator:** Long, bow-rakish tines used to turn dirt in preparation for planting. Another type looks totally different—it has four curved spines

projecting from a shaft in a circle, and two long handles stretching out from the top. You twist it to cultivate one spot.

- **Digging Fork:** Four wide, flat, tines. Smaller fork than a pitchfork. Used to cultivate soil and loosen plants for harvest.
- **Fruit Picker:** This is a little basket on the end of a long handle, used to pick individual fruits (apple, pear, peach) that are out of reach.
- **Hoe, Traditional:** Wide, straight and sharp metal edge. Used to cut a furrow and to chop weeds from a bed.
- **Hoe, Circle:** Metal forms a circle; one edge is sharpened. Used to cut weeds; shape makes it easier to get close to crop plants without accidentally cutting them.

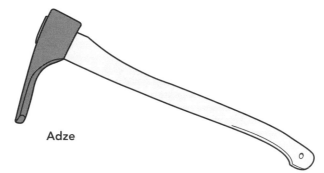

Adze

- **Hoe, Shuffle:** Sort of a cross between the previous hoes, with two sharpened edges. Used with a back-and-forth motion to cut young weeds in soft soil.
- **Loppers:** A shears held in two hands. Used to lop small branches from trees and cut thick bases of plants.
- **Manure Fork:** Self-explanatory; also called a muck rake.
- **Pitchfork:** Four thin and very sharp, pointed tines. Used to move hay and straw.
- **Post-Hole Digger:** Two handles attached to rounded, sharpened half-cylinders are connected with a hinge. Used to dig a deep, narrow hole.
- **Rake, Leaf:** A thin-but-long-tined fork with tines that fan out and turn under at the very end. Used to collect fallen leaves. Can be made with plastic or metal tines.
- **Rake, Bow:** A set of short, straight tines that turn under midway. Used to even out patches of uneven soil and woodchips.
- **Shears:** Hand-held Cutters. Used to trim plants and cut very small branches from trees.

- **Shovel, Digging:** Has a pointed and slightly sharpened edge. Used to break ground and dig holes.
- **Shovel, Manure:** Has a wide bucket and flat, even edge. Used to scoop manure, wood chips and grain. Also, reasonably enough, called a "grain scoop."
- **Spade:** Rectangular, flat sharp-edged shovel with slightly shorter handle. Used to cut a straight line for a hole or garden-bed edge.
- **Trowel:** Hand-held pointed shovel best used in delicate work or tight corners.

This is by no means an exhaustive list, but it will get you started. Anything with a wooden handle can be outfitted with a replacement handle if it breaks. You'll also need at least one wheelbarrow—replacement parts are also available for it.

Cultivation and Planting

Gardening is a decidedly un-democratic process—in order to enjoy a good harvest, one is constantly ripping out weak plants and coddling strong ones. Pulling weeds in favor of crops. But it has to be done. At the very beginning of my gardening days, long before we bought the farm, I was given by my friend Tara a four-inch pot with two broccoli seedlings in it. "Plant them," she said, "and pinch off the weaker one in a week or so." After a week passed, one of the seedlings was a couple of inches shorter than its twin. But I didn't have the heart to kill it! The result was that I never saw any broccoli—the two plants, fighting each other for the nutrients and water in the soil, were both unable to thrive and make a flower stalk. This story, writ large, is why so many farmers are practical people: You simply can't afford to care too much.

There are three ways to have a harvest at the end of the summer: start seeds under special conditions, before they would germinate in the ground, and then transplant them; plant seeds directly in the ground; buy "starts"—plants that some-one else germinated.

Germination

The idea behind starting seeds in February or March, long before winter's end, is that by the time the soil in your garden is dried out and warm enough to encourage growth, you've already got sturdy, healthy plants to put in the ground—bringing harvest day that much closer.

Unless you're into saving heirloom seeds from previous harvests, starting plants from seed *yourself* is more a matter of pride than practicality. Plant nurser-ies carry strong starts for only a few dollars apiece—if you factor in your materials, electricity and time you are probably better off buying nursery starts. But if you do rely on the local nursery, you are at their mercy—you can only grow the varieties they offer, and if they sell out of cucumbers, you're out of luck.

A lot of plants actually do better if you wait and start them in the ground. Corn, peas, beans, cucumbers and melons do not like being pot-bound or transplanted. Carrots, parsley and onions have tiny seeds and tender seedlings that are difficult to handle without damaging them. Beet seeds are actually pods of tiny seeds, so even if you put one beet seed in a pot you will have a cluster of starts all vying for attention. Lettuce can grow under nearly any condition. I never got spinach to thrive no matter what I did.

The plants that I find benefit from being started indoors are basil, tomatillos, nightshades (except potatoes) and brassicas. Basil is a tender thing, prone to sulking in cold weather and burning in direct sunlight. Tomatoes and peppers are finicky plants that thrive in hot weather, particularly hot nights. If you live in a temperate climate, it's a trick to get them to fruit, so starting them early gives them a leg up when it's finally warm enough to put them outside.

Brassicas are tough plants that don't like hot weather very much, so it's best to plant one crop on either side of summer. One crop of broccoli goes straight in the ground in spring. The second crop, which can include more broccoli, Brussels sprouts and collard greens, you'll start indoors in early July and then put out in August so it can enjoy the end of the season. The greens and Brussels sprouts are especially tasty after a frost, which releases their sugars. Chard is a relative of the beet, not broccoli, but can be treated this way as well.

In order to start a germination area, you need a space that can support hanging fluorescent lights and possibly heating pads if it's a cold basement or shed (i.e. you need lots of electricity). It would be great to have a water source nearby. You'll need lots of small pots, fresh dirt and some labeling materials (I used a Sharpie and the previous season's popsicle sticks). You'll need some kind of pan that catches the extra water under your pots. You'll need some clear plastic to cover the seeds until they sprout (at which time you remove it for fear of mold forming.) There are, of course, a number of products you can purchase to this end, but most of it can be improvised.

There are pots so small that they're designed for one plant each and are packed tightly together in eight-plant units. These are called "cells." They are pretty easy to work with, but you have to pay attention so that they don't become root-bound. They make it easy to center a young plant in a four-inch pot because you transfer the cell rather than throwing tiny seeds into a (relatively speaking) giant four-inch pot.

Another option is to start plants outside but in a protected environment. A small box with a glass lid is called a "cold frame." Some are extremely simple and some have temperature-sensitive hydraulic lifts on the lids. These can't be started as early as plants under grow-lights. Or, you could start the plants under grow lights and then transfer them to the cold frame rather than straight into the ground.

Read your seed packets for specific instructions. Plant three or four seeds in each pot to be sure that you get a strong start in each. When a seed sprouts, its first two leaves are called "seed leaves." The plants are extremely vulnerable until they're grown two sets of regular "true" leaves, so treat them with utmost care. Once you have some sprouts, examine each and remove the less vigorous ones. The best candidate has a straight stalk and the best-looking leaves. Don't pull the "loser" plants or you'll disrupt the root system of the good plant—snip them at the dirt level with a pointy-tipped clippers or scissors.

> **#1 Mistake:** Starting big. If you have room under your lights for fifty cells and plant fifty cells, you will be out of room once they graduate to four-inch pots.

> **#2 Mistake:** Under- or over-watering. I've actually had beans that rotted in their pots because they were getting too much water. The soil needs to stay consistently damp. Check them every day, or more than once per day.

> **#3 Mistake:** Going out of town. You can't expect a neighbor or house-sitter to properly care for these starts; it's too labor-intensive.

Young plants are extremely sensitive—to everything. The first year I tried starts (we still lived in Portland), I had absolutely no idea what I was doing. Once the plants were a couple of inches tall, we had a nice, sunny day, so I put them all out in the full sun for the afternoon, thinking they would love it. When I went to fetch them, most had scalded into white crisps. They were not ready for full sunlight.

Ease young plants into everything; this is called hardening them off. Wait until they have four or five sets of true leaves before you start breaking them in to the real world. Blow on them or run a fan on them to get them used to wind. Put them out for an hour in partial shade to get used to full sun. The big test is leaving them out overnight, when the temperature drops significantly. Be sure they're ready. After they've adjusted to all these things, then you can consider putting their roots into the cold ground of reality. If you buy starts from a nursery, they'll already be ready to plant, but maybe set them in the garden in their pots for a couple of days, so can acclimate. Make sure they don't dry out.

Potatoes are totally different. Potato plants make seeds, but you don't use them—you make clones. Potatoes grow from "seed potatoes," which is basically taking existing potatoes and cutting them so that there is at least one eye and so they have enough old potato to nourish the new plants until they grow some roots and leaves. Each chunk should be about as big as a golf ball. Leave the chunks out for a few hours, but no longer than overnight, so that the cut sides can heal a bit before you put them in the ground.

Planting

Every winter I made an elaborate sketch of my garden, trying to determine how much of each thing to plant and where everything was going to go. Partly this was therapy—thinking about spring kept away the winter doldrums. Part of it was insurance. It takes some thought to figure out where to put everything, because plant families must be rotated.

Every year, various insects and fungi attack plants. Some of them drop their eggs or spores into the soil to overwinter. One way to fight that problem is to not put the same plants in the same place every year. The trick is, any plant from the same family counts—so the tomatoes could not go where they had been the previous year, nor where the peppers or potatoes had been. I would spend hours with a pencil and eraser in hand, trying to put everything in a place that made sense. It helps to know how much room each plant needs, but that comes with experience.

Figuring out when to plant things is also tricky—an art as well as a science. For example, it took me years to figure out when to plant my cilantro so it was ready at the same time as the tomatoes, and not weeks in advance. Ditto the dill and the cucumbers.

Each spring, a gardener has an internal battle over putting her starts outside too early. One 70-degree day is the siren's call. Resist! Cold nights will surely follow. Plants that go out too early, if they don't die outright, are stunted and never catch up to plants that are put in later, when the soil and nighttime temperatures are warmer.

Another discipline bummer: When you plant strawberries and blueberries, your plants will benefit from focusing on growing a good root system that first year. That means you need to pinch off all of its flowers the first season. All of them. It just may be the hardest thing you'll ever do.

When you plant starts, give them a little plant food to grow into. I used to dig my hole and then dump a small handful of organic fertilizer pellets at the bottom, so that the roots would hit the food when they started to grow. A nice little surprise.

Maintenance

The challenge to gardening is not only that you can't go anywhere, but that summertime is when anyone who wants to visit you comes to visit. So now, instead of digging that brassica bed like you were going to, you have to take your friends to the local attractions and then out to dinner. Which is, of course, fun…but if someone comes every weekend, which is possible, guess who's not getting her harvest in.

I was well into the second draft of this book, when a friend pointed out I hadn't even mentioned weeding. Ha! That can only be the result of heavy-duty memory repression. You will do a lot of weeding. Every day, if you can. You are creating such a nice, comfy place to live—why would weeds not want to live there? Pulling weeds by hand from moistened soil yields the best results but, depending on the scale of your garden, that may not be feasible. That's where hoes come in. Be very careful that you dig up the weed plant and not the food plant.

Midway through the growing season, it's a good idea to give the plants a little food. Remember, gardening has nothing to do with natural selection and hoping the plants do the best they can—it's about manipulating them into making the most succulent, enormous fruits they're capable of.

Contrary to popular belief (in my experience, at least), it's not that helpful to let chickens into your garden. Yes, they eat slugs and bugs, "aerate" the soil and leave nutritious droppings, but they're not discriminate about where they're digging—I got tired of raking the woodchips from my paths off my beds and back into my paths. Chicken manure is too acidic to be helpful straight from the source. And, they'll decimate anything but mature plants, more by digging them up looking for bugs than by eating them.

Saving Seed

An important part of farming has always been to nurture this year's plants in order to collect a food crop, and also to collect seeds for the following spring. The way this is done is to let some of this year's annuals crop complete its life cycle. Because annuals live only one season, they do not waste time with sturdy stems and bark and all of the things that perennials develop. They are all about the seeds.

Annuals bloom and pollinate each other; their flowers are then pushed out of the way as its fruits develop. If this is a bean plant, for example, the pods begin to form. As the pods grow, the seeds inside the pod grow as well. They mature at the end of the season, and then plant begins to die. It stops transporting water to the seed pods, and they dry out and turn brown. Eventually the pods dry out so much that they pop open, flinging their seeds into the air in the hope that some of them will stay in the dirt (and not be eaten by birds or rodents) and sprout the following spring.

Farmers harvest seed just like they harvest food. They store it in a dry, cool place and plant it in the spring. Sometimes, there will be a seed-swap, where farmers can bring their extra seed and trade it for seeds that they need. There are even seed libraries in the world—places that store all of the world's plant varieties.

The trick with seed storing is that you have to grow "heirloom" varieties. Heirlooms are basically everything that existed before people really got into hybrids.

Hybrids are developed in order to take advantage of the characteristics of two or more heirloom varieties. This is how we get tomato plants that can grow in Alaska. The trouble with hybrids is that they do not reproduce true to themselves. If you save hybrid corn kernels and plant them the following spring, you will get corn—but probably not the sweet, succulent corn you had this year.

People who develop good hybrids make money by selling their seeds, which they "own," like a patent. This one reason why people go nuts about companies like Monsanto—they seem to be attempting to have proprietary rights to the world's seeds for large, cash crops like canola, corn and rice.

Woody Perennials

Because fruit and herb bushes and trees are "permanent" as garden plants go, you need to take extra care when planting them. Choose your young trees carefully— a weak or spindly tomato plant will only set you back for one season; fruit trees can live decades. Look for well-shaped trees that have been pruned to a few main branches with strong, 45-degree crotches. Make sure the tree sits well in its pot or, if bare-root, that the roots are well heeled-in and moist. Check the trunk to see that the graft is healthy, and there are no nicks or cuts. Some trees can self-pollinate; some need another tree of the same species nearby so they can cross-pollinate.

Our 82-year-old neighbor in Portland told Mike once, "No use putting a dollar tree in a ten-cent hole." Any mistakes or shortcuts you make will stick with the plant as long as it lives (which, depending on the mistake or shortcut, might not be that long).

Hopefully, you've already considered the conditions mentioned above, as per the beginning of this section, and have picked the perfect, well-drained site for your bushes and orchard. Mike and I put our trees where we wanted them to be for aesthetic reasons, lining a path away from our gazebo. Aesthetic reasons are not the right choice. We paid for it every spring thereafter by having to dig drainage trenches for them so they wouldn't drown during the spring thaw. Consider the spacing as well—it seems ridiculous to plant apple trees twelve feet apart when they're nothing more than sticks. But if they grow to have ten-foot canopies, they will need that much space.

Next, you want to give them that dollar hole. By hand or with a tractor, dig a hole that is three feet deep and three feet wide (for bushes, two by two). Dig through the soil from that hole so that it is light and fluffy, and mix in compost and/or fertilizer, and any amendments signified by a Ph test. If the soil is clay, and there is a defined edge to the hole, rough it up a bit so that the roots have a better chance at penetrating it when they start to grow. Fill the hole back in about one-third, and tamp it in. Water it.

The level at which you build the hole back up depends on the size of the young tree—you want the place at which the trunk (either its own trunk or its rootstock) and its roots meet to be at ground level once you've filled in all the dirt. You do not want to bury the rootstock. You can kind of hold the tree in the air at the approximate place it will be, and gauge how much dirt needs to go back in. Create a small mound inside the hole, tamp that in a bit, until you get it so that the tree is resting on the mound at the correct level. Drape the roots evenly over the mound, making sure none of them are out of the hole, or go down a ways and then head up again. Fill the rest of the hole. Tamp in the dirt, leaving the surface in a saucer shape that will direct water toward the tree. Build up the edge of the saucer—if you had to cut sod to plant this tree, you can use strips of upside-down sod. Water thoroughly.

We were very naughty orchardists and never sprayed our trees. I say "naughty" because we lived amongst commercial orchards. Our little orchard could have become a safe haven for invasive pests that would gladly decimate our neighbors' crops, so we were supposed to spray our trees. I was on the fence about spraying—most of the things sprayed on fruit trees are natural compounds but I still didn't want to expose myself and the environment to them. For the most part, not spraying never ruined our crops. We had very young trees, so they weren't producing a ton of fruit anyway. We did lose one cherry tree to some kind of boring insect, so I cut that tree into pieces and burned them. I don't know if spraying would have killed that particular pest or not. We never had worms in our apples; our peach tree had a bit of leaf curl, but nothing unusual for the Pacific Northwest.

If you inherited some mature trees with your farm, but they're overgrown and not bearing much, hire a professional arborist to fix them.

Planting bushes requires the same technique applies, but with a smaller hole. The spacing consideration can be a little different: If you want them to grow into a hedge, you purposely space them closer.

Blueberries are fussy little plants with lots of rules. First of all, you need more than one plant in order to get berries, because they cross-pollinate. But, they can't be the same variety. But, they have to be types that bloom at approximately the same time so they have flowers at the same time. No wonder blueberries are so expensive in the grocery. They are also acid junkies. My friend's mom planted her blueberries in pine needles, with just enough dirt to hold water.

Winterkill is a big issue with perennials. During the winter, some of the new, tender branches will not be able to withstand the cold. These parts are easy to identify: They appear gray and withered in the spring. A little winterkill is normal, but don't plant anything that isn't rated to your area. I tried to grow rosemary, a remarkably successful plant in Portland, three years in a row before I finally gave up. It would thrive during the summer but just couldn't fend off the week or so of single-digit temperatures we experienced every winter.

Woody plants should be trimmed during the last winter/early spring, while they're still dormant. Read up on tree-trimming; shaping a tree is an art as well as a science. Always cut shoots (twigs that stick straight up on branches) and suckers (shoots that appear at the base of the tree). Use sharp tools, and clean them with rubbing alcohol or bleach between trees so you don't spread disease. Pruning was something I had to do when Mike wasn't around—he couldn't bear to see so many branches getting unceremoniously whacked. I collected the ones with big buds and put them in a vase in the house, as they could sometimes be tricked into blooming. Later, they were dried for sweet-smelling kindling.

Another painful-but-necessary activity I had to do myself was thinning the fruits. Fruit trees are all about spreading their seeds, not producing gigantic fruits. They will grow four or five apples in one cluster. If left to nature, four or five—small—apples will grow there. Humans like big fruits. So, we remove some of the baby fruits in a cluster, leaving one or two.

Be sure to control grass and weeds around the perennials; these can suck up most of the water that should be going to your plants. Feed them in the spring.

Once the fruit is getting close to ripe, watch it carefully. You may need to throw netting over your trees and bushes when they're small. Why? You are not the only one anticipating these fruits—area birds are also well aware of the impending harvest. And, they're not polite enough to eat one entire apple—they'll take what they consider to be the most succulent bite of each one. Once your trees are big enough, they will take the fruit on the top of the tree and you'll get the rest.

Competition (Pests)

Being organic may be harder than you think. When you're growing such soft, succulent, defenseless fruits and vegetables, you're not the only one who will want to eat them. Insects, animals and even fungi will go after your plants, and if you simply stand by and watch, you may find yourself without a crop.

Mike and I never got totally organized about thwarting hostile takeovers: the first two years, the critters hadn't found our new garden. The second two years, I was in denial and both of us were too busy. The third two years we were being crushed by everything, including garden pests. But, if we *had* gotten it together, we would have employed a technique called Integrated Pest Management.

IPM is a combination of strategies that use plant placement, physical removal and destruction and *natural* chemicals to deter pests. Even organic farmers use chemicals sometimes—the difference is that they use natural compounds and use them sparingly. They also hoe and burn weeds, use diatomaceous earth to kill or dissuade pests, and employ the help of beneficial insects such as nematodes, lacewings and ladybugs. A pest-control method that I do not recommend is those blue-light electric zappers—you'll kill just as many beneficial insects as harmful ones.

One year, I decided to let some of my snap peas go to seed so I wouldn't have to purchase them the following spring. I let a few pods dry on the vine and then picked them and put them in a mesh bag for a couple of weeks. One morning, I decided it was time to shell them and put the seeds in my storage box.

I separated the seeds out and realized that many of them had neat, perfectly round holes drilled into them. It was the strangest thing. Then, I noticed that others had a perfectly round lighter-colored circle, and if I pushed on it with the end of my fingernail, the circle popped off. And the circle revealed…a bug! My peas were full of little black beetles with yellow spots. (That is, the ones that hadn't already been vacated.)

It didn't take much research to learn that they are pea weevils. The beetle had implanted its eggs in the peapod when it was young, and as the pea grew so did the larva inside it. I remembered seeing tiny bumps on the peapods and thinking nothing of them as I popped the pods into my mouth. Just a little extra protein…

Then there was the year I dug up my beets and potatoes (which were in the same bed) and found most of them covered with strange lesions, which, I learned, are "scab." Scab affects root crops and is caused by a microorganism in the soil that in my case might have been there because of my use of not-aged-enough chicken manure in that bed. The organism pokes into the tuber when it's small, and the tuber reacts as it grows by hardening around the organism. For the most part the produce is fine—there have been a couple of spots of "necrosis" (dead tissue) in the potatoes. I peeled them and cut out the bad parts and the rest of it was fine to eat, though I chose not to save any for seed that year.

Integrated Pest Management means harmonizing with nature whenever possible, but not being afraid to defend your crops. The last season I gardened, I faced the reality that if I intended to actually benefit from my labor, I was going to have to kill things. Not aphids. Not cabbage worms. Gophers.

Gophers

In early 2007, I was delighted to see that my usual forty garlic and six shallot plants were poking their sprouty heads tentatively out of the snowy ground. As the weather slowly warmed they grew tall and strong; I was pleased with the fact that while there were still dozens of mysteries to gardening, I had figured out how many garlic and shallot bulbs to plant so that I harvested enough to plant the following year as well as to eat.

After a few weeks, I went to look at them again. They're like the daffodils of the vegetable garden—so early and hopeful; a promise that spring is actually on its way. To my surprise, three were missing. There was no sign of them whatsoever except for small holes in the ground. I blamed the jays (they had pulled up, but not eaten, my onion starts before) and thought nothing of it.

Thereafter, every week or so that I went to look at them, more were missing. Shallots too. In one hole, the top third of the plant stuck out of the hole. I gasped. A gopher! A gopher was pulling plants down into the ground, just like I'd seen in cartoons as a kid! I hadn't realized that actually happens.

I was at a loss. How could I stop this thing? By now the remaining plants were nearly full-sized. I started asking around.

"They don't like human hair," said one neighbor. "Put some hair in their holes."

"Stick a hose down the hole and flood them out," said another, instructing me that the water would fill the tunnels—I'd know when to stop when water came out of other holes or the hole I was using. In the garden, I stuck my finger down one of the garlic absences and was shocked to find my entire hand easily broke through the crust into a huge passageway. The gopher had pretty much excavated the entire bed. I turned the water on for twenty minutes; the hole never filled.

In July, desperate to save my remaining six garlics and single shallot, I took bamboo kabob skewers and stuck them into the ground at an angle, all the way around the plants, creating a little bamboo cage for each. The painstaking effort worked: I had just enough harvest to plant in October for the following year.

As I do each year, in October I took a blank outline of my garden beds and plotted out where everything would go in 2008. I made sure to put the garlic/shallot bed as far from the existing bed as possible, so my little friend might not find them. I planted forty garlics and six shallots, and hoped for the best.

In the spring, I once again eagerly awaited the appearance of the little green sprouts to appear. About a dozen did. That little so-and-so had made his way over and survived the winter thanks to my efforts.

Only slighted daunted, I began my regular spring plantings. I had decided to try something new, rutabagas, which are wonderful in rich winter soups. I planted a row and found them easy to raise; I soon had thinned them to about twelve plants. I was a little nervous, putting a root crop right next to my garlic carnage, but hoped for the best.

One day in May, I went down to water the rutabagas and found a large hole. I sighed and realized I was also missing a potato plant and five leeks. As June wore on, the delight of eating fresh strawberries and raspberries was tempered by the frustration of cataloging what had gone missing overnight. More leeks. Onions. Another rutabaga. I stuck my hand in the dirt to sneak some baby potatoes for a meal and found a huge open cavern underground. I prayed that the critter wouldn't decimate my asparagus just a few feet away.

This was getting serious. "Hoping for the best" was not a winning strategy.

I had been, on trips to the hardware store, venturing further and further down the aisle stocked with various agents of death: bug sprays, ant and roach hotels, rat poison and medieval-looking steel traps with menacing spikes. Until recently, I had always turned up my nose at this aisle and the people in it. *What a bunch of Neanderthals*, I'd thought to myself. Not only that; the traps were scary. They looked like they could do serious damage to the novice trap-setter.

I chickened out and went to the plant nursery, where they had more innocuous remedies. I bought a twenty-five-dollar bottle of repellant made of various biodegradable oils.

"It makes the soil smell bad," said the cashier, "and they'll go away."

When I arrived home to apply it, I saw that our friend Dustin was over for a visit. Dustin has a deep Love of the Earth and Everything Who Lives on Her.

"Why don't you just plant more of everything and share it?" he asked. I thought of my skewer shallot cages.

"If I could get a written agreement that he'd limit himself to 10 percent of the yield, I would," I said. I attached the repellant to my hose and carefully doused all of the root crops and the asparagus bed. It certainly smelled bad; if I were a gopher I would definitely go away.

That night, the gopher ate a broccoli stalk. I reached for other options. My cat had caught many animals but never a gopher. If I caught the rodent in a live trap and relocated him, I would simply make him some other gardener's problem. Or, more likely, he'd find his way back.

At the hardware store, I took a deep breath and picked up a gopher trap. I looked a little like an old metal roller skate, but with spikes instead of wheels. I got a lesson in trap-setting from the clerk (the traps come with an instructional paper diagram, which did not help me in the least) and was on my way.

In the garden, finding an "active hole" was no problem—why, there was a half-eaten rutabaga sitting in a big hole from which a tunnel extended in two directions. Perfect. I put one trap into each end of the tunnel, securing it with a length of string as per the instructions. No one had mentioned baiting the tunnel but I left the rutabaga there for good measure, and then covered the hole with big pieces of bark so it was totally dark below.

The next day, I went down to check the traps. One of the strings was taut. I donned gloves and tentatively peeled away the layers. I pulled the trap out, slowly because I definitely had something and I didn't want the string to break. I sat back on my heels and looked. *I'll be.* A big, fat gopher was clipped in the middle by the metal trap. His yellow buck teeth were the same size as his front claws—huge implements that explained how one creature could construct such a maze of tunnels and eat nearly everything I put in the ground.

Because gophers spend so much time underground, their ears and eyes are small compared to a mouse's. He didn't look like he had struggled.

I had by this time gotten comfortable with setting the trap but had neglected to learn how to extract the dead gopher. Gloves were a mandatory item already, but especially for this. I pushed awkwardly on a metal bar and turned the trap upside-down. Mr. Gopher fell into the brush, where I hoped the bugs and beetles would make good use of him.

Other "Pests"

I use this term reluctantly. Every animal—even my former nemesis, Mr. Gopher, was simply trying to live its life and raise some children. The animals we call pests are only pests to us—it's a similar psychology to calling German soldiers "Krauts" during World War II—it de-personified them and made it easier for a "Yank" to kill one without incurring permanent psychological damage.

A list of other animals that are trying to make a living in your garden follows. It's by no means comprehensive, just a sampling of "favorites."

Aphid

Oh, insidious aphid. I could spend an hour every day turning over the leaves of my broccoli plants, my collards, my Brussels sprouts, my cabbage, and smashing aphids off with my thumbs. There would be hundreds clustered together on the underside of every leaf. I could hose them off. I could spray them with the oil-soap mixture. It didn't matter. I could put a dent in their numbers but never eradicate them. The leaves were scarred where I was successful, making them unfit to serve for dinner.

It doesn't help matters that some ants keep aphids like cattle. They protect the aphids and make sure they are happily sucking the life from your plants, and then "milk" the aphids' honeydew, a sugar-rich excretion, by stroking them with their antennae. You can't make this stuff up.

Every once in a while, I'd see a ladybug on another plant. "What are you doing on this raspberry cane?!" I yell at it. "Get over there to those Brussels sprouts!"

Cabbage Moth

As you garden, you'll see so many wonderful things. Hummingbirds will zing past your head, cats will come and monitor your progress, butterflies will flit playfully across the way. You might see a pretty blue-white butterfly or moth, or a couple of them. So pretty. You must go to the pretty moths and…smash them in your hands! Those are cabbage moths or "small whites." Both lay little yellow eggs on the undersides of your brassicas (you should remove them as well) that grow into pretty green caterpillars that you should…squish in your fingers or cut in half with your clippers! Otherwise, they'll eat your crop to bits.

Deer

Deer love to nip down young plants, tomato vines and young shoots on your trees. I planted a dogwood near our pond—gone. Mike planted maple trees to line our driveway—irreparably stunted. A deer once got into our garden in June and ate every tiny apple, every young pear and every crabapple, as well as the tender young wood. I sat down and cried when I saw it.

Earwig

Who came up with the earwig design? It's like the classic group project—no one wants to be pushy, so the end result is a compromise that has no distinct purpose. You'll find earwigs everywhere in the garden, especially if there is moisture. Cut some peonies, you'll bring some earwigs in the house. Peel back the husk on a fresh ear of corn and you'll startle the earwigs that were hanging out in there. I even have plucked a juicy, fresh raspberry off its core, raised it toward my mouth, stopped because movement caught my eye, and seen an earwig crawl out of the cap! They move quickly, like a centipede, which may be part of why they are so creepy. (They don't, contrary to earwig lore, crawl into your ear. I mean; it could happen, but it's not something they aspire to.)

Earwigs are far more of a gross-out than an actual nuisance in the garden. They even eat arthropods. So, if you can get your natural impulse to recoil-and-smash under control, you might consider just whisking the creatures off your produce and carrying on.

Mole

Moles are pretty cool-looking critters, rather large with no eyes to speak of, funny long snouts and enormous front digger-claws. They damage they do to gardens and lawns is inadvertent; they're not eating roots, they're pushing them out of the way as they tunnel around looking for worms.

Rabbit

One rabbit can do an enormous amount of damage to a garden overnight. So cute and yet so devastating.

Raccoon

Not that there's a lot you can do about it, but as you are watching your corn ripen to the perfect sweetness, so are the raccoons. Your options are to pick early, share, or spend a night in the corn patch with your dog or a rifle.

Shrew

Shrews are adorable, fast and fierce little things, not rodents but members of the *soricidae* family. One rarely sees them but they're there, foraging under the brush for small bugs and worms.

Slug

In the Pacific Northwest, we have slugs the size of a pencil lead and slugs that can stretch across your palm. We also have a lot of good beer. That leaves us plenty of cheap American pilsner to use in our slug traps! Fill a plastic dish with beer and set it in the ground near your most succulent garden plants. The slugs will be drawn to it, get all loopy and drown. Drown in beer? This has got to be the most "humane" lethal trap on the planet.

Another favorite means of dispatching slugs was to pick them off my plants by hand (and turn over a few pieces of wood here and there in the paths), gather them on a tray and place it before the chickens. They disappeared in seconds.

Vole

The vole gets, unfairly, blamed for garden damage. Really, they just eat seeds, like a mouse. They are larger and darker brown than mice, no white belly, and have very small eyes and ears. Vole fights fiercely if threatened. I saw many of them rear up to swat and bite at my cat, even though they hadn't a chance of survival.

I doubt that many people reading this book would consider using mass doses of poison, but if you are, keep in mind that it's difficult to control what consumes it. Our friends lost a beautiful black lab named Maggie because she got into the neighbor's rat poison. Need I add that is not a good way to die? The main ingredient is warfarin, a compound that causes massive internal bleeding, diarrhea and vomiting. Or, you could poison a mouse or a gopher that your cat eats shortly thereafter. Oops.

Chapter 16
Harvest and Storage

For the rest of the time that you live in the country, don't make any big plans in August and early September. You will not be hiking, biking or playing badminton at the beach; you will be harvesting and putting food up for the winter.

This may seem like a bummer, but you'll forget all about the missed ice cream cones and gin-and-tonics some fateful day in February, when it's 20 degrees below zero and you can't get up the driveway because yet another foot of snow fell, and you go down to your cellar and pull out a big jar of peaches. You'll remember how good they smelled when you peeled them; how the chickens went crazy when you threw the skins and pits in to them. You'll eat a couple of peach-halves, or maybe you'll eat all of them. Don't you dare throw out that peach juice; drink it right from the jar. It's not called "nectar" for nothing.

Different plants are used different ways—humans eat the leaves of some plants (lettuce); the stalks of others (celery); the buds of others (artichoke); the rhizomes of others (potato); the seeds of others (almond); the fruits of others (peach). The stalk of the rhubarb plant is delicious with sugar; the leaf is poisonous. Some food by-products can be frozen; some dried; some stored as-is. Do not wash vegetables or fruits before dry-storing them; this will hasten their decomposition.

Pick fruits and vegetables carefully, especially soft fruits like berries and stone fruits. You don't want to preserve anything bruised, which will lead to premature spoilage. Vegetables must be blanched before freezing, and the amount of time you cook them depends on their size.

Most farm folks have a cellar somewhere—in the basement, or maybe as a separate building. Both its temperature and its moisture level are important. One unfortunate truth is that you can't store everything in one place. The gases that emit from apples, for example, will cause your potatoes to sprout well before spring. Check the produce regularly, so you can identify and remove items that are beginning to "go the other way," as we say.

Whether you harvest grains or purchase them, store them in airtight containers. This is less to keep the oats, flour or cornmeal fresh, and more to keep grain/flour moths out. Large canning jars are a good option; moths can get into plastic storage containers with snap-on lids. If you find a strange webby accumulation in your grain (or dog food), or see actual small gray moths flying around, you have a problem. Compost the materials in that container. If you have a really bad infestation, you'll even have to move your breakfast cereals to airtight containers.

Individual Fruits and Vegetables
Apples

Store in flats rather than bushels, no more than two deep. If you can get a hold of some of the plastic inserts from commercial fruit crates, use those. Rot usually develops where two apples are pressed together. Some varieties store better than others. Making applesauce is easy: you just peel and slice them, and then cook them down to a consistency that you like. This can be water-bath or steam canned. Apple slices also dry nicely.

Apples can be juiced in a cider press, which is a medieval-looking device that grinds them into a mash and then presses the juice out. The press can either be electric or human-powered. If the latter, and you're making a lot of juice, this is an all-day affair for a team of people. Some friends of ours had a tradition: buy one ton of apples and invite twenty people over for pressing day. Everyone brought empty plastic jugs and bought into the apple cost; everyone went home with full jugs of fresh apple cider. And their cows and chickens got the apple mash, so everyone was happy. This cider was not pasteurized, so it had to be stored frozen. It was not cheap, either—one year each jug worked out to cost nine dollars apiece or something. But it was a fun day and the cider was absolutely delicious, drinking that felt like eating.

Artichoke

In Portland, we had artichoke plants that were six feet tall and six feet wide. They made a dozen chokes each; amazing plants. If you are also so lucky, cut your chokes when they have gotten as big as they're going to get; you can tell because the blades of each bloom will start to loosen. If you leave it there, it will bloom into an incredible purple flower that reminds you it's in the thistle family.

If you cut it off and steam it, you can peel each leaf one at a time and dip it in butter, and then scrape the base off with your front teeth. Mind the sharp point on each blade. Or you can extract the hearts of many artichokes and freeze or can them (requires a pressure canner).

Asparagus

Treat this plant like a bush or tree—prepare its bed carefully. Asparagus is a perennial that can live twenty years, so take good care of it. That means making a dedicated asparagus bed with soil that has sand and compost added to it, and which is kept diligently weed-free.

Asparagus will reward you with a spring crop of the most succulent, tender shoots you can imagine. They embody the flavor "green." After picking one, steam-cook it immediately and briefly, maybe throw a little butter and lemon juice on it, and oh! Vegetable bliss.

After you plant asparagus, you have to wait a year or two before you can harvest—the plant needs those first, thin stalks to feed its rhizome, which lives underground. In the third year, the plant will send up lots of thin shoots and a couple of fat ones. If the plant has at least four shoots, and one shoot is bigger than your finger, then you have yourself a treat. Grab it near the ground and snap it off. The shoots that you leave will grow tall and willowy, and ferny branches will develop. The female plants will grow red berries as well. Even once the plant gets going, leave some shoots so that the rhizome gets nutrients.

Later, when you have lots of asparagus, you will know where to snap the tender part from the woody part by simply testing various sites along the stalk—it will naturally snap off at the end of the tender part. If, for some reason, you have some left over at the end of the season, you can freeze or pickle the rest.

Avocado

I dream of living somewhere I can have an avocado tree. One tree can produce 1,200 fruits per season! It is native to the Caribbean, Mexico, Central America and South America, but can be grown in California. The fruits are rich in potassium and folate.

You can ripen avocados (sometimes called "alligator pears") faster by putting them near apples or bananas, which emit ethylene gas. These fruits don't freeze well whole or sliced, but can be frozen as a purée. It's still not a great option. Be sure to add some citric acid to minimize browning. The best option if you have an excess of avocados is to make a gigantic vat of guacamole and invite your friends over for margaritas. But, that's just me.

Basil

The best way to store basil is to freeze it—either whole leaves or as pesto. To collect the leaves early in the season pinch or snip the biggest leaves. I tried to have enough plants that I could forgo any leaves that had been burned by the sun or excessively nibbled by bugs. I had small, pointy clippers that were faster than pinching and didn't result in turning my thumbnail and forefinger black. As the season wore on, I also clipped off any flower stalks that emerged from the center of each branch. As soon as the plant starts flowering, it stops making leaves, so you'll get more yield from the plant if you stunt the growth of its flowers.

I washed and thoroughly dried the leaves, and laid them out on a large, clean dish towel and folded the top over them, gently turning it over every once in a while. To freeze whole leaves, put them on a cookie sheet in the freezer, then into a storage bag or container.

Regardless of your diligence with removing the flowers, the plant will stall out in August. At that point, I cut the plants at the stem, shook them out a bit to encourage any spiders to vacate before I rinsed them, allowed them to dry and then meticulously snipped every leaf of every size into a bowl. Wear comfortable shoes; this takes a while.

There are many pesto recipes in the world: I basically chopped up the leaves I had and then did approximately one-third that volume each in pine nuts (smashed in a mortar), parmesan cheese (grated and then chopped) and garlic (pressed). I threw in some salt and a lot of olive oil. It's a consistency thing—you want the oil to hold everything together but not be drippy. Try a little and see how the flavors balance—can you taste the cheese and nuts? Feel a little zing from the fresh garlic? Enough salt? You're ready.

Rip off about six inches from a roll of waxed paper and tear that in half. Spoon a heaping tablespoon onto the center of each square and fold the sides over to make a little, flat bundle. Put the bundles into a storage bag or tub.

Or, freeze the pesto in an ice cube tray and later empty the tray into a storage bag. If you do this you should dedicate the tray to pesto—the strong flavors sink into the plastic even after a thorough cleaning (unless you like garlic-tinged ice). I have read of leaving the garlic out, as it can turn bitter in the freezer; I never had this problem.

Beans and Edamame

There are pole beans, which grow long and tall, and bush beans, which grow close to the ground. And there are snap beans, which are meant to eat fresh, pod and all, and shelled beans, which are dried on the plant and then stored, shelled, in jars.

Green beans typically grow on vines that need a trellis or other support. These beans are picked and left in the pod. You can eat them fresh or cooked, and they freeze well. They can also be canned (pressure canner) and pickled, called "dilly beans."

Shelled beans (including pinto and turtle/black beans) grow as the bush variety. Their pods dry to a golden color; pick them before the pods burst open and fling the seeds hither and yon. It's incredible to open a dun-colored pod and find shiny black or burgundy beans inside. Make sure they are completely dry before you put them in a jar, or they will mold.

Fava and lima beans actually have two shells: the outer pod and a wrapping around each bean. If you blanch them for fifteen minutes, this wrapping will come off easily.

Berries

Harvesting raspberries, blackberries, dewberries, marionberries, blueberries, huckleberries, gooseberries or strawberries is pretty straight-forward. Hold your hand beneath the fruit, so it can drop into your palm—otherwise, some (invariably the biggest one you've ever seen) will get away from you. If you manage to get some back to your kitchen without eating them, they can be frozen in waxed paper sandwich bags that are then placed in plastic storage bags. I don't even wash them, because water clings to the berries and it would be too hard to get it off. I do wash my berries if I'm making jam. I also remove stems and errant leaf matter (and the occasional earwig).

The sturdy berries, like blueberries and strawberries, can be dehydrated (though I wouldn't bother with huckleberries, as they'd become so small). Any of the berries can be made into fruit leather. If you have individual, frozen berries, they are a delicious summertime treat or fancy-drink garnish.

Broccoli, Brussels Sprouts, Collard Greens, Cauliflower

Harvest broccoli before the flowers bloom. Flowers? Perhaps you didn't realize that a broccoli spear is composed of dozens of little flower buds. If left unpicked, they open into small, yellow flowers. But you won't let that happen. Once the shoot looks fully developed but not beginning to open, cut it off with a knife at a diagonal. But don't pull the plant yet—when you cut the main stem the plant will make secondary shoots on the sides.

Before you do anything with brassicas, soak them in salt water for a half-hour to kill the many insects that are hiding out in them (collards probably don't need this). It's not easy, because there are lots of air pockets, and they float. You may have to weigh them down. These brassicas are best blanched and frozen, or cooked and then frozen. If you're blanching Brussels sprouts, subdivide them by size to regulate blanching times.

The sprouts and collards benefit from experiencing a frost, which causes the plant to send sugars out to prevent freezing. Mike would cook the collards with onions, garlic and tomatoes, and then freeze the whole thing—we'd just thaw and eat with some cornmeal-battered catfish, beans and rice. Yum.

Cabbage, Bok Choy

These leafy vegetables can be stored in dry storage or frozen, chopped or as separate leaves. Cabbage is the root ingredient of sauerkraut, which is processed using a bizarre, old-world process of fermentation and controlled rotting. But it's sure good on sausages.

Cantaloupe, Honeydew Melon

These fruits are pretty resilient cut into pieces and stored in the freezer. Not so good canned.

Celery

Don't freeze celery unless it's an ingredient in a soup—it totally loses its integrity. However, you may be able to overwinter the plant in a mild climate. Just break off a stalk when you need one.

Cherries

There are two kinds of cherries: sour, which are used in baking; and sweet, which are eaten fresh, canned or dried. Either kind must be washed and pitted before storage. My friend, Andrea, would store cherries in a vodka-sugar mix, which she called "hooch."

Chives

This is a nice little herb that is fairly self-reliant once it gets going, save needing regular watering. Snip leaves near the bottom and then chop as an ingredient or a garnish in numerous dishes, from casseroles to eggs to soup.

Coconut

Shred or chop the meat and freeze, dry or covered in coconut milk. Good for baking.

Corn

Fresh sweet corn is one of the otherworldly fresh-food experiences. Pick cobs when the kernels look plump, or when a kernel that is poked with the point of a sharp knife drips milky juice. The kernels on a good piece of corn are tender and burst into your mouth when you bite them. They are so sweet that you'll find it impossible to put the cob down; you'll just keep eating until it's gone. Butter is extraneous.

Once you've had all you can eat, put some up for winter. Cobs can be frozen whole, or the kernels can be cut off with a knife. Hold the (cooked) cob near the fat end and rest the small end on a cutting board. Place the knife at the fat end against the bottoms of the kernels, and push the knife down, trying to keep it as close to the cob as possible. Bags of this corn are great to throw into soups or batches of corn bread.

(Corn that is fed to livestock is called "field corn" or "feed corn." Its sugars have turned to starch.)

Cranberries and Currants

These tart little guys are great in baked goods or dried. Cranberries are also juiced. Both berries can be frozen whole, either dry or in syrup. Wash and remove stems.

Dates

These are usually dehydrated but can also be frozen. Dried dates can be pitted or not; frozen dates should be pitted first.

Eggplants

They are so beautiful on the vine, a rich purple. But they just don't do anything for me gastronomically. And they don't store well. It might help if you prepare them first and then freeze the meal, e.g. as eggplant Parmesan.

Grapes

Real grapes are only somewhat similar to the seedless behemoths we are used to buying at the grocery. Grocery-store grapes are the Angus beef of the fruit world; refined but lacking their relatives' bolder characteristics. Real grapes are no bigger than a cherry. Eating one provides two different experiences at the same time— when you crush it between your teeth, the interior sort of bursts from the skin. The two halves float around and possess very different characteristics: The skin is bitter and must be chewed up. The interior is extremely sweet and feels like a bubble; carefully break it without crunching up the seeds inside. Don't eat the seeds, or a grape vine will grow in your stomach! At least, that's what my mom told me.

Grapes can be juiced and made into jelly. They can also be dried into raisins. White grapes varieties make "golden raisins."

Guava

Guava can be frozen or made into jelly. Or, juiced!

Kale

This sturdy leafy green can be sautéed in a number of dishes, frozen, chopped into a pesto-like affair, or—of all things—baked with olive oil and salt to create a "chips" snack!

Mango

Mango freezes pretty well, either in strips or as a purée. Mango is also a delicious juice and dried snack.

Okra

Anyone who has tried okra either loves it or hates it. If they love it, they've had it prepared properly, in a gumbo or other stew. If they hate it, it was served to them as a side vegetable. Okra pods contain goo, which viscosity gives gumbo that wonderful, solid, dense character. It does not lend itself to being served solo.

Okra can be canned or frozen. I blanched and froze mine whole; later, if I was making a batch of chili, I chopped them into half-inch pieces straight out of the freezer. The pods can also be breaded and deep-fried.

Onions, Garlic, Shallots

In the Pacific Northwest, these bulbs are planted in the fall and harvested mid-summer. Onion starts can be planted in the spring as well. Water them until they are nearing the end, when the plants start to dry out. Onion stalks will even fall over sometimes. Dig them up once the plant part has dried (or mostly dried; there can still be a little green toward the center of the stalk). Unless rain is in the forecast, leave them on the ground for a day or two to continue to dry out, and then hang them in a well-ventilated place to dry even further (if you want to braid them, now is the time).

Once they're completely dried and the stalks are golden, you can bring them in the house (or sooner, if there is a freeze in the forecast). These like to be stored in a cool (but not cold) and dry place. I stored mine in a closet, not the cellar with the root veggies et al. I tied them in bundles with twine, and then hung them. You could also store them loosely in a paper or mesh bag.

Oranges, Grapefruit, Limes, Lemons, Tangerines, Mandarins

These fruit are delicious eaten fresh, or sectioned and frozen in juice, water or syrup. Marmalades and curds are also an option. Beware the peel and membranes for fresh eating; they are bitter. A bit of grated peel is sometimes used in baking.

The membranes of grapefruit are particularly bitter. To serve, cut in half against the grain (perpendicular to the blossom-stem axis) and then use a curved, serrated knife to cut the fruit of each along the inside perimeter. These chunks can then be fished out with a spoon. Don't forget to squeeze the excess juice from the rind at the end! Grapefruit used to benefit from a glaze of sugar, but these days, sweeter varieties have taken over.

Oranges can either be peeled and sectioned, or sliced into sections. Their membranes are edible. Tangerines and mandarin oranges slip their skins more easily than the other fruits. Their smaller segments are popular in salads.

Limes and lemons are sourer than the other citrus fruits but extremely useful in tandem with other ingredients. Limes are used extensively in Southwestern cuisine; lemons work well squeezed onto fish and to keep sliced apples fresh. Lemon juice is also used in canning to add acid.

All of these fruits lend themselves to being juiced. Limes and lemons need additional sugar, and are not used full strength (add water).

Oregano

This herb is used in Italian and Greek dishes, fresh or dried. You can also freeze it. To dry, cut healthy stalks with many large, intact leaves, and hang upside-down in a cool, ventilated area. Once the leaves are dry, store in an airtight jar. You can either crumble them all at once with clean, dry fingers, or leave the leaves whole and crumble them as needed.

Parsley

Italian parsley is hard to get started from seed, but once it's going it can thrive. I've even had plants overwinter. It is a biennial, though, so if it does overwinter it will bolt once the weather improves. You can also try this inside. It doesn't like direct sun on hot days. Rather than harvesting the entire plant, just break off leaves as you need them. Once it bolts, save the seeds for next year.

Peaches, Nectarines, Apricots, Plums

Mmm, peaches. They are sublime fresh from the tree, the juice running down your arm. "Cling" varieties have a stone that doesn't separate easily from the seed; "freestone" varieties do. I find peaches to can better than freeze, but it's a personal choice. In fact, all are good canned. Apricots may be dried with good results; halve and remove pits. Plums may be dried or made into a sauce. All may be made into jam.

Peanuts

Not a true nut, the peanut is actually a legume with fruits that grow on underground rhizomes, like a potato. They can be boiled, or roasted dry.

Pears, Asian Pears

A good pear is so good, and a bad pear is so gross. A good pear is firm but not hard; a bad one sort of collapses in your mouth, a mealy mess. Be sure you're canning firm ones. They're also dense, so it's better to slice them than to can halves. You can freeze pears but only if you want a sauce.

Asian pears are like a cross of a Western pear and an apple. They are crisp and have a mild flavor, with a thicker skin, so people tend to peel them before eating. Because of their high water content, people tend not to bake with them. Once they have achieved the right size and color, final ripeness is determined by tasting one. Unlike Western pears, Asian pears must ripen on the tree.

Poached pears (either variety) are served as a sublime dessert.

Peas

As with beans, there are fresh-eating peas and dried peas. Of the fresh peas, there are those bred to be eaten in the pod, such as snow peas and sugar snap peas, and those which are shelled. Sugar snaps are best eaten raw; snow peas are often used in Asian stir-fry dishes. The husks of shell peas become tough as the peas inside grow. Peas can be canned in a pressure canner, but in my opinion turn out better blanched and frozen.

Black-eyed peas are dried and then reconstituted in a soup, or plain—they are served on New Year's Day in the South for good luck. Shell peas are dried and reconstituted as split pea soup.

Peppers

There are "sweet" and "hot" peppers. Sweet peppers include bells, bananas, and cherries. Hot peppers are all the ones used in Tex-Mex and Asian cuisine: jalapeño, habañero and Serrano. The Anaheim and poblano peppers are mild but still considered a hot pepper; poblanos are usually used for *chiles relleños*. If handling, especially chopping, hot peppers, wear gloves or other protection. The spice comes from an oil, meaning soap doesn't necessarily remove it. Don't be like me and rub your eyes after making a vat of chili. And don't be like my friend, Rich, and go to urinate after making a vat of chili.

Peppers are a nightshade and therefore prefer hot weather, especially hot nights. They are also sensitive to other nightshades; if you are a smoker, be sure you've washed your hands between smoking and handling the pepper fruits; you can damage them.

About the only way to preserve peppers is to pickle (sweet) or dry (hot) them. Some can be frozen but their use is limited to being an ingredient in a soup or enchilada or something, not in their original crispy form. My friend Rebecca makes a yummy jalapeño jelly.

Pineapple

This fruit dries well in rings or pieces. It also cans and freezes well. To cut a pineapple, cut the ends off, then use a pineapple-corer and cut off the remaining skin and eyes. Or, cut into quarters lengthwise and then cut the core from the center and the skin and eyes from the edge.

Pomegranate

This crazy puzzle-fruit is packed with ruby-like sweet fruit-nubs studded with slightly bitter seeds, if you can get at them. The fruit-nubs can be frozen in juice or syrup, though I don't know how you'd use them thereafter. Pomegranates are also juiced: the best way to get at the fruit-nubs is to cut the fruit in half, turn the halves cut-side down and then whack each half with a hammer. That makes it easier to take apart. Then the fruit-nubs are cooked and strained. Pomegranates do not dehydrate well, because it's all juice and seed.

Potatoes

Digging up potatoes is one of the best tasks on a farm—all of the action has been taking place below the soil, and you finally get to check it out. All those little potato-chunks that you planted in the spring have sprouted a plant using the nutrients in the chunk as fuel until they could start photosynthesizing, grown tall and possibly even produced berries (don't eat them—poisonous), and have started to die off. What you haven't seen them doing is sending out underground rhizomes from which grow potatoes. They look like skinny umbilical cords. Sometimes a rhizome creates two or more smaller potatoes, and sometimes it puts its energy into one giant one.

To get those nuggets out of the ground requires a digging fork. The trick is to dig up the spuds without driving the fork tines through your biggest specimens. It takes some practice to get the spacing right, but I look for the center of the plant (I recommend lifting the stems because what seems like the center might not be) and then place my fork eight to ten inches out. I step on the fork to drive it straight down a foot or so, and then tilt the shaft backwards, pushing the tines under the potatoes and pushing the potatoes toward the surface.

I would wear gloves since you really have to get in there and sift through the entire area to make sure you get all the potatoes. They will be all sizes, even tiny ones that were just getting going. Put them gently into a basket and cover with a cloth to keep the sun off them. If some weren't completely buried, the exposed portion will be green. The rest of the potato is fine, but the green part is poisonous and should be cut off.

For fresh eating, treat them just like potatoes from the store (except these are going to rock your world with their flavor and texture). You don't need to cook fresh ones as long. Prepare them for storage by placing one layer on a bed sheet and covering them with another sheet so they can toughen up their skins. Do not wash them, and do not let them be exposed to sunlight. Eat the smaller and damaged ones, and store the perfect, bigger ones. They basically need a cool, dry place to live. They do not freeze well. You can store some for next year's seed potatoes—mark them as such so you don't accidentally eat them! Don't cut seed potatoes until right before you plan to plant them.

Pumpkin

Interesting tidbit: The "pumpkin" we buy canned in the grocery is not actually pumpkin; it's other squash types, including Hubbard, that are drier and less stringy. But "jack-o-lantern" pumpkins are certainly edible. Mike decided to make pumpkin pies using real pumpkins one year, which worked fine, but we hadn't figured into the equation having to bake the pumpkin for hours just to get the moisture out. Every window in our house steamed up.

Pumpkin can be canned in a pressure canner (cubed) or frozen (cooked and puréed). The seeds can be eaten as well, and are delicious baked in a single layer on a cookie sheet until golden brown, turning once with a spatula. Some people soak their seeds in saltwater overnight first. I add season salt to mine. Pumpkin is also baked into a sweetbread, like banana bread.

Rhubarb

Its uses are limited, but it is such a wonderful "fruit." Actually a relative of the lily, rhubarb is one of the first plants to unfurl its leaves in the spring, which in itself is a great gift. As I mention elsewhere in this book, the leaves are poisonous and should be put on your garden-waste compost pile. The stalks are tender and juicy for at least a month, and then start to become stringy during hot weather. So, harvest them before summer. Cut a few stalks—you really don't need many, maybe eight or ten. To process rhubarb, simply wash the stalks and then chop them into pieces. I cut them about one inch in length for normal-sized stalks and slightly less for the fat ones, and then store them in waxed paper sandwich bags that are placed in plastic storage bags. When cooking, rhubarb requires the addition of copious amounts of sugar except for the rare tart junkie.

Rhubarb makes delicious chutneys and pancake-toppings, as well as pies and crisps—especially when mixed with a sweet berry. However, it has a tendency to turn brown. This can be minimized by boiling it for one minute and then putting it in cold water. I would do this with larger pieces and then cut the one-inch segments afterwards.

Root Vegetables

Use your digging fork or shovel to loosen beets, carrots, rutabagas, turnips and parsnips, and then pull them out. Cut or rip the green tops off and feed them to your chickens. If you leave the greens on, they will continue to live by drawing nutrients from the root. You can eat beet greens yourself, but I never ate mine because they had leaf miners, a bug that tunnels through the leaves. The chickens considered leaf miners a bonus.

Root crops store best in sand or sawdust that is moist but not wet. You can also leave them in the ground and pull as needed, depending on how hard your ground freezes during the winter. You can also blanch and freeze them, or can them with a pressure-canner. Beets are good pickled; I wouldn't recommend it with the rest of this bunch.

Rutabagas, turnips and parsnips are the forgotten vegetables, spurned by baby-boomers who had to eat them growing up and then wanted nothing to do with them as adults, so they fell by the wayside. Okay—I probably don't want a plate of them, but they're great in soups.

Squash

There are dozens of types of squash; some are even dried to make drums and loofah scrubbers! Of the edible squash, there are two types: summer and winter. All squash plants are enormous vines; plant them somewhere that they can spread out at least six feet. They are also prolific—it won't take long after moving to the country before you start hearing from the people who grow zucchini. Zucchini-growers are notorious for using every method possible to consume and give away their many, many fruits. You might even find a bag of them on your front step one day.

Summer squash (including zucchini) are the tender ones that are eaten fairly young. They don't can well but can be frozen. The blossoms can also be eaten, usually breaded and fried in oil. Zucchini is baked into a sweetbread, like banana bread.

Winter squash are grown to the natural end of their lives; they're not harvested until the fruits are grown and matured, and the vines die down. Be sure to pick them before a frost, though, which would hasten their spoiling. Winter squash can be stored in your basement or other storage, just make sure they were cured in a hot, dry place to heal any nicks in the skin. Do not break the stem off flush with the body; leave a few inches.

Sweet Potatoes

This vegetable has a real identity crisis. It's not a yam. There is such a thing as a yam but it lives in Africa and Asia. They're also not true potatoes—a morning glory, not a nightshade. Sweet potatoes can have white or orange flesh and can be fixed like potatoes, though: mashed, baked, and even French-fried.

Sweet potatoes are not grown like potatoes, they are started with slips being cultivated above ground. Cut a sweet potato in half and stick toothpicks in it to suspend it above a jar of water. As the sprouts grow, you can carefully pick them off and put in water. After the root system is better developed, plant in the ground. You'll have the best luck with a real seed potato, not one you buy at the store.

Sweet potatoes are also not stored like potatoes. They don't like to be stored fresh at all, and only last a couple of weeks in a cool, dark place. Do not refrigerate raw sweet potatoes. The best option for long-term storage is to freeze or can.

Tomatoes

Beware—once you've eaten real tomatoes—by which I mean fresh tomatoes that grew in a garden—you will never be able to put another tough, pinkish-gray commercially grown "tomato" slice in your mouth. It is incredible to me that both items are considered a tomato. A real tomato is so sweet and tender you can eat it raw with nary a grain of salt on it. You can practically cut it with a butter knife. In the summer, the tomato slices on our hamburgers are thicker than our hamburgers.

Tomato plants are easier to grow in Southern climes in the United States—they like hot days but really need hot nights to flourish. Botanists and food-science folks have bred varieties that can tolerate cool nights and shorter growing seasons.

Your best storage bets are to can them, halved and in sauces. If a frost is coming, you can pick anything that has a hint of color and bring it inside—many of those last-resort tomatoes will ripen (though they'll be a little tougher than the summer ones). You can sun-dry Roma-type tomatoes, and then freeze them or refrigerate them in olive oil.

Tomatoes, Green

The best way to eat green tomatoes is fried. They are sliced about ¼-inch thick, breaded in cornmeal and fried in oil. That may not sound that great, but when they're done well (not too greasy) they're sublime—crispy and tart and salty.

Tomatillos

Tomatillos have limited uses, but those few uses are good! I like to include them in a vat of chili, or chop them up to make salsa verde (green salsa). Add garlic, salt and onions.

Watermelon

Watermelon can supposedly be frozen, but I can't imagine it. The rinds can also be pickled. Since you can only eat it in its true form during the summer, eat it every day!

Canning

My friend Ivy makes everything: mittens; Adirondack chairs; the most amazing cakes you've ever seen or tasted. If she gives you something she made, you are very lucky. One year, Ivy gave us a jar of plums that she had canned. Mike and I were still firmly ensconced in city life at this point, and we were afraid to eat them! The botulism scares of our youth must have had their effect.

I'm now embarrassed by the fear and ignorance that kept us from enjoying those plums. I find few things as satisfying as the *pink-pink-pink* of all my lids sealing after I've pulled them from the canner. The purpose of a canner is to preserve food by first heating it to a temperature that kills mold, yeast, enzymes and bacteria hiding on or in it, and then by vacuum-sealing the jar so nothing else can get in. There are two types of canning: boiling-water bath and pressure. "High-acid" foods, like tomatoes and fruit, can be cooked in a water-bath canner. "Low-acid" foods, like vegetables and meat, need more intense cooking, which is done using a pressure canner. Pickling is a separate process.

The terminology is a bit confusing: you are "canning" but you're putting the food in jars. That's just the way it is. The key to safe canning is, as my friend Nancy puts it: "Clean, clean, clean and hot, hot, hot." Use clean jars and fresh, clean food. Make sure everything is hot. The amount of processing time needed increases with elevation; if you live in a place that is more than 1,000 feet above sea level, you'll need extra processing.

Jars, lids and screw bands can be sterilized in a bath of boiling water. If you have a dishwasher, you're off the hook—but you do have to time it so that when your food is cooked and ready to go into the canner, your jars are done but haven't cooled off. If you put hot food into a cold jar, the jar may shatter.

"So let's get this straight," you say. "It's August, and I have to run my dishwasher, cook a bunch of fruit, and start water to boil?" That's right! And, you have to pull the jars, one by one, from the steaming-hot dishwasher, fill them with steaming-hot fruit and put them in the steaming-hot canner, and then run the canner for at least fifteen minutes. In the course of things you'll get scalding drips on your forearms and burn your fingers on the jars. I recommend a tall, cold drink when you're finished.

One advantage of canning over freezing is that no one thinks twice about the canned food if the power goes out in the middle of winter. Glass canning jars may be re-used again and again, unless the rim is chipped. You can even buy them at a yard sale—actually, I recommend this because they used to make them out of thicker glass than they do now (surprise, surprise). Just make sure they're relatively clean and were only used for food. Do not re-use commercially canned mayonnaise or spaghetti sauce jars—they are too thin and may shatter during processing, and may not seal well.

However, you should *always* buy new lids for your jars. These are available as a separate item at the grocery or feed store where you buy canning jars. Back in the day, women reused lids by adding new wax to their rims; this is not recommended. I do re-use lids for dry goods storage, like dried beans in the cupboard. I recycle them once they're looking like the wax seal is totally gone, or they start to rust.

The screw band part of the lid has two purposes: to hold the lid on during the water-bath and to hold the lid on after the seal has been broken. The screw band should not be left on the jars while they're stored, at least not tightly, because screwing it on might actually break the seal.

If you can press the center of a lid up and down after the processed jars have cooled, it's not sealed. That doesn't mean the food is inedible; it just means you need to either re-process that jar to see if it will seal, or refrigerate and eat the food in the jar in the near future, just like any store-bought jar of food that has been opened. You should also, usually, hear a small suction noise when you pry a lid off for the first time.

Sealed jars of food should be stored in a dry, dark, cool place that won't freeze. They should be labeled with the contents and date. And then, they should be enjoyed! Their contents will remain edible for many years, but the flavor and nutritional value fades over time. Once you've got it down to a science, you'll use up everything you made the previous year just as you're canning your new batches.

There are two types of canning described below. The first is for what are called "high-acid" foods: jams and fruits, including tomatoes. The second is for "low-acid" foods: vegetables and anything with meat in it (including meat spaghetti sauce).

Water Bath/Steam

The water-bath canner is a tall kettle; fill it with water so that it will be one inch deeper than the jar, and bring that to a boil. Meanwhile, start preparing your fruit. There are many recipe books for this. Fill your jars, cleaning the rims carefully, and put them in the water bath for a period of time that is recommended by the recipe and/or the manufacturer of the canner.

Hot-packed fruit is cooked; raw-packed fruit is simply chopped up and put into the jars, and then hot water or syrup is added to fill up the airspace. You have to poke them around a bit with a rubber spatula to make sure the air is out (a few tiny bubbles are acceptable). I just used water for my peaches, and they turned the water into peach juice with no extra sugar. If you are cold-packing, really shove those peach slices in there because they will shrink during processing, and then you have a few slices floating around in a sea of water.

Tomatoes are right on the cusp—they are okay to can, if you add acid in the form of lemon juice or citric acid, but some people pressure can them because they may retain more of their nutritional value that way. Can only fresh, unblemished tomatoes.

Instead of a water-bath canner, I bought a steam canner from a local hardware store. The steam canner, the booklet explains, is a superior product—steam is hotter than hot water, and the steam canner requires less water and less clean-up. However, it isn't condoned by the United States Department of Agriculture. One of my reference books states that they aren't recommended because "processing times for use with current models have not been adequately tested." The friend who loaned me the book added that a judge at her county fair had told her that newer fruit varieties may have lower acid than the heirloom varieties Grandma canned.

The concerns are that the steam is not hot enough to bring the centers of each jar to the requisite 212 degrees Fahrenheit, and that these new hybrid fruit, with their speculated lower acidity, might require a higher temperature in order to be safe to eat. *So, test them!* I say. But, I doubt this will ever happen—the USDA has bigger fish to fry. Moral: Use a steam canner at your own risk.

Because I use a dishwasher and this illicit steam canner, I don't need the classic set of canning tools: a jar-lifter, which grasps a jar and pulls it from the canner; and a lid-magnet, which pulls the lids from pot of boiling water. I do use a canning funnel, which keeps the food off the rim of the jar (and off the counter), and a rubber spatula to work air bubbles from the food. I also have a couple of clean, wet and heated dishcloths, and a timer.

There are massive canners for sale; keep in mind that the canner shouldn't extend more than four inches beyond the burner. Also, the canner I used totally ruined the enameled finish around that burner because it was so hot for so long.

Pressure

A pressure canner is like a steam canner except the steam is locked into the canner, which makes it even hotter, at least 240 degrees, to kill all the beasties. These devices are the ones that can explode. Simply because of the safety issue, this is something I would not buy second-hand, unless it were a recent model that came with its instruction booklet. You can have the gauge tested via your extension center.

This higher temperature makes it possible to preserve "low-acid" food like meats and vegetables. If you are canning something like salsa or soup, follow a recipe that has been published in a USDA-approved recipe book. Do not skimp on processing times, especially for dense foods like pumpkin. The contents of the entire jar, not just the outer edge, must reach 240 degrees Fahrenheit in order to kill the bacterium that makes botulism.

Most raw-packed vegetables shrink during processing, except starchy vegetables like corn, lima beans, peas and potatoes, which expand slightly.

Be sure to allow steam to escape the canner for ten minutes before closing the valve. Keeping the canner at the correct pressure can be tricky—you have to watch your burner and your gauge carefully. If it drops below pressure, you have to start over with the processing time. Once the food has been processed, let the canner cool naturally—don't pour cold water on it or anything else. This could spoil the food and the canner both.

Canning 101

To learn how to can food, start with fruit jam. Jam is the most forgiving of the canned foods: it's easy to make and is completely salvageable. If it doesn't set, use it as syrup, or add more pectin and cook it again. If the lid doesn't seal, refrigerate that jar and eat it first, or steam/boil the jar again.

Always use clean, ripe but not overripe ingredients. Cut off any bruises and stems. Wash carefully and thoroughly; the bacterium that causes botulism is in dirt.

Jam is a simple concoction: fruit, sugar and pectin (and sometimes lemon juice). The thing that makes the fruit set into a gel is pectin, which is found in apples. You can use apple pectin to set jam; it's just a lot easier to use the boxed, powered pectin. These boxes come with a ***very specific*** set of instructions. It can look sort of intimidating, but really, jam is easy. There is nothing to stop you from experimenting with natural pectin sources and sugar-substitutes like honey. Really, the only way you could ruin jam is to make it set so hard you couldn't get it out of the jar.

You may be shocked to learn just how much sugar goes into jam—more sugar than fruit in conventional recipes! There are low-sugar pectin boxes—I tried one and couldn't tell the difference in the jam except that it set a little harder, so I would recommend it. There are even kinds that use chemical sweeteners instead of sugar.

Ladle the cooked jam into a jar. A canning funnel will help immensely. Leave a "headspace" at the top of the jar—don't fill it all the way to the top. This gives the food an opportunity to expand without forcing its way out of the jar and compromising the seal. Don't leave too big of a headspace, either, or the jar may not seal properly. For jam, about one-quarter to one-half inch will do. Place a lid on the jar, making sure that the rim is clear of drips, and then slide a screw band over it, hand-tight. Do not over-tighten the band, as this will prevent steam escaping the jar during processing. Do not tilt the jar so that the food could come in contact with the seal.

Process the jars thoroughly. If the processing time is listed in your instruction booklet or recipe as fifteen minutes, that means fifteen solid minutes. So, if you turn the heat down too far and the water stops boiling or the steam column shrinks, you need to bring it back up to temperature and start the timer over. Once the jars have been processed, put them on your counter on a dishcloth and let them sit there and cool down for at least twelve hours.

You will need different amounts of fruit for a batch, which is the number of jars that fit in your canner at one time (approximately six quarts or twelve pints). I would not put jam in anything bigger than a pint jar; quarts are for bigger items. There are no preservatives in what you're canning, so once you've opened a jar you have to eat the contents a little more quickly than something processed and sold in the store.

The first year I had to guess how much fruit to use, but I kept track for future years. I found an enormous colander at an estate sale; when I had filled it with raspberries, I knew I was ready to make a batch of jam. One year, I recorded that I bought twenty-six peaches, which I sliced, and they filled nine pint jars. Some people measure by the pound; you'll just have to do some experimenting with the fruit and equipment you have available.

I once made my grandma laugh out loud. I was making raspberry jelly, and phoned her because it wasn't working out.

"Well, tell me what you've done," she said. I explained that I'd cooked the raspberries and added the pectin, like you're supposed to do, and now I was trying to filter it through some cheesecloth, but it was clotting up on the cheesecloth rather than running through it. Then came the laughter, a real hearty chuckle.

"What did I do wrong?" I asked, embarrassed. She got a hold of herself and explained, "You strain the fruit *before* you add the pectin, dear."

It's hard to be a country novice.

Freezing

People realized a long time ago that cold inhibits decay. Thirty miles from our farm, in the mountains near a town called Trout Lake, was a place called "Cheese Cave." It was an underground cavern in which Trout Lake's dairies stored their cheese. In the Midwestern states and Northeast, ice was cut from the lakes in the winter, packed in sawdust and used throughout the year.

Modern freezers—also called the "deep-freeze" to differentiate it from the freezer in the kitchen—are set to 0 degrees Fahrenheit, instead of 30, and make storing food pretty easy. They self-defrost and are designed to run efficiently and quietly. They have drawers and baskets that facilitate finding the food once it's in there. If you plan to store a large amount of food, using a separate freezer is ideal because it minimizes the number of times the door is opened and allows you to run it at a lower temperature than you can if you, for example, eat a lot of ice cream. If you have nowhere to put a deep-freeze, check with the local grocery or butcher—you may be able to rent a meat locker.

Two tricks to keeping the door closed as much as possible:

1) Label everything well. Include what it is and when you put it there, and any other directions or notes (I.e.: "Tomato soup, needs milk!").

2) Make some kind of list or diagram of the freezer's contents that hangs near it.

Then, you're not opening and closing drawers trying to find that elusive pound of bacon. Don't forget to cross something off the list when you use it! If I put in six waxed paper bags of raspberries that are stored in one big plastic bag, I made six marks on the list so I could cross them off one at a time.

The thing that is your enemy in the freezer is air. Freezer burn occurs when moisture evaporates from the surface of frozen food. Did you know that water evaporates in the freezer? This is why ice cubes shrink if left for a long time. Avoid freezer burn by drying food *thoroughly* and then wrapping the food well, eliminating air spaces. If you're using plastic bags (which I recommend), use bags that specify they're freezer bags. Bread bags and other plastic bags are not sufficiently nonporous. Lightweight aluminum foil and waxed paper by themselves are also insufficient.

Vegetables do well in the freezer—just blanch, drain and throw them into a storage bag. Tomatoes can go in with the skins or without. Eat whatever you store within a year—it won't go bad, but its flavor, physical condition and nutritional value will deteriorate over time.

A friend freezes her blueberries and raspberries on a cookie sheet first, and then bags them. The effect of this isn't noticeable until they are thawed again. The cell walls of fruit break open when the water in them expands; when they thaw, they become mush. If you freeze the berries individually they freeze faster, making smaller ice crystals that are less likely to destroy the berry.

I found this rather inconsequential since we used berries in crisps, pies, milkshakes and smoothies. So, instead of going to the trouble of freezing berries individually I used waxed paper sandwich bags and zipping-type plastic storage bags: I scooped berries into a waxed-paper bag, rolled up the top and put it in the plastic bag; I could fit three in each quart-sized bag. And that way, I always had the same amount of berries: Two bags of berries and one of rhubarb were perfect for a crisp.

To minimize the impact of adding new food to the freezer, get it cold in the refrigerator first. Space new packages out in the freezer until they're frozen, and then pack close together. If you're filling an empty freezer, get it extra cold first. If you fill it and then turn it on, it will struggle to freeze everything properly. The last thing you want are thick packages that are only frozen on the exterior.

If you are storing things that have a strong flavor, wrap them thoroughly. We once received a goose from a friend who hunts and fishes—he was cleaning out his freezer of last year's bounty. It was a generous gift more in spirit than in flavor, we learned, once we ate it and it tasted of salmon.

It is possible to use glass in the freezer but I wouldn't recommend it; the last thing you need is a bunch of shattered glass in there. There are dozens of types of plastics in the world, and this is one place I use them.

Drying

Dehydrating food is one of the oldest ways to preserve it. "Jerky" is marinated, dehydrated meat. Vegetables don't turn out that well; I'd stick with canning and freezing. Ditto "vegetable fruits" like avocados and olives, with the exception of small, whole Roma-type tomatoes. Most fruits dehydrate really nicely.
You can dry fruit a couple of ways: in a commercial dehydrator, or outside. Some friends of mine owned an old commercial gas range; its pilot light was so large that they dehydrated fruit in the oven.

Using natural elements to dehydrate fruit is a bit tricky. First of all, you have to live in a place that has hot, breezy, low-humidity summers. It takes a few days to completely dehydrate, so those conditions have to remain constant the entire time. The fruit should be covered at night to minimize re-hydration from the dew point changing.

Food should be elevated on a screen to maximize ventilation. Although hardware cloth might seem perfect for the job, it is galvanized, and that coating could come off onto your food. Same with metals that react to acid, like aluminum and copper. The best option would be a food-grade plastic or stainless. You can increase the effect of the sun by placing reflective material under and around the screen.

Move the fruit around with a spatula every once in a while to make sure it's drying evenly and not sticking to the screen. Once the fruit is dried, kill any critters by baking at a low temperature (160 degrees or so) for a half-hour, or freezing for two days.

You can treat your fruit with sulfites or juices to limit discoloration. Or, you can ignore the discoloration—it's just aesthetic.

Seed-laden fruits like berries and guava have the best results if you make them into a "leather," which means to purée them together and then dry the paste in a thin layer on a sheet of plastic. The leather peels off the plastic to eat.

There are specific varieties of corn intended for popcorn. The best varieties for sunflowers are the ones with big seeds. Let these dry on the "vine" as it were. You may need to cover them with cheesecloth or netting to keep the birds off them.

Chapter 17
Harvesting From the Wild

Before humans developed cultivation, this was our way—gathering edible plants, and catching and killing animals. Any time you walk past a plum tree and pull off a fruit, or cut firewood out of the forest, you are getting back to your hunter-gatherer roots.

The main rules in wild harvesting are Permission, and Leave No Trace. First, permission: If you are on public land, make sure you have a permit to take what you're taking. If you want to go on private land, ask the owner first.

Second, leave no trace: If you are harvesting mushrooms, do it in a way that leaves the parent fungus unharmed. If you are fishing, obey the rules about size and number of fish. The goal with wild harvesting is to allow everything to reproduce so there's more for next year!

Wildcrafting Plants

Most old folks have a story about wildcrafting, though they didn't call it that. It's the last vestige of our hunter-gatherer roots—walking out into the forest, or along the edge of a meadow, and picking the edible bits.

"We went out 'nutting,'" says my grandma: Their family packed a picnic lunch and went out "to the woods," public land between Illinois farms, where they made a day of harvesting wild black walnuts and hazelnuts. Mike's grandma used to dodge highway traffic to get at her secret stands of wild asparagus. My great-grandfather used to terrorize his wife by eating the slimy, black mushrooms he found in the woods.

On the West Coast, wildcrafting is alive and well—if anything, there is currently so much commercial wildcrafting going on that it's threatening some species and occasionally resulting in violence as people fight over "territory."

That notwithstanding, you owe it to yourself to have a wildcrafting experience. It's cheap, it's a good outing, and it results in some delicious food.

The best way to get into wildcrafting is to go with someone who already knows the ropes. Then, you can learn how to identify the right plant (and not a poisonous look-alike) and how to harvest responsibly. It will take time to be invited, as people don't tend to share their secrets. You can also check with your local Forest Service or other public land manager to get an idea of where to start. The only trouble with this is they steer all newcomers to the same spots. Find out the fee (usually minimal, like five dollars) and restrictions for the type of food you want to harvest. Or, ask a private landowner if you can wildcraft on his/her land.

Plant foods that can be found in the wild:

- **Blackberries:** Himalayan blackberries are, by far, the most popular invasive species in the Pacific Northwest. The berries are ripe when they surpass full shininess and have become slightly dull in color. Watch yourself: The canes bite back with thick, sharp thorns. We dress in full sleeves and trousers, even though these are ripe in August.
- **Thimbleberries:** When these divine berries ripen in July, they are extremely fragile; pick with your hand under the berry so if it falls off, it falls into your palm. If it doesn't come off easily, it's not ripe.
- **Salmonberries:** These are a really pretty orange color but not as flavorful as other berries.
- **Strawberries:** Smaller than a grocery-store berry and a thousand times more flavorful.
- **Huckleberries:** A smaller, purple relative of the blueberry that is found in alpine country. They take a while to pick because of their size but are worth it.
- **Grapes:** Smaller than cultivated grapes, with bigger seeds and tougher skins, but yummy. And the plant itself is so beautiful.
- **Miner's Lettuce:** A delicate green that can be added to your garden salad.
- **Lamb's Quarters:** Extremely nutritious relative of spinach.
- **Mushrooms:** The most popular of these in the Pacific Northwest are chanterelles, lobster and king Boletus, but there are dozens of others. Mazutakes made a big splash a few years ago when they sold in Japan for $600 per pound! Morels are prevalent in most of the United States.
- **Asparagus:** The stalks are a bit thinner than cultivated varieties, but the flavor is there.
- **Fiddleheads:** These are the curled-up new leaves of the fiddlehead fern. They taste a bit like asparagus.
- **English and Black Walnuts, Chestnuts and Hazelnuts:** All nuts have an outer husk that must be removed; dry them in a single layer and then use gloves to coax the hulls off (this will stain and otherwise menace bare hands). Chestnuts need to be roasted as well.
- **Stinging Nettle:** Do not touch this with bare hands! The plant grows hundreds of stinging spines on its leaves, a good defense until someone figured out that once you cook the leaves, the spines lose their effect.

Cooked nettles are full of vitamins and taste a bit like earthy, nutty spinach.

- **Dandelion:** Young leaves can be included in a salad; the flowers can be made into a wine. Neither of these impresses me, but on the other hand they're everywhere, so you might as well do something with them!
- **Taro:** This plant's root will make you sick if you eat it raw, but mashes into a food staple on the Hawaiian Islands.
- **Paw Paw:** Found in the Southeastern United States, these fruits can be used in recipes that call for bananas. Some people pureé and freeze the meat.
- **Crabapple:** High in pectin. Cook the apples until they're soft, and squeeze out the juice to use in cooking jam.
- **Ground Cherries:** Similar to tomatillos but must be allowed to fully ripen before eating. Can be stored in husk or dried.

There are also dozens of medicinal uses for wild plants. Get expert advice before you delve into this—you wouldn't want to eat a leaf when you were supposed to eat a root.

Hunting Animals

My family was the "pioneering" one on my dad's side: while the rest of his siblings lived in their hometown of Appleton, Wisconsin, we ventured some 250 miles west to the Minneapolis area. We always returned for Thanksgiving and Christmas or New Year's, which entailed a five-(or more, depending on the weather)hour drive through towns like Menomonee, Neillsville and Steven's Point. En route when I was in the sixth grade, we had stopped at a gas station for a potty break. Strapped across the hood of the pickup at the adjacent pump was a huge buck. His bloody tongue lolled from his mouth, piquing in me disgust and righteous indignation. I glared at the camo-bedecked man pumping gas and said, out loud, "Stupid hunters!" on my way into the building.

As we pulled away, my dad instructed me to keep my opinions to myself in the future.

"But why'd they have to kill that deer?" I cried.

He tried to explain to me the notions of using the animal for food; that deer no longer had natural predators and there would be too many of them if people didn't shoot some of them. None of it swayed me. All I could think of was that beautiful animal in such an ignoble position, and the men bragging about it to each other. Stupid hunters.

"In that case," said Dad calmly, "keep your mouth shut, because if you piss them off they're going to come after me, not you."

So, I learned not to express my disgust with hunting and hunters, but I still felt that way, for years afterward. Until I actually made a friend who hunted. Not for trophies but for sustenance. Erik told me how he and his friend hiked in for hours, and then camped, and then hiked more. How they watched for tracks and listened; they became so attuned to the environment that they could hear a junco knocking snow off a branch. How they spied a herd of elk and, without a word to each other, split up so that one would creep around the animals (which would take an hour) and then flush them down the slope toward Erik. Erik waited patiently, hunkered down in the brush. His legs were numb but he dared not move. He saw his friend flush an elk, which came running straight toward him. How he tried to quell the adrenaline rush that threatened to shake the bow and arrow from his hand. How he took aim, and shot. The elk fell. He would eat. He thanked the elk for falling.

Now this, to me, seems a heck of a lot more noble than going to the grocery store and picking out a plastic-encased slab of "meat." Erik and his friend worked their asses off for that animal. I don't know if this argument would have made a dent in my disgust if my Dad had presented it back in 1980, or not.

I realize that not even this story will sway the staunch vegetarians out there. Which leads me to a mantra that plays a lead role in the Community, Family and Culture Section of this book: Do not assume you know better.

Weapons

There are three ways of hunting, using the state of Oregon as an example: firearms, archery and falconry. Within these three categories, there are additional restrictions and guidelines. Firearms are further characterized by form (rifle; shotgun; pistol) and caliber; archery by form (compound; crossbow). Leg-hold traps and snares may also be legal in some states but have been banned in many states, including Oregon.

Different targets require different bullets. Why? Ask the poor turkey that got in the way of my friend Ian. Ian had a clear shot at a buck and fired at the exact moment that a turkey flew into the trajectory. It disappeared in an explosion of feathers.

The goal of the hunter is to dispatch an animal with one shot, in such a manner that it limits both suffering of the animal and damage to its flesh. If the firepower is too heavy, the animal is rendered "hamburger," meaning there is meat to claim but it's all smashed up. If it's too slight, the animal will run. It may be lost altogether, if it runs into a ravine or other route that you're unable to traverse. Or, it may be wounded but not killed, requiring more shots. Either way, it will certainly suffer.

What the novice would call a bullet is actually a "cartridge" or "round," comprised of a tube that is closed on one end and then filled with gunpowder and a bullet or "shot" (small pellets) to cap the other end. When you pull the trigger of a gun, a primer lights the gunpowder, which explodes and causes the bullet to shoot from the gun (and then the tube, called a "shell," pops off to the side).

There are literally dozens of options, but the basic ammunition types include:

- **Birdshot:** Because birds are so small, hunters fire a shotgun at them. This releases a number of steel balls at once, increasing the chance of killing the bird while not tearing giant holes in it. There are different sizes of shot—the smaller numbers are actually the larger balls. Shot is commonly fired from a 12- or 20-gauge shotgun.
- **Rimfire:** Small-caliber bullets used to shoot squirrels and other small animals. The name simply refers to the fact that the primer is activated via the rim of the bullet rather than the center.
- **Centerfire:** These shells are larger, for large game like deer, elk and moose. Most guns are center fire. Shotguns can also shoot slugs, by which I mean bullets. (Though slugs have certainly driven many a farmer to want to go after them with a shotgun!)

Licensing and Reporting

All hunters are required to carry a license; your state also likely requires various "tags," i.e. permits for specific species and genders. There are numerous limits on when, where, what and how many may be hunted—check your state's game regulations (either a booklet or website). There may be a lottery for a particular tag, meaning the Fish and Wildlife people are limiting the number of animals of a particular species that can be taken that year, and there is more demand than supply.

Your state's game regulations will also include guidelines regarding reporting the animals you harvest. These numbers are used to track populations and to help determine the following year's limits.

These conventions may be frowned upon by a local, if you happen to go hunting with one. They may tell you that it's their God-given right to hunt, and it's none of the government's business. Just smile and nod, and buy your permits anyway.

Trespassing

In addition to knowing the land you plan to hunt on because it will help you find your animals, you also need to know if you are on public or private land—there's not necessarily a fence. If you plan to venture onto private land, be sure to ask permission of the landowners. It's not necessary to give them a gift, but if you happen to bag an extra goose or duck, it's nice to share. Or, drop off a bottle of whiskey.

Safety

Any time a human goes into a wild place he's putting himself at risk. Injuries and deaths occur each year: exposure to the elements, snowmobile accidents, accidental shootings. Accidental shootings often make it onto the front page of the newspaper but are actually quite rare, particularly fatal shootings. And even then, most occur when loading or unloading a gun, or mishandling it—not mistaking another hunter for a deer, although it does happen. This is why hunters (and hikers, and anyone who doesn't want to be shot in the woods in the autumn) wear "blaze orange" clothing.

If you bring dogs on a hunting trip they are also at risk, even if you give them a nice, orange vest to wear. Domestic dogs defend their person's territory; wild animals defend theirs—if conflict arises there is a good chance that your dog will lose. This may mean getting a mouthful of porcupine quills. This may mean being mauled by a bear. Keep your dogs close to you at all times. In some places it's illegal to hunt with a dog, unless you're bird hunting. You might consider booties to protect your dog's feet against rough terrain.

Gun Safety

Always treat any gun as a lethal weapon: Any gun should be assumed to be loaded at all times, until a visual inspection of the chamber shows there is no ammunition. Even if someone tells you a gun is unloaded, confirm that yourself. A gun should never be pointed at someone; hold it straight up or down, keeping in mind that if you're indoors and there is a second story above you, pointing it up is not safe, either. When handing a gun from one person to the other, open the chamber. Just as drinking and driving can be deadly, so can drinking and handling a gun. Never climb up an embankment or a tree, or over obstacles, with a loaded gun.

When shooting, make sure that not only is there nothing else between you and the animal in your crosshairs, but nothing behind it that you wouldn't want to hit. Never rest your finger on the trigger. All children are required to complete a firearms safety course before they receive a permit to hunt. These courses are recommended for adults as well.

A .22 rifle might seem like a less-dangerous weapon because its bullets are so small. Not necessarily so. Those bullets can travel up to a mile; they can ricochet off trees, roads and other obstacles—even the surface of a body of water—and go in directions you weren't intending. And, while a more powerful rifle will put a bullet straight through a person, the .22 can bounce around inside his body and do more organ damage.

It is recommended to protect your vision and hearing when shooting a gun—though it is short-lived, a gunshot is 140 decibels, louder than a jet at take-off. Your eyes could be damaged by a flying cartridge or a branch. I know you won't, but wear goggles and earplugs.

Another safety consideration is related to the significant kick that a large-caliber rifle or shotgun gives when it's discharged. This can bruise your shoulder if you're not ready for it. There's also an avoidable, unfortunate affliction called "scope eye," which occurs when you have your face too close to the viewing scope, and the recoil causes the scope to bruise—or even cut—a neat circle around your eye. To avoid this, adjust the scope properly. The rifle should be against your shoulder when you shoot. A kneeling position is more stable than a standing one.

Practicing shooting a gun is one thing, but it will never completely prepare you for the real thing. When you have been waiting to shoot a deer for twenty-four hours, and there suddenly is one standing right in front of you, the adrenaline rush can be somewhat debilitating. This is sometimes called "buck fever." Your heart races; you forget basic things like taking the safety off; you may shoot prematurely. When this happens, you won't hear anything and, if you do shoot and hurt your shoulder or eye, you won't feel pain right away.

In the thrill of the hunt, don't lose your bearings. People get lost in the woods every year, simply because they are so focused on tracking an animal. Be sure to bring a full survival kit, which includes a map and compass, a set of dry clothes, adequate food and water for at least overnight, matches and temporary shelter.

Butchering

Hunters who travel into the outback butcher in the field so there is less to carry back; scavengers like vultures and coyotes will take care of the rest of the carcass. Most hunters travel part of the way using a four-wheeler, motorcycle or snowmobile, but there are places these machines can't go. There's a good chance you'll have to haul the carcass by hand at least some of the way. Gut it (this is called "field dressing") and then turn it on its back so that you keep the interior as clean as possible as you drag it by the antlers. There are also clever wheelbarrow-like deer-carriers.

If you're really in a steep or remote area, you may need to "bone it out," which means cutting as much meat off the bones as you can and only taking that. There are backpacks designed specifically for hunters, with separate compartments for personal items and for raw meat.

The main challenge is to cool the meat as soon as possible to postpone spoilage. Once you're back in camp or home, hang the deer in a canvas bag (not a plastic bag or tarp). The meat cools faster skinned. Open the bag at night to help with cooling, and close it during the day to keep flies from laying their eggs.

Birds and fish can be cleaned and processed in the field or at home. Wild game birds are often stripped of their skin to avoid having to deal with plucking feathers. Large animals like deer and elk can be taken to a professional processor who has the room and equipment to handle many animals at once. He will cut the meat into pieces and grind sausage, and freeze it—an advantage because putting that much meat into your home freezer will bring down its temperature significantly.

Cooking Wild Game

While this is not a cookbook, I will note that the flavor of wild game differs greatly from babied domestic animals. Wild animals have not been bred to stand, more or less placidly, in a field and eat, eat, eat for months on end. They live much more dire lives—evading predators, eating when it's possible, mating, and generally not living very long (though, a friend pointed out, they live a lot longer than domestic food animals…). They run, jump or fly with purpose. They use their muscles, making them tougher than livestock muscles.

There are two things to making wild game edible, even delicious. One: Marinate it. If it smells particularly "gamey," you can even soak it overnight in salt water (called "brining"). Two: Add fat. Wild game is extremely lean; their lifestyle is not conducive to creating large fat reserves (except those that hibernate). Mike made a duck once in the oven, and I think he rubbed an entire stick of butter over it as it cooked. I've seen venison steaks wrapped in bacon for the same reason.

If you're cooking a wild bird, check it carefully for shot pellets—you don't want to break a tooth during dinner.

Fishing

There are different fish species in different parts of the country: salmon, steelhead and rainbow trout in the Pacific Northwest; bluegill, walleye and perch in the Midwest; smallmouth and largemouth bass, muskellunge and brook trout in the Northeast; catfish, stripers and panfish in the South; halibut, snapper, flounder, mackerel and tuna in the oceans. And many, many others. Most of them are caught using a rod-and-reel; some are caught with flies; some in nets or traps. If you're a Native American, you might use a dip net or spear. Unless you're fishing on a stocked pond on your own land, you probably need to buy a permit or license to harvest fish. There will be limits to the type, number and size of the fish you can take home, as well as the type of equipment you can use. Responsible fishing ensures that there will be more harvestable fish next year, and that endangered species are spared.

Don't let fish bounce around too much when you're landing them; this can bruise the meat. Kill a fish by hitting it soundly on the head; some folks have a small wooden or aluminum club for this purpose. Or, put the fish in a cooler with ice, though there is debate about whether this is humane, as it's hard to tell whether it's suffering or not. Maybe it just goes to sleep.

Fish are extremely perishable; one piece of equipment should be a cooler, with ice, in which to store fish. If the weather is cool, you can use a stringer, immersible basket or "live well," which is essentially an aerated bucket full of water. It can also be used for live bait.

If you used a boat, be sure that you have followed any precautions necessary to prevent the transfer of invasive species from one body of water to another. There are also many outfitters that will take you fishing; some, especially the ocean-going vessels, have the machinery to process, shrink-wrap and freeze your catch before you even get back to shore. You just pop the packages in your cooler and drive home.

Ice Fishing

In Northern climes, there is a phenomenon called "ice fishing." This involves cutting a hole in the ice of a frozen lake, and attempting to lure a fish using a line dropped into the hole. Shockingly, this actually works.

Ice fisher-people protect themselves from the elements by building a small shelter around their hole. Where I grew up, dozens of little houses popped up on nearby Medicine Lake during the winter. Nowadays, the ungainly wood shacks have been replaced by svelte tent-like structures that can be hauled out by a cross-country skier, not a pickup. And, of course, some people go over the top and build fish houses that are equipped with kitchens and satellite television.

Crustaceans and Shellfish

I find it ironic that some vegetarians are willing to eat crustaceans—at least mammals are killed quickly! Sea animals are unceremoniously tossed into a pot of boiling water. But, they're so yummy.

Catching crabs and lobsters requires some investment in trapping equipment, not the least of which is a boat. Make sure that you are permitted and aware of commercial outfits in the area. Commercial fishing practices trump individuals.

Clamming, on the other hand, is pretty easy—but it takes a lot of clams to make a meal. The local Department of Fish and Wildlife office will have information about which beaches are open to recreational clam digging, usually in late fall and early winter. Clams are hunted on tidal flats (when the tide is out); look for small holes in the sand that betray their whereabouts, and start digging. You want the tide to have just been out for a short while, so the sand is relatively soft. Shovels have been the digging tool of choice for years, and then people realized they could shove a length of PVC pipe around the clam to extract it. This idea has been commercialized, with glorified pipes for sale (they do have nice handles on them).

Crayfish (also called crawfish, crawdads and mudbugs in different parts of the United States) are technically freshwater crustaceans, but are used in many of the same dishes as seafood. They look like tiny lobsters and are eaten the same way—the tail is the main item, and then the claws, if they're big enough. Some people, particularly in Louisiana, also suck the herb- and spice-saturated fat from the head.

Mussels are harvested by prying them from the rocks or piers on which they're anchored. This anchor material is called the "beard." When you get mussels home, rinse them and rip out the beards, making sure each mussel is closed tightly. If you can press it open and closed with your fingers, it has died and should be discarded.

Seafood is delicious boiled and served with pasta and vegetables. Crabs, lobster and crawdads can be served alone; it helps to have cracking devices and picks to extract every tiny strip of sweet flesh from their hard shells. Soups and chowders are also a good use of clams and lobster. Mussels can be sautéed in a brine (try white wine or coconut milk, garlic and herbs) and served with bread, or served on pasta. If you want a bit of everything, make an étouffée or paella.

Section Five
Community, Family and Culture

Community, Family and Culture

Just like someone who doesn't realize she has an accent until she moves to another part of the country, you may not realize that you will experience culture shock in a small town. The mantra of understanding rural culture: Do not assume you know better. Say it. It will recur in this section. Don't assume you know better.

Most of the unique features of a small town are double-edged swords: what you love about it is also what you don't love about it. For example, it can be really fun to go to the grocery store and see someone you know in every aisle. But, some days you just want to pop in there, pick up some tampons, red wine and chocolate ice cream, and get the hell out. That will also be the day that you didn't bother to change out of your greasy sweatpants or brush your teeth. That will also be the day that you see your neighbor, your boss and your kid's teacher. The operating euphemism is the "fishbowl effect."

The thing that most people talk about, when they are extolling the value of small-town living, boils down to basic kindness. When my sister and her husband moved to a town twenty miles outside of Portland, I phoned a couple of Portland-area florists on a Saturday afternoon to see if they would deliver an arrangement to her on Sunday. They laughed. I went online and found a flower shop in her town, St. Helens.

"Well, we're not open on Sunday," said the owner, "but if she's not too far away, I can just take it home with me and drop it off tomorrow." She brought it to my sister's house, on her own time, because it was nice to do.

Chapter 18
Small-Town Etiquette

Let's start with some good country manners:

1) If you need to pass through a gate that is closed, hop out of your rig, open it, drive through, hop out, close it and continue. If a gate is open, leave it open.

2) Never return a dish in which someone brought you food empty. Bake cookies; pick strawberries; throw a jar of jam in there. At the very least, include a hand-written thank-you note. It's about more than the dish.

3) Refrain from lecturing strangers about transporting their dog in the back of a pick-up, for hanging a deer carcass from their backyard swing set, for leaving their car running while they're in the store, or for burning trash. At least at first.

4) Wave at oncoming cars (detailed in the Vehicles and Driving Chapter).

5) Because the garage and parking area are around the side of the house, most people use the back door, and you can too. Unless you are at a stranger's house. Doorbells are generally unnecessary because the residents likely saw or heard you come down the driveway, and their dogs will alert them of your arrival.

6) Park in such a way that you're not blocking the driveway, particularly if it's circular. Pull off to the side unless you're just staying a minute.

Colloquialisms

As you get to know a town, keep your ears peeled for sayings that are unique to the town or the region. A friend returned to her hometown in Arkansas for a visit, and one of the neighbors looked her up and down, and said, "Well, you've been grazing in the right pastures."

There are different types of regionalisms: pronunciation (such as "spicket/spigot" or "creek/crik"); vocabulary ("draw/holler" meaning "small valley in the mountains," or "bubbler/drinking fountain"); and sentence construction. Mike and I did some backcountry camping in the Smoky Mountains in 1995. We had hauled our dirty, tired selves back up to our van after five days and were slowly undoing all of our straps and buckles, when a family pulled in next to us in the parking lot. The patriarch was a really friendly guy who spoke pretty fast, with a thick (to us) Tennessee drawl. He asked about where we'd camped and where we were headed. We said Chattanooga, where we planned to get a motel room.

"Yep," he said brightly, "dembedsleepgood."

We smiled and nodded, and parted ways. All the way down the mountain, Mike and I tried to decipher the man's words. Finally, we got it: "It's nice to sleep in a bed, especially after you've been camping."

A local quirk may be as simple as calling a gravel road a "rock road." Or, there may be special names for local landmarks (for example, your house will probably bear the moniker of a previous owner). Colloquialisms are, to me at least, one of the best parts of living in the country. Old-timers speak colorfully and playfully. And they wink a lot, especially if they like you.

Be judicious when employing these phrases yourself—you want to fit in but not be obnoxious about it, nor impose yourself on the locals before they've accepted you.

Chapter 19
Town Personalities

The two best ways to get to know a community, other than living there, are to phone the chamber of commerce and ask for their packet, and to subscribe to the local newspaper. Monitoring the newspaper's website may not be sufficient, as most small-town papers work on a shoestring and have minimally developed websites. Visiting during different seasons isn't a bad idea either, but keep in mind that you still won't get a completely accurate read because tourists are treated differently from locals.

When Mike and I first moved to Oregon, Mike asked a co-worker about various towns to visit; we wanted to explore our new home state. She pulled out a map and ran her finger down Interstate 5: "Okay, that's a hippie town; that's a redneck town; that used to be a redneck town but now it's a hippie town…" And so on, all the way into California. This was intriguing to say the least; no one would ever do that using a map of Minnesota. (Maybe one could point out German towns and Scandinavian towns, but German- and Scandinavian-Americans would be the only ones who could tell the difference.)

Each town has its own personality; it's important to get a read on a town before you hitch your wagon to it. If its personality doesn't match yours, you are going to have a hard time assimilating. And, be sure you understand—you are the one who has to change, not the community. If it's not a good match, you are the one who will have to go.

The locals won't respond to your arrival with a tickertape parade: "Hooray, a cultured person is finally here to save us from our squalor!" No. The locals probably haven't heard of your favorite band, probably haven't seen live theater (unless you count church skits), and probably haven't read *The New York Times*. And, they don't care. If they feel that you think you're someone special and they're not, you are not going to get very far at all.

Okay, so here are a few general personalities; try to find one that meshes with your interests and values.

Farm Town

The United States was, for about one hundred and fifty years, a nation of farmers. Think about it: Why is the weather report on the news, over and over, every single day? Does it matter if you are commuting in the sunshine or rain? Does it affect your ability to finish that quarterly report, answer the phone or do data entry? Will you have to cancel your meeting? No. The people who care about the weather work outside.

As many recent books have documented, the corporatization of farming has changed farm culture. What used to be a more-or-less natural state of being in harmony with the land has become a commoditized, mathematical, chemical process that works in spite of Mother Nature rather than in conjunction with her. Farmers' children who plan to take over the family operation now go to college to study business management, food science and animal science to augment what they learned growing up.

Farm towns may have other buildings—churches, a school, a tractor dealership and so on—but at the heart of those towns is a diner. It is there that people will gather, after they've got their livestock fed, for breakfast and coffee. It is there that they'll discuss local politics, the latest farm practices, and keep up on what's new in town (also known as "gossip"). If you want to make inroads with the town elders, start showing up for coffee in the morning.

The things that matter in a farm town are: tradition, family, community, farming.

Ranching Town

These are similar to farm towns, but instead of cultivating the land (except to grow hay for their livestock), ranchers raise animals as a "crop." Dairies are technically farms because they don't raise the cows for meat per se (although old milk cows do find their way into the slaughterhouse). There are dairies across the United States; beef cows are raised in two regional operations:

- Cow-calf ranches in the Western states are where mama cows give birth to and care for calves until they are weaned.
- Yearlings are shipped to large feedlots in the Midwest, where they are "fattened up" for slaughter.

Some people also specialize in raising breeding males and/or females.

In the West, there is a colorful history of cattle ranchers warring, literally, against sheep ranchers. They would mess with boundaries, poison each other's animals, sometimes shoot each other in cold blood. Supply-and-demand being what it is, cattle ranchers won out, even on land that is better suited to sheep. Americans like beef better than lamb.

Fishing Town

Fishing towns have many things in common with farming and ranching towns. They are, naturally, located on the coasts of the United States. There are wide variances in "flavor," depending on the region—a Maine fishing town is nothing like an Alabama fishing town is nothing like an Alaska fishing town. Similarities include being very active in working with federal and state authorities to manage animal populations, water pollution and the like; knowing how to repair nets and motors, and tie a hundred different knots faster that you can say "Davy Jones' locker;" and being very independent and self-reliant.

Commercial fishing men and women struggle every season to negotiate a good price with the corporations that buy their fish or other seafood; they tend to eschew trade unions but still work collectively to accept or reject deals. Like farmers, they have to leverage the purchase of expensive equipment (boats, nets, winches, processing equipment) and rely on Mother Nature to bless or condemn their harvest.

A fishing town is going to be, shall we say, odiferous. Hot, still days can be challenging. Winter is also a challenge—ever seen rain blowing sideways at twenty miles an hour? The salt in the air will make it difficult to garden, and will attack your car, your mower and anything else made of metal.

Fishing is considerably more dangerous than farming or ranching. Once the season is open, the boats go out—regardless of the weather. If a boat goes down, it is a community-wide affair.

Industry Town

The industry may vary—coal, automobile, logging, ranching—but the impact on the town is similar. Everyone either works in the industry or in a helper industry, such as a parts-manufacturing business in an automobile town. Back in the day, the company owned everything. Workers were required to lease their tools from the company and rent their home from it. They were paid in scrip, not real money, which was only viable in…the company store! Not a bad deal—for the company.

Things have obviously improved since the late nineteenth century. Today's industry towns have chain stores and restaurants, and workers receive U.S. dollars as compensation for their efforts. People who don't support today's unions must at least respect the impact they had on the plight of the working person a hundred years ago.

I lived near a modern version of an industry town—a company that designs unmanned drone airplanes, which are purchased by the United States Air Force, owned a number of buildings in our town. Because the work itself and the missions for which the airplanes were used were proprietary, the company was shrouded in secrecy. Most of the windows were covered. Their employees were paid well; indeed, the company attracted people to the area from all over the country. It was far from a complete take-over of the town, and yet they leased, among many others, the former community center building…

College Town

This is a town—or in most cases nowadays, a small city—that has as its main industry either a private college or a satellite branch of a state university. These towns take on the flavor of the school. If it's a conservative Christian school, there are likely more churches and religious businesses (bookstores, etc.) and fewer bars in the town. If it's a liberal arts college, there's probably a co-op grocery and a tattoo parlor. Any college town is going to have at least one café and brewpub, and possibly a few clothing/shoe stores, restaurants, and a music store. There are likely many venues that offer live music, at least on the weekends.

There will usually be a district that is full of student housing. I'd recommend buying a house elsewhere, unless you enjoy loud music at one in the morning and vomit in your flowerbeds. Bless their hearts.

Tourist Town

When Mike and I considered the implications of moving to a rural area, the fear of having to jettison our cultural life was tempered by the fact that Hood River is a town with a great tourist draw. Tourism translates into shops, restaurants and, to some degree, arts opportunities that true small towns can't offer. Cafés that have baristas with formal training, and real pastry chefs. Good surgeons (at least for sports medicine). Yoga studios, massage therapists, and florists that have quince branches and orchids, not just carnations. You get the idea. We felt like we'd be able to eat our *petit four* and have it too.

For the most part, that stood the test of time. The only thing we hadn't considered was the crush of tourists throughout the summer months (and, to a smaller degree, the winter months for skiing and snowboarding). It got so that we didn't even go downtown between Memorial Day and Labor Day. It was too aggravating to find parking, or to just try to cross town while stopping every block for a stream of pedestrians or cars going two miles an hour in search of a parking spot. One could almost hear a collective sigh of relief when the kids went back to school.

Your town may have special deals that are just for locals. It might take a while to find them. Where we lived, there was a free pass to a nearby, prestigious regional museum; one simply had to check it out from the library. A sporting-goods store offered locals a discount on their birthdays. We received a book of coupons in our post box that was good for the winter months, when the "summerfolk" had returned to their cities.

Sports Town

These towns are usually built around skiing, snowboarding or other recreation in the mountainous states on the eastern and western edges of the continent. But there are other towns, such as the ones on Tennessee's Pigeon River, which offer whitewater rafting, mountain biking and other sports.

The Columbia River Gorge is known for its mountain and water sports: windsurfing, kiteboarding, whitewater rafting and kayaking. Mountain biking and climbing are also big. Hiking. Cross-country skiing. Vacationers come to try a sport for the first time; professional athletes have a second (or third home) in the area for their off-season training days. This has created what I call a "Culture of Dude."

In a Culture of Dude, the streets are lined with bicycle shops, skateboard shops, windsurf/kiteboard shops, ski/snowboard shops, and second-hand gear resale shops. There will be taquerías and brewpubs. (The real businesses that local working-class people go to, like Safeway and Wal-Mart, will be on the outer edge of town, out of sight of the quaint downtown.)

Because the only people who can afford this kind of lifestyle are trust-funders and successful businesspeople from big cities who are vacationing, there are a lot of well-groomed Caucasians wearing $200 down vests and $100 T-shirts and stretch pants, with mats roiled under their arms or in quiver-like slings on their backs, on their way to yoga.

Cafés host premieres of documentary films that feature the most extreme of these extreme sports—athletes engaged in death-defying feats from the tops of mountains and waterfalls. Local bars will have live music, either an eighties cover band, a funk jam band, or a Reggae jam band. No one in attendance will listen to it; instead, they will talk loudly over it, discussing the day's weather conditions—wind speed, snow depth, etc.—in terms of how it affected the day's sport.

Because of the F-U-N element of a sports town, the personality of the town can be a little shallow, built around recreation followed by partying. Going to the bar on a Friday night in Hood River sometimes felt like returning to high school, and not in a good way. On the other hand, Dudes are good-hearted, funny, optimistic people who are fun to hang around with. And not stupid—most are college-educated and well read.

The people in a Sports Town may be single-minded, but they are inspirational in their single-mindedness: The philosophy is akin to Lance Armstrong's Live Strong campaign. Live life to the fullest; love friends and family as much as you can; when you die, die doing something fun. These sports are all dangerous; there are a couple of deaths every year. Injuries are shrugged off and joked about—deaths are a community event.

Exurb/Bedroom Community

If a small town is close enough to a city, it may become an exurb, or bedroom community, meaning the people who live there make their living in the city. The homes are only populated at night and on the weekends. If enough city-generated income is spent in the town, it can still appear to thrive—sort of a living ghost town. The parades will still happen; the kids will still attend the school; the restaurants will stay open (a couple of them, at least). It's sort of small-town living the way that Las Vegas is a city—it's real; it takes up space on the planet. But, it's a reality based on developers' interpretations of what people want.

I tend to be someone who avoids "what people want," but that's just me. An exurb can provide a safe, rural-yet-cultured place for you and your family. Not too close to the city and yet not too far away.

Economically Depressed Town

Many small towns are completely run-down; they're usually former industry towns in which the industry has vanished. There was a factory; a mine; a mill; a smelter that kept the town going. When that industry contracted, the inhabitants lacked the imagination or resources to train into a new industry.

After a few years of "getting by," the town starts to deteriorate. No one can afford to fix up the house, do anything with the yard, or have the garbage collected anymore. Sometimes, these people are called "white trash." Hopeless and ambivalent, they leave broken cars where they lie and burn their garbage, including decrepit furniture and plastic wrappers, rather than pay to take it to the dump.

The children of the wealthier families go to college and never return. The children of the poorer families tend to get knocked up, perpetuating a cycle of poverty.

In many such towns, the drug trade becomes supplemental income to the monthly welfare check. While Hood River was a thriving town of orchardists, tourist-industry suppliers and trust-fund athletes, many towns to the east (in both Oregon and Washington) were limping along. One can feel the oppressive atmosphere when driving through.

An enticement of buying property in such an area would be that you could get a lot of land for almost nothing. But you could also be a target for theft, maybe even of crime that was sanctioned, or at least ignored, by local law enforcement. And you would be a target for derision, because you are not economically depressed.

I don't recommend moving to one of these towns unless you have a reason, meaning a job. Or better yet, a business that will result in hiring locals. There is a practice of wealthy people purchasing huge parcels of remote land and then basically walling it off from the community and never being seen in town. I find this rude and demoralizing for the existing community.

But, maybe you can't win either way. I know of a successful musician who, when he built a rather fancy house in a depressed town, thought he'd be smart about it by introducing himself to neighbors, and donating money and musical equipment to the local schools. He surely won over some people, but not everyone. He's had intrusions such as slashed tires, landscape sabotage—even a cherry bomb set off near his house! A few of the locals didn't cotton to his swooping in and being all magnanimous. Makes them look bad.

Chapter 20
People

Mike and I have been walking into strange small-town bars and diners ever since we embarked on camping road trips in our early twenties. You get used to the quiet that happens once you push open the door—everyone in the place turns to see who's there, and when it's someone they don't know, they stare to try and feel you out. While this is slightly unnerving, we've always walked in with a smile and we've never gotten hassled. On the contrary—once you exhibit some interest in the place or its people, the locals will usually warm right up and tell you anything you want to know: the main industry, how to find the nearest motel, what a "pasty" might be.

We were camping in the Upper Peninsula of Michigan, and kept passing small storefronts that advertised "Pasties." The only pasties we knew of adorn otherwise naked torsos, so this piqued our interest to say the least. The buildings were too small to be strip clubs. We stopped at a bar, bought a couple Leinenkugel beers and, after we had been there a while, inquired about the pasties.

"It's pas-ty," laughed the bartender. The first syllable rhymes with "glass." Turns out, it's some kind of pot-pie-sandwich.

But I digress. My point is that locals are friendly and generous with visitors—it's each other they can be perfectly horrible to.

If you become a person who gets involved in local decision-making, I salute you. You are the kind of person who makes this democratic country great. That is, unless you get involved in local decision-making because you want to make sure that as decisions are made, they work in your favor.

Unfortunately, many decision-makers have this motivation. Assisting them are the people who go with the flow, don't make waves, sit on their hands—pick your cliché. The fence-sitters might privately disagree with a powerful, unscrupulous person, but when push comes to shove and there's a vote, they refuse to stand up for their beliefs. Why? Because they have seen what happens to outspoken people.

Outspoken people have the nerve to have at heart the common good, rather than political and financial gain, and to act on their conscience. They point out when someone is bending a rule, even if that someone is serving on the same council or board; even if that person has been nice to them, maybe even done them a favor at one point or another. They say what they think, even if the opinion is unpopular.

Outspoken people are very, very strong people, or else they don't last long in the community. Because once a person has piped up once too often about the wrong issue, person or business, the guillotine is set—it's just a matter of time until the blade drops. Maybe that person will lose her job and be blacklisted (unofficially, of course) from getting another. Maybe that person's son won't get picked for the varsity team, even though he's one of the best players. In extreme cases, maybe that person's dog will get poisoned, or his rig or home vandalized. Because community in the country is a condensed version of community in a city, so are the politics.

If you are an outspoken person, watch it. I'm not suggesting that you change— indeed, humanity relies on people like you taking a stand on things. But, as a new-comer, make friends before you start making enemies. While you should start being involved with the community immediately, wait a couple of years before you take on any civic offices, school boards, or community groups. Resist the urge to respond to the bone-headed and uncharitable letters to the editor that you read in the news-paper: chances are good that you'll meet these folks in person. When you do speak out about something, be strategic about it. Start with individuals before you present your ideas before large groups.

The unscrupulous people will probably be some of the most charismatic in town. The existing outspoken people may at first appear to be unpleasant, but it's probably a result of having been worn down by the rest of the town. The unscrupu-lous people will treat them like whiners and troublemakers. The fence-sitters will secretly applaud outspoken people but will usually abandon them if challenged.

There is one other archetype, which is extremely rare: the diplomatic phi-losopher. If you have the good fortune to work with a diplomatic philosopher, take advantage—listen, observe. This person is somehow able to meet everyone halfway; create consensus; break a smile onto anyone's face. He can present many sides of an issue in a measured, emotionally detached manner. His presence is calming rather than confrontational. Even if a power monger still does everything she can to cir-cumvent a diplomatic philosopher, she will respect him. Diplomatic philosophers are the standard, in my opinion, to which everyone should aspire.

Neighbors

Rural people take care of each other in a way that may seem unreal to you. In some communities I've visited, it seems like the locals would rather hold a bake sale than apply for government support. When someone is sick, friends and neighbors mobi-lize. The word gets around, and plates of food appear on that person's doorstep. Someone will cut some firewood for him. Someone will paint his fence. Same if a baby is born. Same if someone dies.

One of my friends characterized it this way: "Your neighbors are your lifeline. Especially in the winter." Another said, "You may not like someone, but if they're hard up, you help them out. And they'd do the same for you."

I went to a memorial service for a neighbor who had lived nearly his entire 84 years in our valley. The funeral parlor was packed to the gills. After the service, the family announced that there was a reception at the Eagles Club down the road. Anyone who wanted to come was invited. There was enough food there to feed a school. Not grocery-deli cheese plates, either—homemade casseroles, desserts, chicken wings. A ham.

"Who made all this?" I asked when I was in line.

"I did," said a woman in her fifties, a family friend. "Well, my daughter-in-law made the brownies and the scalloped potatoes."

Neighbors will help you retrieve a tractor that's hung up in mud. They'll plow your driveway. They'll help you cut up a tree. Make sure you're reciprocating, either with labor, diesel money or food. Neighbors really like pie.

I saw announcements in the local newspaper and taped to the bulletin board in the post office: "Please join Joe Neighbor for a birthday celebration." An open invitation for the whole town to his home. Imagine that in a city.

You may have neighbors, and even random strangers, come down your driveway. Just as some people prefer email, some phone calls and some texting to communicate, in the country some people would rather just talk to you in person. We also had the occasional white van carrying Mormon missionaries. Twice we had someone selling something: once an Indian with a fish he'd just caught, and once a delivery guy who gave us a big spiel about having an order cancelled so he could give us a great deal on some frozen steaks. *Caveat emptor* is all I can say.

While there are testosterone-laden individuals everywhere, "rednecks" are associated with the country. Entertainers use the redneck stereotype as fodder for hilarious comedy acts and movies. However, this is one of those situations in which it pays to give the guy a chance—don't assume that because he is missing teeth, burns his garbage in the backyard and hollers at his kids that he lacks redeeming qualities. He might even have a respectable job.

And don't be paranoid about him. City people think that every rural person who's wearing dirty clothes is a character out of *Deliverance*.

Friends of mine had just moved into a tiny house that they planned to refurbish. As they moved in, they saw a redneck neighbor checking them out. They waved. He didn't. They continue to move furniture in as the man watched. As the evening wore on, they started to get creeped out by him. They were awoken the following morning by a loud bang. And then another. He was shooting at them! They dodged along the walls, keeping out of sight of the windows. Another—bang!

After a couple more rounds, they started to doubt their original assessment. One of them snuck out the front door, heard another bang and followed the noise. Pinecones were falling onto their metal roof. Their neighbor came over that day and introduced himself. Now, they're friends.

If you happen to find out you live near someone who's truly unfriendly and maybe even dangerous, proceed carefully. Ask other neighbors about him or her. Get some back story. Most anti-social people just keep to themselves, but if you have an active situation (say, they're dumping garbage on your land, or they put in a fence that cuts into your property) document it and contact the person in a *non-confrontational* way. Do everything you can to deescalate the conversation. After your first encounter with the person, bring a friend or another neighbor with you as a witness.

Notice I haven't said "involve the authorities" yet. Most neighborly disputes are resolved without the help of the sheriff, for two reasons:

1) He's not going to come out unless someone's life is in imminent danger.

2) He might be related to or otherwise involved with the neighbor.

But once you have established a real problem and the neighbor has made it clear he's unresponsive to your requests, you may need to contact the police or sheriff, or even an attorney, and hope for the best.

Trust

When all was said and done, the papers and the financing had gone through, and we were finally the official owners of our country property, we contacted the sellers to arrange Moving Day and where to leave the house key.

"There aren't any," they said.

We had seen locks on the doors, but it turned out that the previous owners never locked the house. Ever. Not even when they went out of town.

Neither, it turned out, did we. The front door's deadbolt was engaged only because otherwise the wind blew it open. I found myself being embarrassed if someone rang the doorbell (which itself was an anomaly; friends just parked and came in the back door) and I had to unlock it, like I was some sort of paranoid city-slicker. Mike and I snickered when people from the city came to visit and locked their car in our driveway.

A friend in a remote town in northeastern Oregon lived in an even more lax community. I was visiting one summer, waiting for him to come home from work. I sat on the front step, drinking a beer, when a guy came down the driveway. "Just using Jon's table saw for a minute," he said and disappeared into the work shed. After he left, another guy came with a lawn mower. "Borrowed this last week," he explained as he dropped it off. During my visit, friends left their dogs in Jon's shed while they went to a nearby pub, and went into his house for God-knows-what. And he probably had equal access to their homes. It just depends on local culture.

Not that I'm daring you to leave your house unlocked. We had a hidden driveway that was very steep; strangers did not casually come down it. Some friends of ours lived off a secluded but more traveled road, and got robbed in the middle of the day—the thieves did a sweep and grabbed the laptops, the iPod and the camera, just like would happen in the city. People who do lock their homes have a key hidden somewhere that their friends know about.

I was sitting in a café/store in rural Oregon, eating lunch. As people came and went, the gals behind the counter had something to say to each of them: "You get that hay in? Going to the fundraiser for the school on Friday? You having the usual?" When there's one café in town, it becomes a hub of activity. A guy came in to buy soda and chewing tobacco. "Do you mind if I pay for this later?" he asked. "I left my wallet at home and I've only got five bucks on me." No problem; bring it in next time you're in town.

With every rule, there is an exception. Here, the exception is yard sales. I have experienced it personally, and heard of many other instances: You start your sale at 9 a.m. By 8:30, there are twenty people waiting to have at it. Most people just want to get a jump on your wares, but others want to rip you off—maybe a couple, or an adult with some kids. One of the people will distract you, and the other will make off with the most expensive things he can get his hands on, in our case the splitting mauls and some other hand tools.

One strategy is to hire or recruit many friends at the beginning of your sale. Enough so that you have one-on-one coverage, if possible. If the sale is an estate sale, you have one entrance into the home so you can control how many people can get in. Keep the expensive things near the check-out table. The people who stole from us, we learned later, own a second-hand store in a neighboring town. Because we were moving, they banked on us not noticing the theft or, if we find out who did it, having neither the time nor the gumption to drive twenty miles to try to get our stuff back. And they were right. By the time we had our moving sale, we were too busy and emotionally overwhelmed to go fight with some backwater yokels over a few tools. In order to not be consumed with rage, I decided to consider it a "donation" to a struggling economy.

Privacy

At home, you will have lots of privacy: Finally, you can walk around nude if you're so inclined. You can go to the barn to check for eggs in your pajamas (or, maybe even nude! Though I would wear boots). You may have shades on your windows, but you really won't need them. You won't need to lock your cars. It will be a great time to learn a musical instrument—no one will hear you practice.

Elsewhere: Did you enjoy high school? The alliances and the rivalries? The epic parties where everyone was there? The embarrassment the next week when the story circulated of you having thrown up on the football captain at that epic party? The X cheating on Y with Z? Then you will love living in a small town.

The first couple of years of small-town life are really fun because everything is new: You're meeting new people and learning new things. You're on an adventure. Call it the "honeymoon period." The next couple of years, after you've met all the town's players, you start to pick up on who's friends with whom, and—perhaps more importantly—who isn't friends. You learn about people's pasts. You learn whom not to cross (hopefully via a friend and not the hard way), and what the repercussions of it are. After a while, the honeymoon is over.

I have always struggled with the idea of "gossip." I am a student of the nuts and bolts of life, which means I want to talk about "real" things: relationships, health problems, feelings. When I talk about real things I bring into a conversation situations that I have been in, as well as situations others have been in because they're relevant to the discussion. I guess that's the difference: anecdotes are salient to a topic, and gossip is telling a story about someone else just because it's juicy or, worst case, with malicious intent. In any case, you will experience gossip. I had a friend who knew someone who worked at the hospital; I learned more intimate details, without asking, about people I hardly knew than I know about some of my closest friends.

A Hood River community group once held, with the most sincere and good intentions, a seminar for mothers and pre-teen daughters. Some of my friends fit that category and attended because they wanted to keep the lines of communication open with their daughters as they enter their teenage years. The mothers and daughters were split up into small groups; at one point the mothers were instructed to tell the groups about a bad choice they had made as a teenager. The mothers all looked at each other. They balked at sharing the information, not because of their daughters but because they all knew they would be giving each other ammunition to use against themselves at a later date!

Confiding in each other is one of the most important human interactions. It's the best way to cope with our inner turmoil and to keep a fresh outlook on our lives. When you confide your innermost thoughts and feelings with someone, you create a bond. You also trust that person to keep those thoughts and feelings to him- or herself.

The bottom line is: Choose your alliances carefully, especially close friendships. When you develop close friendships, nurture them. The worst scenario is to have a falling-out with a trusted friend (or your spouse). Maybe he will keep your secrets to himself, and maybe he won't.

Isn't it sad to have to think about friendships like some sort of war game? Yes, it is.

Dating can be just as bad. One benefit of living in a small area, if your town is large enough that it is possible to meet "new" people, is that it's pretty easy to find out about a potential date from others who know her. Date carefully; your maneuvers, as it were, are terrific grist for the rumor mill.

The best source of gossip is the local newspaper. When I lived in Washington, all of the police reports and courthouse records were published every week. Birth announcements and obituaries were a major feature. In the newspaper of neighboring The Dalles, the hospitals listed their admittances and discharges. The hospital records and obituaries are intended to be a public service—this way you can see if someone you know, or their family, needs a meal or a greeting card. I can only assume that the police reports and courthouse records were intended to shame people into behaving themselves. So keep in mind that if you get a speeding ticket, a DUI or a divorce (unless you file in a neighboring county), everyone will know about it.

If you are a business owner or any kind of local celebrity, your lack of privacy will be breathtaking. People thought nothing of stopping a friend of mine, who was a computer technician, in the grocery store, at the gas station or anywhere he went, to ask him questions about their computers. And expected on-the-spot answers. In one town, the school superintendant was afraid to order food at any of the local restaurants for fear the teenagers working there would spit in it. Two women who worked locally for Child Services and had recently removed a young girl from her home couldn't go to the local deli, because the girl's mother worked there.

Locals

The world is populated by people who stay and people who move. I have friends from high school who live less than a mile from their parents' homes, whose kids are now going to our high school (in some cases, with the same teachers!). In most parts of the world, people stay (unless they're forced out, which is a different story). Many people can trace their history back dozens of generations in one area. If you're reading this book, you are most likely a person who moves.

The fun part of being a person-who-moves is that you get to experience other cultures, even if you're just traveling within the United States. But, once you leave your "homeland," you've severed an umbilical that can never be reattached. And wherever you land, you may never truly belong. This is less apparent in a city, where there are lots of movers who create new bonds, and achingly real in the country.

"You've got to have three generations in the cemetery; that's the only way you fit in." This spoken by someone who moved to her little Midwest town in 1975 and ran the library there for twenty-five years. And she'd grown up in a town that was less than an hour away. If you're on the East coast, you might need ten generations instead of three. The most direct route "in" as a newcomer is to marry into an established family.

I met a woman who had grown up in a city, and whose mother had been raised in rural Oregon. This woman, in her mid-thirties, and her husband had just purchased eighteen acres in a different rural area. She was in the beginning phase of country life, when you're introducing yourself every time you go into town, and generally trying to make a good impression. She said that without fail, people looked disappointed when she said she was from Portland, but they perked up again when she mentioned that her mother grew up in Burns. "It's like a wall comes down," she said. It is the country version of "street cred."

After living on the farm for a while, I started to attend the council meetings for our unincorporated little area. I had met some neighbors who invited me to a meeting. The council met at the firehouse to field questions from citizens and figure out who needed to get involved (County? Forest Service? Department of Natural Resources?). The meetings had been contentious for the past couple of months because the committee had also been asked by the county to recommend a re-zoning of the area, and after six years of assessment they had submitted their recommendation, which allowed for much smaller parcels to be carved out in a number of areas—areas that opposing voices accused would jeopardize the bucolic nature of our valley and benefit the council members personally. As I attended more and more meetings and got to know the players better, I learned the incestuous connections—this person was that person's stepfather; this person's daughter had married that person's son and then divorced him because he cheated on her; etc. At times the proceedings felt like I had stepped into someone's kitchen during an argument. And the future of the valley was in their hands!

Those of us who were rather new to the area were not well received by the council. In their minds, it was their valley and those of us opposed had essentially invaded their privacy by even attending the meetings. More than once, members spoke to the audience directly and scolded us for voicing opposition to their plan, saying, "You weren't even around when we started this process, and now you're coming in at the last minute to try and stop it!" Well, true—because we just found out about it…

So, keep in mind that when you dip your toe in the water—and I say "when" and not "if" because I do think it's important to be on top of what's happening in your community—there might be sharks. Wade in carefully; learn who's related to whom by blood and by marriage, and who owns what businesses. And, understand that even if you end up being the mayor and town hero, and they erect a statue in your honor in the town center, you're still not from there.

Minorities

How you are treated as an incoming minority, of any type, may differ from how minorities who were born in the area are treated. This is, in some way, a sign of open-mindedness on the part of the rural person—the fact that you are a Stranger trumps whatever Otherness you might embody. Unless you live in a particularly progressive town, minorities are generally considered a liability, maybe a challenge. Don't take it personally: anything different is suspect.

The best defense is offense—while you're still new to the area, invite neighbors over for a housewarming party. Bring cookies to the neighbors' houses and introduce yourself. Present yourself as someone who's interested in being an asset to the community—and interested in the community as it is. "Tolerance is a two-way street," says my friend Monica.

College towns are a good place to start looking, as most of them (though it depends on the college) are more liberal than average, and may host support groups that wouldn't exist in a town that doesn't have a college. Even a community college can improve the tolerance level of a town.

If you're a white minority in a predominantly Spanish-speaking community in the Southwestern United States, learn the language and research customs of Hispanic culture, particularly interpersonal communication. Any effort to meet people halfway is appreciated.

After a few years, you may find that you've won people over, and they will actually defend you even if they don't like your "kind." As a friend explained it, "I may be a lesbian, but I'm *their* lesbian."

But, this is just getting along with your neighbors—what about getting a job or a loan? The United States Department of Agriculture is still working out settlement payments, decades after the fact, to minority-group farmers who were denied or obstructed from the loans that make commercial farming possible. If you suspect you've been the victim of discrimination, follow the same channels you'd follow in the city—file legal complaints; write letters to the editor; engage your state and federal representatives.

Religious

You'll probably have to do some sleuthing to find non-Christian worship services, if they're even available. Sometimes people hold services in private homes. If your group grows to a size that requires renting a space, a church may, ironically, be a good option. Churches often rent our their meeting rooms to public groups during the week.

There will be little to no accommodation to your holy days in the schools. Small-town schools are still Christian-holiday oriented—it may read "Spring Break" on the calendar, but it's really Easter Break. If you can finagle some educational opportunities here and there, go for it. It will not hurt anyone to learn what Passover is.

Dealing with a religious majority can be daunting. I have a friend whose children attend the public school in her town, which has a high population of an ultra-conservative denomination. She and her husband have two children; they're not anti-religion but have never gone to church on a regular basis, and have a *laissez-faire* attitude about one's belief in God. One of her kids came home from school and asked her, "Are we on Jesus's side?" When that son went on to middle school, my friend learned that the "science" teacher at the school did not present evolution in his curriculum. At all.

As editor of a local magazine, I was once challenged by the publisher for wanting to run an essay by a local geologist who, shockingly enough, referred to the geological history of the area in terms of millions of years. He wanted me to change the word "millions" to "many" or "thousands," because evolution "is just a theory." I still have a scar on my chin from my jaw hitting the floor.

Unless they're looking for conflict, people are smart enough not to mention extreme views right off the bat. But you may be surprised, once they get to know you and open up a little bit, to learn what they really think about certain issues. Remember the mantra.

Racial

Regional differences come into play here—I remember a black professor I had who remarked during a lecture that his son, his son's black friend and his son's white girlfriend were planning a road trip across the southern United States. My professor thought they were crazy to even consider it—two black men in a car with a white woman; they were just asking for trouble. That was just twenty years ago, in the early 1990s.

After decades of civil-rights struggle, I think it's finally safe to say that, for whatever it's worth, the racism you experience will be subtle. More the sideways glances when they think you're not looking than name-calling or overt sabotage. I have friends who live near Ithaca, New York, who told me that their gay and African American friends have experienced more harassment within the city limits than outside them. Unless you're up against a deeply hateful person, the fact that you're a good neighbor is more important than anything else.

The most challenging racial makeup to have at this point in time is Arabic, Persian, Sikh, or anyone who can be confused with being a "Terrorist." Bigots whose lives are run by Fear are not overly concerned with Accuracy. Your best defense is to have advocates within the community, so make friends with whomever you can. Be the lovely person that you are, and your neighbors—most of them, at least—will respect that.

If you belong to a particular denomination, look for it in the town you're considering. If you're Latino, look for services (most common in Catholic churches) conducted in Spanish.

Sexual/Gender

When most people think about "gay" and "rural" at the same time, they think of Matthew Shepard, the University of Wyoming student who was brutally tortured and left to die in the wilds of Wyoming in 1998. Since his murder, a theater production has been written and awareness has grown. Homophobia is far from conquered, but steps have been made.

Don't assume the rural = homophobic. The first state to decriminalize homosexual acts was Illinois, in 1961. And one of the first states to legalize same-sex marriage was Iowa. A lesbian friend of mine who grew up there says it boils down to a Midwestern "live and let live" mentality. As long as you're feeding your livestock, paying your bills, and being a good neighbor, there's nothing to talk about. "It's none of my business," one of her relatives said when she came out to him. And that was that.

However, it's still true that most children who realize they are attracted to the same gender keep a tight lid on this information until they graduate high school and leave their hometown for college. Until the last ten or fifteen years, they left their hometowns for good. There was a small window of time—the 1980s, mostly—during which young men went back home to die of AIDS in the arms of their mothers. And that was the only way they could go back. My friend Tom, who came of age during that era, said that his boyfriend's parents allowed him to return to Kansas from San Francisco but would not let Tom, nor any of their other gay friends, visit him as he was dying.

Nowadays, it's possible to move back to your hometown with your partner and become respected members of your community. Moving to a town in which you have no family ties might be a bit trickier, but it's certainly as easy as it's ever been.

One means of gauging a town's gay-friendliness is online research—there are even databases and indexes that you can search by postal code. Or, look for one or more churches that go out of their way to advertise that they welcome people of all sexual orientations. This is a more likely indicator than seeking out a LGBT support group, which is unlikely even in otherwise neutral or supportive towns.

I once spoke to a group of young people who had all moved to Portland from small towns. All five said that it was easier to be a lesbian in a small town than a gay man. Being a straight woman, I can't speak to this further but I can see the logic—manliness and capability are valued in the country. A butch woman who can take on "men's work" would be less of a threat to the status quo than an effeminate man (not that all gay men are effeminate). One of the men in this group said that he wanted to do all of the things his father had done: build a house with his own hands, raise children, go to church, work on a farm. He just wanted a husband instead of a wife.

If you are someone who enjoys an outrageous, in-your-face queer community, you'll feel an emptiness in a small town. Gay- or lesbian-only clubs are rare. Flamboyancy is a spectrum, just as sexual orientation is, and those on the high end of the scale tend to migrate to cities.

Mainstream Culture

The level of cooperation in a rural area can be astounding, but this is not to say that everyone likes each other. More than one person has put it this way: "You get along, because you have to."

The thing that keeps everyone united is mainstream culture. If everyone's roles are defined, order triumphs over chaos. I was ostracized at one of my country workplaces—not because I wasn't doing a good job but because I was Different. My main offenses:

- I was childless.
- I did not attend church.
- I had limited interest in typical community events, like '50s cover bands, lip-synching contests, or high school sports or theatrical performances.

And, worse, I wasn't interested in assimilating. One day, I went in for a routine meeting with the executive director (the one who'd hired me had already been ousted…another story) and was told I was being "laid off." It was a traumatic experience.

The most shocking thing was that I had moved to the country with an open mind. I didn't have much in common with these folks, but I was glad to know them and learn from them. I didn't hold our differences against them—and they were not affording me the same courtesy. And most of the people I considered allies turned their backs on me—out of self-preservation, yes, but it was still cruel. I was accustomed to marching to my own drummer, and learned the hard way that in the country, there is only one drummer.

You can't even be a hermit—"keeping to yourself" is viewed with suspicion as well. A friend once said of some new people, her voice rich with the tone of approval, "They've come to the church group and the school meeting and the potluck—they're just jumping right in!"

Being a good neighbor and making friends are not necessarily the same thing. A friend who moved to the Northeast from the West Coast found making friends a very different experience. "On the West Coast, you're innocent until proven guilty. You make friends with someone and then, as you get to know someone, you decide if you're still compatible—if it doesn't work out, it's no big deal.

"It's the opposite on the East Coast. There, you have to prove yourself over a period of time. It may seem like you're friends, but then they don't invite you anywhere and refuse your invitations, until, and it might be years, then all of a sudden you're friends. They think the West Coast is really fake; that everyone pretends to be your friend but you don't really know each other." She found she had to work hard to earn someone's trust, but once she had it she would never lose it.

Sports

If you've never rooted for a college or professional sports team, now might be a good time to start. You don't have to truly be interested—it's just a vehicle for building relationships. And, if you didn't guess already from the preceding section, I'm only speaking to men right now. Even if it's a co-ed party, the women will end up in a separate room (usually the kitchen) and be completely oblivious to the game. But they'll keep the bowls of chips full!

High school sports might be even more enthusiastically followed. Some school districts have even adapted a four-day school week to accommodate the kids traveling on Friday for sports events. (They also claim cost-savings for the building maintenance, utilities etc.). Attending these sports events is another way to make inroads with the community.

Gender Roles

I once sat in an admittedly feminine-themed rural café with three male friends who were passing through on their way to Portland. We were the only customers. A woman walked in, saw us there and exclaimed, "Well, I'll be! Three men in a café!" The issue was not that they were drinking coffee, but that they weren't drinking it in a diner, where men gather. I can only imagine her hypothesis of why I was alone with them.

If you like pointing out the differences between women and men, you will love the rural social scene. Do you say things like:

- "Oh, isn't that just like a man!"; or

- "We're women—we just talk and talk about anything!"; or
- "We're women—we love to shop!"; or
- "You know men…[insert complaint here]."; or
- "It's a guy thing."?

Do you think that a mother-daughter event equals a tea party, pedicure or shopping excursion, and a father-son event is either a sporting match or hunting trip? Then you're in good shape.

There are some exceptions. Art and music are pretty safe for all children, though *art* becomes *craft* in adulthood, at which point it becomes women's work unless there is a lathe, band saw or spot welder involved. And only men are in bands that play out on the weekends, unless a succubus, home-wrecker female vocalist moves in from out of town.

I drove one friend's husband crazy. He liked me most of the time, but I confounded him! I used tools and swore and did men's work. On one hand, he admired this and wished his wife would help him out once in a while. On the other hand, it was *wrong!* And I kept giving his wife Ideas, like she should try to get a job if she was bored at home all day, and it wouldn't kill him to cook his own dinner a couple of nights a week.

Bottom line: If you are someone who, male or female, does not prefer to live according to traditional gender roles, you will have to learn to hold your tongue and participate in activities that don't interest you in order to fit in. If you figure out a way around this, please let me know.

Chapter 21
Children

This may be the primary reason you're reading this book—you want to give your children or children-to-be the best upbringing possible. It's true that a rural area can be a great place to raise kids—they can run around outside; they will be raised by the proverbial village and not get away with as much mischief; they can learn to be responsible for themselves and others; they can learn to appreciate nature. They can learn hard work and to understand death as part of life.

But, moving to the country is not a panacea. Country schools still have bullies; still have good teachers and not-so-good teachers; still have parents of other kids who are jerks; still have sexual abuse and teen pregnancies and drug problems.

Most country kids also grow up with a certain naïveté that city kids lose early on. City kids learn how to fend for themselves in a crowd; they've seen homeless people; they have friends who are a different race than they are; they know how to take the city bus and drive in traffic. Your kids may go a little more berserk when they go off to college than the average city kid because they're over-stimulated. Or, they may be terrified of the city and refuse to go there at all.

Babysitting and Day Care

A lot of this can be true anywhere, but it's food for thought: You will be at a great disadvantage if you move to a town in which you have no family members, particularly retired parents. This is not to say it's impossible, of course, just more difficult. Because there are so few teenagers, babysitters are expensive and hard to secure. If your area offers babysitter training (the American Red Cross is known for this), make sure your babysitter has completed this. If some organization offers training in your area, you might be able to get recommendations from them of teens who have completed it.

Many weekend parties end up being early evening barbeques—the kids can entertain themselves and the adults are, barring the occasional breakdown in pint-sized diplomacy, left alone. Plus, there's a lot of work to be done the following day, so no one can afford to waste it being tired and hung over.

Parents also kid-swap, so for example one house takes all five kids on Saturday afternoon and the other house takes all the kids Sunday afternoon. That way, each set of parents gets an afternoon to themselves. Or, two of the parents will take the whole group skiing or to a movie. You get the idea.

Summertime camps are popular for this reason as well. Plus, it gives the kids a chance to socialize with children they've never met before, which is rare in a small town.

Be very selective when choosing daycare—many down-and-out people try to make a few extra bucks after they've had a baby by taking on a couple others, without having any particular aptitude for it. Make sure your daycare provider is licensed, and tour the facility before signing a contract.

Many communities are creating daycare cooperatives, meaning the parents all pay a fee to fund the facility, materials and a main caregiver, but also take turns helping in the daycare. There are also Montessori schools, which I describe below.

Education

Whatever extracurricular activities exist for children in the country—graduation party, Easter egg hunt, sports—are there because the parents put in many hours of preparation and, usually, fundraising for it. I once read a diatribe in the Letters to the Editor section of our newspaper that ripped into urban transplants for dropping their kids off at Little League practice and leaving the coaches responsible for them (instead of staying to help). There is an expectation that when your kid is involved in something, so are you and your spouse. Your role is more than chauffeur and half-interested cheerleader.

What is true of extracurricular activities is true of school itself. While parents have volunteered in the classroom and in the library for decades, more and more people are choosing homeschooling, "unschooling" and small private cooperatives for their children. Most parents provide alternative schooling during the elementary years and then send their children to public high school, for a lot of reasons: their children's studies have exceeded a level at which they have mastery; they want their teenager to experience the socializing of a school; they or their kids are just plain tired of homeschooling. Some families go all the way.

Because children learn in different ways, and because the pressure to conform can be even harder in a small, rural school than an urban, diverse school, alternative education opportunities may serve your family well. On the one hand, the "socializing" aspects of a public school environment may be beneficial. But if your child is experiencing bullying, or is "different," which can mean anything from being transgender to being outspoken or artistic—why does he need to experience that kind of trauma?

Homeschooling

What used to be the bastion of the Darwin- and Sex Ed-averse Religious Right has become a popular way to educate children who simply don't thrive in traditional classrooms, or whose parents have alternative work schedules. Or whose public school is sub-standard, at least by their standards.

I have a friend who started volunteering in her son's fourth-grade classroom because he wasn't doing well. She was sort-of-considering pulling him from school but was afraid of "screwing up" his education if she took responsibility for it. After a few days in his classroom, she realized, "Well, I can't do any worse than his teacher is!" She ended up homeschooling him through graduation, and both of them thrived.

In the Columbia River Gorge, a number of parents spend one or more months in Baja California in order to extend their wind-sports season. They pull their children out of public school with two months' worth of curricula and homework assignments (the teachers are accustomed to doing this for the children of migrant workers) and bring them along.

If you plan to homeschool, you may still need to register your children at the local public school—it's illegal for children to not be educated starting at age five. Check with the state laws. You may find that you're not treated very well by the school administration. If this is the case, don't take it personally. You are costing them money—schools are reimbursed on a per-child basis, and if your child doesn't attend the school, they don't get paid.

However, you don't get paid, either. You will need to provide all educational materials, including a computer and textbooks. The legality of homeschooling has been debated for decades; check your state for its laws requiring teaching certification for parents. Many states have mandated that home-schooled children have access to public school's extracurricular sports and other amenities, such as the library.

Curricula can be found on a number of websites. There are also books made specifically for this type of education. Many homeschoolers form groups that meet regularly for socializing and to complete group projects. Or, you might be able to meet with other homeschoolers via a church or social group. By law, your children have access to various public school amenities—for example, they are eligible to participate in extracurricular activities such as sports and drama. They are also required to submit to the standardized-testing system whenever their public-schooled counterparts are. One friend's son received an ROTC scholarship for college through his public high school.

An advantage to being the child's only teacher is being able to integrate lesson plans across subjects. For example: if you teach a unit about the pyramids of Egypt, your child can study the physics of making the structures; she can study the arts and culture of ancient Egypt; she can study the history of the dynasties during which they were built; she can study pyramid-related vocabulary. She can write an essay and a fictional story and a poem. The best part is that you don't move forward until the child has mastered the lesson. Talk about No Child Left Behind.

Bookstores carry hundreds of books directed specifically at homeschooling parents—everything from *What Your Third Grader Needs to Know* (Doubleday Publishing) to *The Secret of Handling Money, God's Way* (Moody Publishers). And then there are thousands of general-interest books to supplement their studies.

Before you commit, consider the impact that homeschooling will have on you. You are giving yourself an unpaid, full-time job. You will never have time to yourself unless you plan carefully. You will have to create curricula, and/or research and purchase lesson plans from others. When the kids get older, you have to stay at least one step ahead of them academically. Teaching addition? Fine. Teaching geometry? That can be a lot.

Do your kids learn well from you? Such is not always the case. Sometimes personalities get in the way. Do you have a separate room in your house to make into a schoolroom? Doing homework at the kitchen table is one thing, but might become unsustainable day after day. Be honest in your assessment of how well home-schooling might work in your family. Then again, if it doesn't work you can always re-enroll your child in the public school.

Unschooling

This concept is considered a variation of homeschooling by some but not others—the premise is that children are naturally curious and do not need to be "taught" in a pedagogical sense but guided through their education. Radical unschoolers feel that homeschooling is merely recreating the school environment at home, while unschooling is using a completely different learning style that has similarities with Montessori (see below). However, while Montessori provides a less regimented environment than traditional school, in which everyone in the class learns a lesson at the same time whether he is ready for it or not, Montessori does still have method. Unschoolers are anti-method.

Online Schooling

A recent player in the alternative education field is online learning, also called "distance learning." This is another learning opportunity that is self-paced and, at least to some degree, self-directed. This can be a great alternative to accommodate a teenager who works or has health issues that keep him out of school.

Some online schools are run by existing public schools or universities; some are charter schools and some are totally independent and receive no government funding. Be sure the program you're looking at is accredited and issues a valid diploma. Some programs are free because they are part of the public school system—some even provide textbooks and computers (on loan)!

If you know an adult who didn't graduate, there are also GED programs online.

Montessori

Montessori is a specific teaching style developed in the early 1900s by two-time Nobel nominee Dr. Maria Montessori. The curriculum supports the notion that children are naturally curious, and learn more thoroughly and deeply with encouragement rather than coercion. Equal value is given what might be called "book learning" as well as emotional and psychological health, even "grace." Testing and grades are replaced with personalized lesson plans and assessments by the teacher. Indeed, in some schools the teachers aren't even called "teachers" but "guides."

Many parents appreciate the tenets of Montessori. If enough of them support it, a new school can emerge. Registering a new school may be an even bigger challenge than registering kids for homeschooling. Friends who opened a school in their town found that the school district was "making calls" to the city and otherwise trying to impede their progress in having the building permitted as a school. Remember, every child represents a dollar amount to the public school. Its primary concern, ironically, may not be the net gain for the community—it's the net loss to the school's bottom line.

Montessori teachers receive specialized training and use approved Montessori materials with their students. The curricula and materials are expensive, meaning you will most likely have to charge more per student than the local schools, meaning your prospective student pool is the subset, within the group of people who value this kind of education, of those who can afford it.

These friends who opened their school had to come up with the initial funding themselves, which meant digging into personal savings; asking the grandparents to pitch in; etc. And even five years later, the parents are still responsible for bringing the snacks and working two hours per month cleaning, landscaping, etc.

Most Montessori schools are pre-schools, with students being welcome as soon as they're out of diapers through age six, and then moving to the public school for first grade. There is a "lower elementary" curricula that serves children six through nine years of age, and another curricula that serves children to age twelve. There are two types of Montessori philosophies: the original, which is called "Association Montessori Internationale," and what my friend calls the watered-down version, "American Montessori Society." His school follows the curriculum of the Internationale model.

College Prep

If your high school junior or senior excels academically, she might find it challenging to be in a small school. On the one hand, her school may enjoy small class sizes and she may receive a lot of individual attention. On the other hand, her school may be understaffed, in which case the teacher-to-student ratio may be similar to an urban school. And because there are fewer students, achievement levels vary widely within one grade and there are fewer opportunities for higher-level ("talented and gifted") study.

One option for high school upperclassmen may be to take college-level courses at a local community college. Caveat: Your child's university may not accept the transfer credits, in which case she'll have to re-take 100-level courses. Is it better to be bored in high school or college? High school is less expensive…

Urban and rural community colleges have in common that they are an incredible opportunity, but hit-or-miss with the faculty. As with health care, the professionals in your area may be dregs who couldn't get a job in a larger market if their lives depended on it, or superstars who forewent a decent salary in order to share your corner of the world. Or anywhere in between.

It's also difficult for teenagers to find meaningful jobs, since the adult workforce is underemployed already. However, people are generally eager to help students, so if you see an internship opportunity that doesn't officially exist, try to work something out with the business owner.

Bus Shelter

Driving around, you'll see little open-faced sheds near the road; these are shelters for school-aged children who are bussed into town. Another newbie story: On the main road into White Salmon, Mike and I noticed shortly after moving to the area one such bus shelter that was painted yellow. The words "White Salmon Lions" was painted on the side in gigantic letters. "Wow," we thought, "now there's some school spirit."

Not long afterwards, our neighbor, Sue, invited us to a football game at the high school, a home game featuring the Columbia High Bruins.

"I thought it was the Lions," I said.

"No," said Sue. "It's a grizzly bear."

I explained my confusion, which—and I was starting to cringe every time this happened—made her laugh. "The Lions are a social-service club," Sue said. "They built the shelter as a community-service project. You know, the *Lions*? Eyeglasses?"

Fundraising

Every month or so, Sue's daughter came down the driveway with a catalogue and a large paper envelope. She was selling magazine subscriptions, chocolate, candles and other things to support her school. Even though Sue kept her from accosting us with every fundraising campaign, I found it astonishing that children were being taught to constantly beg for their educational programs.

Perhaps I have the wrong attitude, and it's about children learning to be invested in their education and understanding that things cost money. But to me it seems like a shakedown when everyone is already paying taxes to support schools. Whether your children are in a public or private school, be ready to fundraise for music, for sports, for class trips, for a senior party.

4-H

As fashion-punk teenagers in a suburb of Minneapolis during the late 1980s, my friends and I used to go to the Minnesota State Fair to gawk: at the rides, at the farm animals, at the cute guys. What was infinitely more fascinating to me than the animals in the enormous livestock barns were the strange creatures who were attending to them: human beings my age who, instead of wearing a "Dead Kennedys" t-shirt and combat boots, or some outfit designed by Esprit, were dressed in plaid shirts and jeans and, instead of mousse-ing their hair into something resembling an explosion, had perfect, simple, gleaming French braids down their backs. And they seemed happy that way. I watched them, brushing down their horses and cows, in awe.

These were 4-H participants, farm kids who buy an animal, raise it and then sell it at auction for slaughter at a fair or rodeo. Or, if it's a horse, the kid competes in races and other shows. Many kids help pay their way into college with the proceeds of their 4-H projects.

Children between the ages of nine and nineteen can participate. Before you sign your children up for 4-H, make sure it's something *they* want to do, or else guess who will be feeding the goats at 6 a.m.? This can be an amazing experience for a child—they learn responsibility, compassion and reward for hard work.

Not all 4-H projects are large animals—even ducks or rabbits can be raised. A child might pursue agility with an alpaca or a llama. In fact, many 4-H projects aren't animals at all. There is also a science, engineering and technology program to encourage the exploration of those areas. There are "citizenship" projects as well. The Hs are Head, Heart, Hands and Health, meaning that developing a well-rounded character is the goal of the organization. 4-H has no affiliation with schools; it's managed through the local extension service.

Future Farmers of America

If your child really takes to 4-H and shows interest in a career in agriculture or ranching, he can sign up for Future Farmers of America starting in ninth grade. Nowadays called the National FFA Organization, this extracurricular club serves teenagers until the age of twenty-one. The organization provides curriculum that one takes throughout high school; they have specific projects every year, including community service projects.

Mike and I used to hire an FFA kid to come and till up the back half of the garden in the spring; it was easier than renting a disc and cheaper than hiring an adult. So, the job wasn't perfect but it was close enough, and it was great to see a seventeen-year-old bouncing around on a tractor with ear buds in.

Safety

Farms are so wonderful but not particularly safe places. They're working places. Imagine letting your kids loose in a factory. The modern "helicopter" parent will finally feel vindicated because there are, in fact, hazards all over the place—tools, old bundles of barbed wire, biting and kicking animals, and water tanks and unfenced ponds. Teach your children what to avoid and how to safely handle tools and animals, and make sure visitors are aware of the hazards.

Raising children in the country can mean that you are providing the best food money can buy—food you grow yourself. You may even can some kinds of baby food, the same as you would jam. Most of my baby-toting friends have invested in a food mill, which grinds up just about anything into a nice paste. This is scandalously less expensive than buying organic baby food in the grocery.

If you are allowing your children to enjoy Mother Earth by foraging wild berries, miner's lettuce and whatnot, you need to show them the difference between what is okay to eat and what is not. And, most importantly, teach them: *If you are in doubt, do not eat it.* It's too easy for a kid to mistake an edible berry for a poisonous one. Most of the time, the inedible one will be so bitter she will know right away. Teach your child that if she eats something questionable to come home immediately with a few samples in hand. That way, if you don't recognize it and the child does in fact get sick, you can bring it to the hospital for identification.

Even some of the food in your garden can be dangerous. Rhubarb stalks are tart—my friend used to get them as a kid along with a baggie full of sugar—but the leaves are poisonous. Potato plants grow seed pods that look a lot like unripe tomatoes, and they are poisonous, too.

Chores

On a farm, everybody pulls his weight. Country kids have chores nearly as soon as they can walk. A three-year-old can throw kitchen scraps to the chickens. A five-year-old can check for eggs if the nest is accessible and there's not an aggressive rooster. A six-year-old can paint a fence. An eight-year-old can bottle-feed goat kids. A ten-year-old can learn to drive a riding lawn mower, tractor—or even a pickup. It's legal so long as they are on your property; check for specific laws governing your area.

I once asked a fifth-grader if he could find his mom or dad to move their rig, because they had parked me into a driveway.

"Oh, I can do that," he said brightly, and hopped into the cab (the keys were in the ignition). I had to laugh—of course he could.

Young kids usually start out helping in the garden with weeding and feeding the dogs and cats, and then move up to mucking out the stalls. There are even kid-sized tools for them. As they get older, they can bottle-feed any orphaned or abandoned animal babies (which are on a two-hour schedule, just like human infants), drive the tractor, water the garden and harvest garden vegetables. It's not unusual for older kids to get up at 5 a.m. in order to get their chores done before school.

Chores are not assigned as some kind of "learn the value of money" lesson—they are essential to the survival of the farm. Mike and I often joked about getting a bunch of teenagers to live with us, so we could get everything done.

Chapter 22
Amenities

Library

Most small towns have a library, thanks in part to Andrew Carnegie, who spent a portion of his vast steel fortune to build libraries throughout the country in the early twentieth century. Few of these are intact one hundred years later—they are too small and not ADA accessible. But libraries themselves are going strong.

Modern country librarians are quintessential rural pioneer-types—they can figure out a way to do anything with almost no budget; they're scrappy defenders of free speech and privacy; they welcome new technologies before many of their patrons have even heard of them. They know every kid in the area and what books they like to read; they are constantly on the lookout for new programs. The rural library focuses on the future, as Kid Central, and houses the area's past as told in books, photographs and publications.

Most libraries are formally connected to other libraries in the area; this allows them to engage in interlibrary loans, thus expanding their collections exponentially. Many wisely have made themselves independent tax districts, which means they are not susceptible to city budget cuts. They raise money with levies.

If a library serves a rural area with many small outlying communities, it might have a mobile unit. Klickitat County was served by an RV outfitted with bookshelves; a woman drove it around four days per week unless there was too much snow.

Public Transportation

Many small towns have some sort of skeletal bussing system. It may only run once per day in each direction. It may run from one town to the next, or into a city, or just from one end of town to the other. You may have to "order" a pickup so the driver knows to stop for you. It may be available to anyone, or just to senior citizens who need transportation to a medical appointment, social service appointment, or other service (e.g. grocery shopping).

If your town has a bus system, it's probably big enough for a few taxis as well. Most people rely on family, friends and neighbors if they can't drive themselves.

Grange Hall

The Grange is a farmers' association that was organized in 1867 as the Order of Patrons of Husbandry. It's the place where farmers gathered to discuss issues and organize lobbying efforts, and also where social events were held: the Fourth of July picnic; the Saturday-night square dance; the bake sale. Many rural communities still use their original Grange Hall, which is the old-time equivalent of a community center. Whether it's a practical or a sentimental choice, many square dances and other traditional arts are still held in grange halls.

Membership Clubs

If you've visited a small town you may have noticed buildings with curious insignia on them, perhaps an Eagle or the letters "I.O.O.F." These buildings belong to what one of my friends glibly refers to the "animal clubs." Membership-based organizations help provide a framework for rural society—they offer a way to access the town's established citizens, to be an active philanthropist and to spend free time.

The oldest fraternal organizations (for example, the Oddfellows was formed by a fraternity of knights in 1452) served the role that insurance does now. If you were an Oddfellow who hit hard times—say your house burned down—your brothers would help until you got back on your feet. In fact, each Knights of Columbus chapter still has one member who is an insurance agent.

Until recently, many of these organizations thrived on the basis of clandestine membership. The downfall of exclusivity is that the un-chosen tend to go on with their lives. Nowadays some of the formerly secret societies, whose members have literally died off, have loosened their restrictions in order to attract new members and collect hall-rental fees for events held by outsiders.

Some groups are more religious than others; all are co-ed unless noted differently. A few have websites but, if you're interested in learning about one, your best bet is to find someone who is a member.

- **American Legion:** Organization founded by veterans of World War I and chartered by Congress to provide support for veterans of war. Fights for veterans' legal, health care and other rights, and provides places to gather in the form of social clubs.
- **Benevolent and Protective Order of Elks (BPOE):** Social club known for its good works, such as creating hospitals for children. Their "clubhouses" often have amenities such as swimming pools and workout rooms.
- **Fraternal Order of Eagles (F.O.E.):** Originally started by six theater owners in Seattle, this social organization sponsors a lot of recreational activities, such as dances and bowling tournaments.

- **Freemasonry (Masons):** There are four sub-groups of Freemasonry—Scottish Rite, York Rite, Ancient Arabic Order of the Nobles of the Mystic Shrine (Shriners), and Order of the Eastern Star. Women are welcome only in the last group, which is for "Masons and their wives." The Shriners, who have funded hospitals across the United States, Mexico and Canada, are known for rolling through parades on miniature cars and motorcycles, wearing red fezzes. In spite of this and other imagery, they claim no connection with Islam.
- **Jaycees (United States Junior Chamber):** International youth organization that sponsors programs like Relay for Life, Support Our Troops and Outstanding Young Farmer. Being youth-oriented and savvy, they offer membership benefits such as reduced-rate car rentals, credit cards, etc.
- **Kiwanis International:** Social-service club dedicated to improving communities by helping children.
- **Knights of Columbus:** Fraternal order for "practical" Catholic males only. Not surprisingly, they are outspoken opponents of abortion rights.
- **Lions Clubs International:** The largest service organization with numerous programs, the best known of which is probably their re-distribution of used eyeglasses to poor countries. Lions donate their time, and accept grant applications from local nonprofits.
- **Independent Order of Odd Fellows (I.O.O.F.):** Benevolent society with a mission "to improve and elevate the character of mankind." Female members are called Rebekahs; people eight years or older "who believe in a Supreme Being, Creator and Preserver of the Universe, and are faithful to their Country" may join.
- **Rotary International:** Rotarians are business leaders who work together to raise money to support local scholarships as well as international projects, such as polio vaccinations. Even this seemingly secular group leads its meetings with a prayer.
- **Soroptimist International:** Organization for professional women that seeks to improve women's lives in the United States and around the world. Some groups directly fund programs and projects in their communities.

Local News

If you see a fire on a nearby ridge, how can you find out what's going on? Unless you know someone on the ridge you can phone, it may be difficult. The newspaper comes out once a week, so you'll eventually read about it, but you want to know *right* now. Most community newspapers have a website, but it is put together by an overworked and underpaid skeleton crew that can barely get the print edition out in time. Your town may have a website but, again, it's likely not anyone's first priority to keep it up-to-date. Local radio is alive and well in rural areas; there may even be a community station. This is your best bet.

When was the last time you attended a city council meeting where you live? Urban people are used to letting news outlets recap the proceedings; rural people are more likely to witness the news as it's made—or to get directly involved. Town council members are not career politicians; they are truly the butcher, the baker and the candlestick maker.

Other news sources: There will be announcements of community events, lost pets and funerals posted at the post office, library, church, and maybe a commonly visited market or gas station. Some organizations may mail out newsletters.

Probably the fastest way things get around is word-of-mouth—just be sure the facts are straight before you pass the news along yourself.

Shopping

I am a "Buy Local" gal, through and through, but it's tough to do that in rural America. Well, it's tough to do that in urban America, for that matter, when nearly everything is made in another country. It created a real conundrum for me—should I buy something made in China from a local shop, keeping some of my money in the community? Should I use the gas to drive 140 miles round-trip to Portland to buy something made in the United States there? Should I go online?

Most of my friends did not share this inner conflict, especially if they had kids—if they needed magic markers or new galoshes, they unapologetically drove to the local Wal-Mart. I honestly think Mike and I were the only people who refused to step foot in the place.

Chapter 23
Community Events

Festivals, Rodeos and County Fairs

Like urban areas, small towns host numerous social gatherings, from seasonal festivals to harvest celebrations to holiday parades. Most businesses participate, often donating goods or services.

Many communities also feature some kind of "arts walk." Since there aren't numerous art galleries such as an urban area can support, local businesses usually host local artists as well. Many communities have an arts center of some kind, which may house a gallery/gift shop as well as a workshop area, maybe even a theater. Programming usually includes a lot of content for children.

Rodeos and county fairs are traditional community events. Everyone expects to see everyone else there, because people come in from even the most far-flung ranches. Rodeo events include:

- **Barrel Racing:** The rider and horse wait on a starting line at one end of the arena. On the other end, and on the sides, are barrels. The horsewoman must race across the arena and circumnavigate all the barrels before racing back to the starting line. This is typically a female-only event; I've seen girls as young as five compete, which is about the cutest thing on the planet. They're all decked out in cowgirl outfits, and use crops to tell the horse to go, since their legs aren't yet long enough to get around the saddle.
- **Calf Roping:** A calf is released from a chute and the rider must chase it down, jump off his horse and tie the calf's feet together as quickly as possible. (They actually use this skill when they gather up the new calves in the spring to brand them.)
- **Bronco Busting:** A cowboy or cowgirl mounts a horse that likes to buck in a chute; the chute is opened and the horse jumps out, trying to get the rider off. The rider stays on as long as possible, usually just a few seconds.
- **Bull Riding:** Same as bronco-busting but more dangerous. Bulls are even less amenable to having a rider, and bigger. And they have horns.

You might find this whole thing disturbing—*they are torturing those animals!* Not really. The horses and bulls used in rodeos are familiar with the routine, and get treated well before and after the event. I would even go so far as to say that most enjoy the challenge of trying to dislodge the rider. The horses that ropers and barrel-racers ride are their own, so those are prized possessions, even family members. The calves, well, they'd probably opt out if they could; I'll give you that.

The County and State fairs are amazing. There will likely be some rodeo-type events in an arena, but there is so much more—the canned fruit, the art, the competitions in homemaking and leatherworking, the 4-H auctions. These fairs are where the kids who participated in 4-H that year bring their animals to sell them. They have a small ring (dirt floor "stage") surrounded by bleachers and a table at which the judges sit. One by one, each child brings his or her animals into the ring and walks it around so the judges can determine how healthy it is, and an auctioneer takes bids on the animal. This is a pinnacle in the country child's year—they earn real money from their hard work.

I have seen both extremes in size: the Minnesota State Fair, which houses thousands of chickens in its Chicken Building, and the Klickitat County Fair, which had about twenty chickens in its competition. Big fairs will wow you with the scale of things; small fairs are utterly charming, and people are more than happy to answer any question.

Fourth of July

Be ready to see more red, white and blue than you could ever imagine. Small-town America considers the Fourth of July holiday to be a celebration of small-town life as well as of our nation's founding. If there is a fireworks show, a local social-service club like the Lions probably raises the money for it, and your donation is welcome. There will likely be a parade as well as barbeques, fun-runs and anything someone takes a fancy to. Hooray for the United States!

Halloween

In the city, Mike and I developed a Halloween tradition that we absolutely loved—we made a batch of chili and drank hot toddies all night on our porch while we passed out candy to neighborhood kids. It was a great social event and an opportunity to bundle up enough to enjoy the cool fall evening.

We moved to our farm in August; in October we started thinking about what that year's hot drink of choice was going to be. We decorated the front porch with corn stalks and jack-o-lanterns, and then it hit us. We lived on a state highway. The houses were hundreds of feet from each other. No one walked our "neighborhood;"

it was too dangerous. But, there were kids. *Were they driven from house to house by their parents?* we wondered. *What do they do?*

I asked my neighbor, Sue, who explained that most kids were driven into town, where the businesses all handed out candy. Some might also go door-to-door in the neighborhoods there, but mostly they congregated at a party at the school.

In many towns, established trick-or-treating hours keep home- and business-owners from having to remain at their posts the entire evening. Towns often have trick-or-treating from 4 until 7 p.m., and then the children go to a party held by the school or other organization.

A friend who lives in Wyoming told me that in one remote town, they have "Trunk or Treat"—because the homes are so remote and far-flung, everyone drives to the parking lot of the grocery store and the kids go from one rig to the next.

Christmas

Notice, I did not write "The Holidays." In rural America the winter holiday is not Solstice. Not Hanukah. Not Kwanzaa, though the kids might learn about these fringe celebrations in school. It is Christmas.

Mike and I try to focus on Winter Solstice as our holiday, rather than Christmas, but without children for whom to create a tradition, it really doesn't stick. And the rest of our family celebrates Christmas. As a Solstice celebrator, I finally got an inkling of how non-Christians must feel, however, because it is relentless, this Christmas! Decorations and advertisements and grocery displays and window paintings and community events. It's all anyone talks about for weeks.

Wherever Mike and I have lived, we've made a tradition of shopping at local businesses for holiday gifts before we resort to online or big-box purchases. I encourage you to do the same; support your neighbors! This may be more of a challenge if your town does not have a lot of shops. And don't be fooled by "fake-local"—I once went into the local plant nursery, which in December is transformed into a magical, festive "Christmas Central." I had a bunch of gifts—beautiful handmade ornaments, candles and the like—in my arms, when I turned one over and read the sticker: "Made in China." I investigated further. Everything I was holding had been made in China. I put it all back, and asked the shopkeeper if they had anything that was locally made. She shook her head and smiled, "I wish I could." I am still stymied by that answer.

School Events

Ask anyone why they love a small town, and they will likely call it "a great place to raise kids." It's the proverbial village that it takes to raise a child.

If you have children, I don't need to explain why it's important and fun to be involved in school events. If you don't have children, I might. Because children create opportunities to meet new people, it is all the more challenging to make it in a small community if you don't have any. I can't tell you how many conversations were stopped short when someone asked me how many children I had, and I said none. They hadn't asked *whether* I had, but how many.

Some simply couldn't fathom the idea and made some cloying remark like, "Well, not yeeet!" It got to the point that I would simply tell a perfect stranger that I'm infertile, which is none of their business, so that they could, at least, pity me for being unsuccessful and then we could move on. I preferred pity to judgment. If you happen to be child-free happily and by choice, don't bring it up.

Children are the grease of the society's machinery: relationships are forged, jobs are recommended, and salaries are compared while waiting in front of the school and cheering on the soccer field. In a larger community, the chance that you'd meet someone in this context who can actually recommend a job in your industry is slim; in the country there are only two or three degrees of separation between anyone.

Therefore, even if you don't have children, it is in your best interest to get involved with school activities, at the minimum attending a few public events. This includes sports, science and art fairs, band and choir concerts, and theater productions. Or, better yet, volunteer as a coach or activity leader.

Recreation, Arts and Culture
Recreation

Living on seven acres provided some great recreation opportunities, and limited others. When Mike and I lived in Portland, it was an all-day affair to go cross-country skiing: Put gear in car; drive sixty or ninety minutes to a Sno-Park (that was if we already had a parking pass; otherwise, we had to go to a store on the way up and buy one); unload; ski for a few hours, eating granola and dried fruit on the trail; drive sixty or ninety minutes back to Portland.

When we lived on our farm, we had two options: Drive twenty minutes to a Sno-Park, ski and be back home in time to dig into the pot of soup that was on the woodstove. Or, step outside, slap on skis and ski around the pasture. The latter was awesome! No driving, no permits, no nuthin'. Our neighbors opened their gate between our properties, and then we could each ski on the full twelve acres. We also snow-shoed that way; it was fun to go down to the woodlot and see how the snow had changed the landscape. Tufts of snow fell from the upper branches, covering the sleeping ferns and silencing the creeks.

On the other end of the spectrum, I used to be a bicycle commuter. In my twenties, in Minneapolis, I would ride my bike until the temperature got below 0 degrees Fahrenheit. Zero! Right before Mike and I moved to Portland, I traded in my trusty, 40-pound Diamondback for a new, sleek one. I rode it quite a bit in Portland as well.

After six years in the country, I realized I had not ridden my bike. Not once. The reasons: We lived on a state highway with fast drivers, steep hills, blind curves and a negligible shoulder. I have never been interested in putting my bike on a vehicle, driving my vehicle to a trail, and then riding my bike on the trail. So, I never got on it.

Ditto hiking and running: Our options were to "walk the P" (perimeter of our land), from which you could maybe squeeze one mile if you did every fence in the place, or get in the car and drive to a trailhead. We couldn't walk very fast on a P-walk, either, because of the slope and uneven ground of our land.

The upshot was that while I was getting a lot of exercise hauling wood and digging garden beds, I got almost no aerobic exercise during non-snow months unless I used a workout video or drove somewhere else.

Fine Arts

Most communities have some semblance of an arts group, be it a loose committee that arranges an arts fair once a year, an amateur theater company or orchestra, a writers' group that meets monthly, or a full-fledged nonprofit that occupies a building in which there's a gallery. The beauty of small-town arts is that if you're motivated to be a big fish in a small pond, the possibilities are limited only by your imagination and your budget.

And by that, I mean *your* budget. The detriment to small-town arts is that, generally speaking, your efforts will garner little or no wages, and may even require money from your own pocket.

If there is no artists' cooperative in your town, consider starting one. Everyone who becomes a member pays his or her share of the rent, and everyone takes turns working in the space. The more, the merrier—and the less each person has to pay. If you register the group as a nonprofit organization, you can apply for grants and enjoy tax-exempt status (for the organization, not the individual artists).

When I lived in the country, I had a lot of friends who were writers. We were all busy with our jobs, families and farms, and didn't get a lot of time for creative projects. We didn't get to hang out very often. Being a multi-tasker, I came up with an idea: Let's make a date with each other, once a month, to write. It was called Time to Write. We gathered at 9:30 a.m. and then wrote from 10 until 12:30. Then, we enjoyed a potluck lunch. There were anywhere from two to a dozen guests who were working on projects that ranged from poetry that revisited a childhood in WWII-era Germany to a novel featuring telepathic horses. While I haven't reconvened the group since returning to Portland, it still exists on Facebook (where everyone decides their own parameters).

I believe that these efforts hark back to a time in the United States when everyone was creative in some capacity: they made quilts; they carved wood; they brewed beer; they played a fiddle; they recited Shakespeare and Tennyson. People farmed all summer and then got together during the long winters and entertained each other. If they wanted something, they had to sew, build or cook it.

As more and more people moved to cities, they became accustomed to "having done" rather than doing—hiring out a plumber; going to a restaurant for a meal; buying household items. Rural people began to use their harvest surplus to purchase things they would have made themselves in previous generations, or done without. Nowadays, most people—urban and rural—never develop their latent artistic talents because they're lulled into complacency by the television. This leaves the playing field more open for those of us who want to pursue art, but there are fewer Others interested in watching, listening to or—most importantly for the working artist—buying it.

Having land usually means outbuildings—music to an artist's ears. You can finally get out of the spare bedroom or the basement, and into your own studio! You can finally make as much noise as you want to, at any hour of the day or night! Make sure your new hidey-hole has grounded electrical outlets, heat and a sink if you need one. If you work in a toxin-producing medium, such as photography or glazed pottery, you're going to have to figure out what to do with the waste product, because it suddenly doesn't just go down the sink and "away"—it becomes part of your property and possibly your groundwater.

Restaurants

This may seem odd, but consider how often you rely on take-out meals. Thai, Middle Eastern, Mexican, Indian. By the time Mike and I returned to Portland, we were so glad to have quick meal options other than boxed mac-n-cheese and frozen pizza that we ate phô or burritos ten times in two weeks. Find out if there is a pizza shop in town that delivers to your house. If not—are you willing to devote that many more hours per week to driving into town for take-out, or to making meals at home?

If going out for dinner is important to you as a recreational activity, and/or you are a staunch vegetarian or vegan, seriously reconsider your move. Because unless you live in a resort town, there will be *nothing* for you. I mean it. Average American restaurants have hamburgers; turkey sandwiches; fried chicken; fried fish;

French fries; coleslaw; the most flaccid, uninspired salads you can imagine; and pickle slices.

None if this food comes from a local source; it came from a regional supplier that trucks everything over, frozen or hermetically sealed. The soup came in a large plastic jar. The hamburger patties were in a giant plastic bag. Even the carnitas in the Mexican restaurant and the eggrolls in the Chinese restaurant came from a supplier. If the chicken-noodle soup is advertised with a hand-lettered sign as "homemade," they probably mean "home-assembled."

Occasionally, there will be a blessed, wonderful exception. They will make their soups and piecrust from scratch; offer organic, vegetarian entrees sourced from local growers; brew good coffee. Their food may even be better than anything you could make at home. The trouble is that you will want to go there every time you go out, and "too much of a good thing" is real. Hood River is a tourist town, so we had about ten awesome restaurants to choose from. Despite that, after six years I could hardly stand them.

If you like corporate fast food, the adjustment won't be so bad, as all but the most remote rural areas host at least one McDonald's, Pizza Hut, or Taco Bell.

Other Cultural Opportunities

If your town has a bookstore, rejoice. Even if their regular stock does nothing for you, the owners will happily order a title. Hopefully, there are readings held, though it's hard for small towns to attract big-name writers, or even medium-named writers, unless the town is close to a larger city that is on their docket.

Television is available by either cable or satellite. Rural television packages require the same kind of *caveat emptor* as they do in the city. There is usually a super-cheap package, with just the local network channels, that they provide but don't advertise—you have to ask for it.

Many small towns have a community band or orchestra. These concerts are charming, if not rigorously precise. Ditto community theater. The set and costuming may be minimal, the acting mediocre, the selections pedestrian. On the other hand, they might be pretty darn professional; the ticket cost almost nothing; everyone in attendance has a great seat. And it's fun to see friends expressing themselves.

There might be a bar that has live music on weekends, a Grange hall that hosts a square dance once a month. And, again, if there is something in particular you want to see—make it happen.

Adult Education

Because of various initiatives over the past few decades, community colleges and other adult education programs exist in dozens of communities, offering everything from formal associate's degrees to technical degrees, to Spanish-language and English as a Second Language programs, to cooking and crafts classes just for fun. Our area had both a community college and a thriving adult education program that offered computer classes, field trips to bigger cities to shop or see a theatrical performance, and small-business administration. These classes were taught by regular people in the community, not career educators, and were extremely reasonably priced.

Consider teaching as well as taking adult education classes. If there's something you're good at, share it with others.

If you're looking for a career change, the community college may also be a source of real job training. Columbia Gorge Community College specialized in training for two quickly expanding fields: nursing and wind turbine technicians. The liberal arts offerings were less compelling, but good just to get out of the house and into some interesting conversations.

Complex Political Issues

All across the United States, there are contentious land-use issues, whether it's oil drilling, coal or mineral mining, development and affordable housing, transportation, or wildlife. Find out what issues are relevant for your potential new home before you move there. And then, keep your mouth shut for a while and listen to how those issues play out. Even if you have well-researched views.

We happened to live in one of the most contentious land-use areas in the United States. The Columbia Gorge is a National Scenic Area, an act of Congress that President Ronald Reagan allegedly signed into law while holding his nose with his other hand. This act is intended to preserve the natural beauty of the area by limiting the scope and type of development that can occur within it. But, this is also the Wild West, a place where people don't like being told what they can and cannot do, particularly on Their Land. The result is the Act is constantly being challenged, not in obvious ways like trying to amend it, but in having it creatively reinterpreted to suit those in power (and those in power generally have residential and housing developments up their sleeves).

And that's just the start. Dozens of dams were built on the areas' many fast-moving mountain rivers during the 1920s and '30s in an effort to harness their power to generate electricity. However, the "progress men" didn't consider the salmon that were suddenly unable to return to their spawning grounds to reproduce (salmon famously hurl themselves up rocky waterfalls to do so). Billions of dollars have since been spent on salmon restoration, but a movement has been growing to breach some of the smaller dams that only generate a few households' worth of electricity. The arguments against doing so have been astonishing, from concern that the debris flowing out with the water will kill all the fish, to outrage that a "hundred-year-old" ecosystem would be destroyed (as opposed to the million-year-old one that preceded it?).

Upriver on the Columbia, a uranium-processing facility called Hanford was built in the 1940s that helped launch the atomic age; now, its underground concrete waste-storage tanks are leaking into the groundwater. In an effort to supplant hydro-electric power, wind farms are going up while locals argue about whether the towers are an economic boon or an eyesore (even a health risk and environmental hazard). Rural zoning is constantly being undercut and challenged by people who want to subdivide. The bridge between Hood River, Oregon, and White Salmon, Washington—the locus of outdoor recreation in the Columbia River Gorge and possibly the entire Pacific Northwest—does not allow bicycle or foot traffic. Additionally, it's a toll bridge, owned by the Port of Hood River, that was paid off decades ago.

There is no end to points of contention in the Gorge. And in the ring are a number of people from a variety of backgrounds: fourth-generation orchardists; liberal environmentalists; trust-funders who "do" sports and not much else; Native Americans. Both mature, rational people and reactionary, stubborn people. People with honorable intentions and people for whom backroom deals is a sort of hobby.

Moving to the country was a significant lesson on the one hand—in Portland I would never have made an effort to get to know my neighbor who shops regularly at Wal-Mart, or the one who throws her recyclables in the trash. Out here, I have to. And I've found that I really like my Wal-Mart neighbor. Even when we disagree on something, it's with respect and understanding.

So Lesson Number One: Do not assume anything about anyone. Even if they're burning plastic bags in their backyard, they might share your views about the president. And in any case, it's best to keep the lines of communication open. This lesson can be learned in the city as well as the country—a bad neighbor can really make life unpleasant.

Lesson Number Two: People do not like to be told what to do, especially by the Government or Environmentalists.

Lesson Number Three: Do not assume you know better. Or, at least try to understand the reasoning behind the opposite point of view. Generally, it's self-preservation. Just because you have a master's degree in biology doesn't mean you corner the market on best land-practices. Your neighbor might have a master's, too, and in any case probably knows that land like his own body. Most farmers/ranchers and environmentalists have similar concerns about sustainable land use, but because most environmentalists have descended upon country folk like so many kvetching nannies—and been backed on ballot measures by an urban, liberal majority—the walls go up and no communication takes place. Or, worse.

Mike was once on a documentary shoot that dealt with the sticky wicket of water rights. A water master had led the crew to a junction of three irrigation ditches, which was on an old rancher's property with an easement. Regardless of the water master's legal right to be there, the rancher came blazing across her field toward them, skirts whipping around her ankles, carrying a rifle.

"What the hell are you doing, Carl!" she yelled.

"Now, Vera," the water master said. "I'm just showing these fellas how the ditches are managed."

She would have none of it, cursing the water master and the crew alike. She pointed at Mike and volleyed her final epithet: "And I don't like you sonsabitches with whiskers!" Then she turned on her heel and marched back to her house, where she continued to monitor the group from the front porch, rifle on her lap.

The easy synopsis of such an encounter is "Those country people are loony!" But it's not that simple. From the view on the front porch, their lives are nonstop work—all summer in the heat and all winter in the cold. They are not driving to work in a warm car, stopping for a hot latté and a scone on the way, and sitting in a comfortable chair in front of a computer all day. In their eyes, that is not work at all. Bucking hay for ten hours in the hot sun—now, that's work. So for a bunch of soft, pasty-skinned pansies to pass legislation that makes their life even harder—say, to re-introduce wolf populations into an area where ranchers depend on their sheep to make a living—well, they think those people can go straight to hell.

Environmentalism

The term "environmentalist" has come to mean both "bleeding-heart liberal commie tree-hugger who has no right to get in my business" and "enlightened, educated and morally superior lover of the Earth who knows better." Whom does this leave out? Rural farmers and ranchers who love the land, who have the experience and knowledge to act as responsible stewards, and who don't appreciate the input of thousands of clueless urban intellectuals.

This is a bit of repetition from the preceding section, but it bears repeating: Do not assume you know better. Urbanites embrace the idea of "wilderness;" ruralites know exactly what they're protecting. A third-generation rancher who has spent her entire life—every afternoon as a child; every working day—on a particular parcel is going to know more about it than any city environmentalist who might come to study it. And certainly more than someone in a voting booth in a city, who's never even seen her or her neighbors' land, or maybe never even left the city. As far as a country person is concerned, a city is Fantasyland, where people buy food from a store and have no idea where it came from, and leave their garbage on a curb and have no idea where it goes. They think the people in a city live like children, with everything being done for them. Worse than children—country children know how to cook and drive, and get up every morning at 5:30 a.m. to do their chores.

"People think we're out here running cattle for the money," a man in Eastern Oregon once told me. "That's not true. We run cattle so we can live out here. When you've been here a couple of generations, it's just like the Indians—the land becomes a part of you."

Now, I comprehend the inadvertent racism here—this guy is enjoying land that was brutally requisitioned, to put it nicely, from the very Indians he claims kinship with. It may even have been his own great-great-grandfather who helped evict the Indians, who eventually landed in a postage-stamp-sized reservation twenty miles away. But if urban environmentalists don't try to understand the purview of rural environmentalists with real compassion and without judgment, why should ruralites try to understand urbanites?

Guns

Note: Types and use of firearms is discussed in the hunting part of the Food Section.

Some friends of mine moved to Vermont, where they happily discovered a publicly funded preschool program. One day, four-year-old Peter came home with his weekly library book, in this case, a magazine—*National Rifle Association Magazine*. My friends returned it, saying to the preschool staff, "This must have been a mistake." No, no mistake. The school found it perfectly legitimate to let a small child read about guns. Not even read—Peter couldn't read yet, just look at the pictures.

My friends decided to take on this issue, writing letters of complaint to the principal and superintendant. They were not against hunting, they carefully explained. They just thought that a child ought to be old enough to complete a firearm safety course before he could check out literature about weapons. As it was, Peter would recognize a gun and like them—what if he saw one at a friend's house? He had no idea about gun safety, and could become one of the annual casualties of accidental shooting.

The school did not share their view, and ever after my friends were stigmatized as those Pinko Liberals Who Don't Want Us to Be Able to Have Guns. Teachers and other parents would glare at them when they dropped Peter off in the morning.

Rural people are extremely supportive of Second Amendment rights. Men, women and children as young as five all have guns in some rural areas—less so in towns, but there's most likely at least one in every house.

And, they use those guns. Country folks' casual, regular use of weaponry may be disturbing to the average pacifist, so prepare yourself if you fit that description. While non-criminal urbanites who carry firearms do so to protect themselves from potential attacks by other humans, in the country the additional motivation is shooting animals.

Hell, Mike and I even had a gun on our farm. An elderly .22 single-action rifle, to be sure, but it was operational. We had bullets. Some of our urban friends became uneasy if they noticed it hanging over the door (on pegs built into the wall for it). They'd say with surprise, and just a hint of judgment, "Is that a…gun?" But, it made sense to us to have one in case we had an animal that needed to be put down. We'd both shot a gun before, so we knew how. For the record, we never used it. Mike mentioned target practice a couple of times, but we had too much work to do to be goofing around, ruining a piece of plywood.

Some urban environmentalists can open their minds and find it morally acceptable to hunt for sustenance. But what about cold-blooded murder? In the country, if you go out and shoot cougars or gophers on your land, that is considered a defensive (not offensive) act, because those critters might ruin your crops or livestock. I know people who feel it's a public service to kill snakes and coyotes—or even wolves, an endangered species—at any opportunity. Live trap-and-release is generally snickered at.

What if you're killing purely for sport? I once taught a writing workshop at a rural elementary school. Extremely rural; two-kids-in-each-grade rural. In the course of my four hours with one class, I was regaled with lively tales of shooting sage rats and crows, stabbing geese, pulling the legs and tails off lizards, and burning ants.

"Hey, Frank," said one kid, working diligently on his prose piece, to the boy next to him, "did we pour oil or gas on those anthills?"

Maybe video games aren't so bad after all, I mused. I was a guest and there to teach storytelling, not compassion, so I checked my reaction. By the end, I was a little shaken by the brazen disregard for the suffering of another being, even a lizard. Killing was one thing—doing it for sport, and enjoying the act of killing, another. Granted, these were young, immature boys showing off for the new city lady, but I could see them in some of the adults around town. Not most, but some.

Loving the Earth while destroying it while preserving it—that is the complex web woven in rural places.

Chapter 24
Making a Living

The best strategy for making it in the country is to bring your own money—whether it's an inheritance or money you earned yourself. Failing that, you'll need to "wear many hats." You're not going to make a lot of money at any one thing, so you have to diversify. Maybe you answer the phone at an insurance company, fill in as a tutor in the elementary school, and sell knitted hats and scarves at a local knick-knack shop. And sell extra eggs to a local restaurant. And rent out your tractor on the weekends. And serve on the city council. You have to be willing to do just about anything. Forget your "skill set."

I know a lot of people who were able to bring their city job to the country with them. I know only a handful who were able to sustain that arrangement for more than five years. So, if you plan to stay in the country for more than five years, you'd better have a viable Plan B.

Relying on an Urban Economy

When Mike and I moved to our new home in the country, we were still fully dependent on Portland's economy. Mike worked full-time, but on a fairly flexible schedule, for public television. I was a freelancer with clients that were all in Portland. At first, this was the perfect arrangement.

Creative Industries Pitfall Alert: The revolution of the Creative Class has not reached rural America. While most skills—plumbing, nursing, horseshoeing, childcare—have a monetary value in the country, writing, editing and graphic design do not. If you're in a business or board meeting and it's decided that a newsletter, brochure or other item that requires any of the aforementioned skills comes up, inevitably someone will volunteer their wife, daughter or cousin to do it for free. It would almost be seen as fiscally irresponsible to pay someone to perform these jobs. When I became the editor of a local magazine that had been in existence for three years, I was its *first* editor. Up until that point, the publisher hadn't felt he needed one (and still wasn't convinced after I started). I served on a board that needed some Spanish translation and suggested a friend, who had done such work professionally and was a native speaker. The board voted to have a trustee's spouse do it, even though she wasn't a native speaker. Spanish is Spanish, right?

The locals won't respond to your arrival with a tickertape parade: "Hooray, a cultured person is finally here to save us from our bad design and writing!" No. If the locals think that you think that you're someone special and that they're not, you are not going to get very far at all.

I think this was the hardest lesson for me to learn—here I had years of experience writing newsletters, press releases and website content, and no one would pay me a decent rate for my work. I had run a statewide book-awards program, which had a six-figure budget, and yet the only way I could coordinate something via the art center was to volunteer. It just didn't compute.

Commuting

If you live in a place that has real winter and plan to continue to drive to a major city to work, make sure that you have an employer who is okay with your taking snow days. Ideally, you'll have both a four-wheel-drive vehicle (winter) and a gas-efficient vehicle (rest of the year). We had a Subaru Forester, which was great in the winter. But when gas topped four dollars per gallon in the mid-2000s, we were feeling it.

After a couple of years, Mike had tired of the commute—not the sixty-mile drive through the Columbia River Gorge, actually, but the six-mile drive in bumper-to-bumper traffic into Portland proper. I wanted to get more involved in the local community. So I started taking more local clients, even though the business owners were less sophisticated (that is to say, they appreciated and understood the need for my skills less) and/or paid less for the same work. I went from earning $50 to $75 per hour as a freelancer to being lucky if I could get $40. Most people wanted to pay me $20 (or were expecting me to volunteer).

If you plan to continue to make a living via an urban economy, be ready for either a brutal commute, or being away from your home for days or weeks at a time. I do know people who have driven sixty miles to and from work for twenty years, and people who go to a city on Monday and don't come back until the end of the week. But spending that much time in the car and/or away from your home and family can take its toll. I recommend not doing the math.

Telecommuting

If you plan to bring your work with you, make sure that you can get high-speed Internet and that your cell phone works *in the room that will be your office*. You'll want to keep a phone with the urban area code on your business card, and it's no fun to have to race to the dining room every time you have a phone call in order to get a good signal. If your computer breaks, there is no tech person to call. In fact, decent help may be an hour or more away, especially if it's a Mac.

To some degree, telecommuting works. But face time is real, and no amount of conference calls and real-time video is going to change that. Unless you are really, really good at what you do, you are expendable, and your employer will need a reason to prefer the hassles of working with you to the convenience of working with someone who can be in the building every day.

Surviving in a Rural Economy

Various factors combined to make it necessary for us to sell our farm in 2009, one of which affected most Americans—the recession that began in 2008. By early 2009 the job market in the Columbia River Gorge was, I estimate, a third of what it had been when we arrived in 2003. On May 15, 2009, I copied down all the job listings in the local newspaper:

- Executive sales secretary/assistant for local billboard company in a town twenty miles from my house: $15 per hour + benefits
- Plant supervisor, inventory control, rollform operator or hand-roller (screens) for a door/window insect screen manufacturer in a town twenty miles from my house, compensation not listed
- Bilingual (English/Spanish) clinician for a juvenile detention facility in a town twenty miles from my house, compensation not listed
- Settlements clerk for a public utility district in a town fifty miles from my house, compensation not listed
- Meat-wrapper and butcher in a town fifty miles from my house, compensation not listed
- School bus driver in a county sixty miles from my house, $9.35 per hour
- Commercial truck driver, in a town 180 miles from my house, compensation not listed
- Online sales for local newspaper in a town eighty miles from my house, compensation not listed
- Seasonal part-time communications dispatcher for state department of forestry in a town twenty miles from my house, $11.44 per hour + benefits
- Pantry person and breakfast cook at a local restaurant, compensation not listed
- Preschool teacher, no details listed
- Foster parent in neighboring counties, $1,300 per month tax-free
- Property maintenance for local small business, compensation not listed
- Real estate risk-management assistant for local bank, compensation not listed
- Reporter/photographer for local newspaper in a town twenty miles from my house, 10 cents per word and $15 per photo

- Advertising sales person, "1K to 15K per month DOE"
- Seasonal laborer for a neighboring county, $11.02 per hour
- Weed control technician in a town fifty miles from my house, $10.46 per hour
- Overnight caregiver for local resident, compensation not listed

…and that's it, at least as far as the equal-opportunity, non-health care jobs that were listed in the newspaper. Meanwhile, the real estate industry and chambers of commerce were running ads in magazines in Portland, Seattle and beyond, tirelessly luring more people with their promises of "living the dream."

Job-Seeking

Nepotism…is real. The people who have good jobs in the community not only will do everything to keep those jobs, they will do everything to hire their family, friends and friends' children. If no one who fits this description is available, *then* maybe you'll get the job.

One exception is high-level white collar jobs, such as physicians, hospital administrators and lawyers. But that's only because the people hiring don't have family or friends who are even remotely qualified, and/or the company has corporate headquarters in a city.

Unless you land a full-time job with the state or local government, chances are you won't find a job that provides health care benefits or paid time off. Most small businesses can't afford it, and many jobs in the country are part-time or contract gigs.

And, of course, there is backlash. It might seem logical to try to get one of the government jobs, or a job at the local college if there is one. They pay well and offer benefits. But then, you are making yourself Better Than the Locals. Some friends who moved to a small town near Ithaca, New York, were asked by suspicious neighbors, "You're not going to work at Cornell, are you?" If the local government agency (in the West, you can pick your agency, but we'll just say U.S. Forest Service by way of example), you are going to be categorically distrusted just for walking through the door.

Interviewing

Hiring practices can be a little more lax than you're used to. In 2009, I landed a paraprofessional (read: not-teacher) position at the local elementary school. The job was to provide reading and math tutoring to a handful of second-graders, Monday through Thursday, for 1.75 hours per day (2:15 to 4 p.m.). I was vaguely qualified because I am a writer and have been volunteering for another school-based reading program for many years, and said I could perform basic math. When the principal of the school phoned to offer me the job, I asked what the pay was (up until this point it had been neither posted nor mentioned during my interview).

"Um, I think it's eleven-something," she said.

I was in no position at the time to negotiate, so I accepted, hoping that the "something" was closer to .99 than to .01 (it ended up being .70).

I got a call from my new supervisor, who had also been at my interview, about when to report for duty and where to fill out paperwork. She didn't know my exact wage, either. "But Sally at the main office will."

Fundraising and Volunteering

In addition to fundraising for the schools, there are silent and live auctions, fancy dinners, golf tournaments, relays and dozens of other fundraising strategies for the area's nonprofit organizations, and for national efforts as well. Local firefighters will descend upon a downtown intersection once a year, holding up traffic with big rubber boots in their hands, collecting money for the Muscular Dystrophy Association. The "Fill the Boot" campaign may seem silly, but their proceeds are nothing to sneeze at—$13,600 in Hood River in 2007.

There are goat swaps: someone from a nonprofit brings a live goat to a local business and refuses to leave until the business pays them to take it to another business, which they get to pick. The goat makes the rounds that day, and the nonprofit makes some money. Another farm-themed fundraising idea is donkey basketball: Donkeys are outfitted with rubber shoes and two teams play basketball while riding them in the school gym. Quite entertaining.

Local storefront businesses receive what I consider an unfair number of donation-requests from the schools and local nonprofits (unfair because there are so many other business that don't have retail storefronts and don't get asked as often). You might consider creating a donations policy: The number of requests for funds can be a little exhausting, not to mention expensive, so pick your most cherished organizations and branch out from there. If you must say "no," do it carefully: any bad blood will haunt you for a long, long time.

In my opinion, everyone should do at least an hour of volunteer work per month. It keeps things in perspective and helps those organizations that can't fund themselves fully, but serve important roles in the community, remain functioning. Whether it's an official volunteer program or an informal agreement is irrelevant. There is no limit to the volunteer opportunities in existence, but here are a few ideas:

- **School:** Most schools welcome parents and other adults to help with both in-school tasks as well as public events (particularly fundraising events).

Call the school's office to inquire. If you work directly with children you will be required to have a criminal background check.

- **Church:** Ditto your church. You might help during the services, or behind the scenes by putting address labels on the newsletter or folding the programs.
- **Firefighting:** Most rural fire districts are served by all-volunteer staff. (The chief is usually a paid position.) Training requirements vary but are usually provided by peers. Because firefighters often respond to medical calls, you'll also need to complete formal CPR training, usually offered by the hospital.
- **Search and Rescue:** S&R is usually volunteer as well; there will be some cross-over with the firefighting roster. Advanced training, and general physical fitness and strength are required.
- **Hospital/Hospice:** These facilities usually have well-developed volunteer programs, likely even a paid volunteer coordinator. There are numerous opportunities, some offering direct patient contact and some being completely behind the scenes.
- **Political Campaigns:** If you feel strongly about a particular party or candidate, help them out!
- **Other Nonprofits:** Dozens of other organizations need your help, particularly social service agencies such as children's advocates and domestic violence shelters. There will be both grassroots-types of organizations and local chapters of national groups like Big Brother/Big Sister and CASA. If the United Way has a local chapter, they can direct you to all of their beneficiaries.

There is particular need in many communities for bilingual volunteers.

Interning

Internship programs are not as developed as in the city because they so closely resemble the vast amount of volunteer work that is done. If you or your child pursues an internship, be sure to establish parameters of what is done and what hours are worked.

Bartering

Our neighbor, Jim, plowed our driveway. This was mostly a favor to us, but Jim also welcomed any and all opportunities to use a tractor. He would sometimes go from house to house, plowing driveways, for the fun of it. Mike and I tried to compensate him for his time by giving him gas money, hot chocolate and cookies, and not complaining when he flattened something out in the yard (picnic table, horseshoe post) in his tractor-driving exuberance.

Bartering can be an effective means of surviving with little income. The idea is simple: I help you put up and shed, and you help me put up a shed! Or, if you make lots of jam and your neighbor has lots of eggs, trade a jar of jam for a dozen eggs! Things get a little more complicated from there: Is an hour of yard work worth the same as an hour of therapy? On the open market, you could pay a teenager or immigrant $15 in cash to rake your leaves. A therapist is going to charge anywhere from $50 to $100 per hour.

A few communities have taken this one step further and printed local currency. This concept has had me scratching my head since it appeared in Hood River a few years ago. I like the basic concept, which is to keep local dollars local, but have never understood why one needs to create different currency to accomplish that aim. The only benefit I can see is to avoid paying taxes, but to me Taxes = Services (like schools, libraries and roads), so I usually support them. And in order to acquire some of the local currency and be listed in the official goods-and-services directory, one has to fork over $40—in U.S. funds—to the founders of the organization.

Another form of bartering is trading daycare and grocery shopping among a group of neighbors. Rather than each family driving twenty-five miles to the grocery to grab a couple of items, take turns. This saves on gas and time for everyone.

Welfare

There are a number of types of assistance for the chronically poor. Some have been poor for generations; some are from middle-class families, who are choosing a sort of vow of poverty by endeavoring to live solely on the local economy—favoring bartering and growing their own food to seeking full-time employment with a business. This doesn't mean they're not working; on the contrary, if this book communicates nothing else it should communicate that living in the country is a full-time job in itself. It means they're choosing to not donate daylight hours to someone else's success. The notion of purposely including government hand-outs as a line-item in your monthly budget might be an affront to those who are trying to raise their families out of poverty. I'm just the messenger.

Assistance programs and qualification guidelines vary from state to state. The obvious ones are earned-income tax credits, school lunch subsidies, food stamps and health care for children. There are also housing vouchers, programs to help someone buy a car so they can get to a job, child care reimbursement and asset-development programs, which help people to save money for a house down-payment or an educational opportunity. I've seen at least one program that supplied a limited-use cellular telephone.

Opening a Business

If you want to do business, either as a bricks-and-mortar operation or as an independent contractor, your first step is to join the Chamber of Commerce. In a struggling economy, which most rural areas have, any sign that things are improving is welcome. So, if you are considering opening a new business, people will fall over themselves trying to help you, especially the Chamber of Commerce. You may even be eligible for financing that you couldn't get if you tried to open the same business in the city.

UNLESS. Unless you plan to open a business that competes with an existing one. Then, you might find walls going up overnight. There may be "this town's not big enough for the two of us"-type of complaints to the city council. There may be a smear campaign fed into the town's rumor mill. You might be surprised at who knows about your business all of a sudden—not just your business-business but also your family business. Be ready to have a stiff upper lip, thick skin, and any other symbol for toughing it out.

I didn't join the chamber and lived to regret it—not by getting my kneecaps broken but because the other businesses in town looked in its directory, not the telephone book, if they wanted to hire a writer. But it was expensive! They didn't have a rate for a sole proprietor. I felt a little bit over a barrel.

A good chamber will provide lots of membership benefits, including a directory, newsletter and membership get-to-know-you events. The Chamber in Hood River promoted the town in nearby metropolises Portland and Seattle to attract tourists and sports fanatics, and managed a comprehensive website on which members could list upcoming events and festivals.

If you have a business that regularly sends and receive packages via overnight shipping companies, make sure there is a shipping office near you and that they will deliver to you. If you are too far out, you might have to receive packages via a downtown business. A friend of mine who makes gift items from recycled bicycle parts, from a shop that's about ten miles out of town, ships and receives FedEx from the gas station. There is probably only one pick-up per day, probably not on weekends; overnight delivery is unlikely.

Businesses that thrive on summertime tourist income can suffer through the winter—if you plan to harness the power of the visiting dollar, make sure you're putting money away to keep you solvent during the lean months.

Farm-Based Income

If you're thinking romantically about small-scale farming, remember: It may be small, it may be organic—but it's still a business. The children of commercial farmers who plan to take over their parents' operations go to college; even after spending their lives on a farm they need to learn the latest in biotechnology, food science and economics if they want to compete in a world market.

What's more, a small farm is not a business that you make money at; it's a business you try to keep afloat. It's a lifestyle choice: Do you want to *be* a farmer? Every day? Think about it before you commit. It can be a rewarding lifestyle, but it is an unrelenting lifestyle.

Before you plant a cash crop, research a niche market, including the estimated cost versus return. Have your soil analyzed; you can only grow what your soil will support. Friends of mine examined the economy in Hood River and determined that while they wouldn't be able to compete in the orchard crops, and they didn't have the right conditions to grow vegetables on a large scale, the burgeoning wedding industry there would support cut flowers like peonies, lilies and irises. They advertised to area florists and wedding planners, and *voila!*—started taking orders.

Other ideas for niche markets: asparagus; nursery stock; firewood; mushrooms. Someone in the next valley over put her child through college growing ornamental Chinese lanterns and selling them to florists in Portland.

Until about the mid-1990s, organic food was only available at "co-ops" and "health food stores." Thanks to books like *Fast Food Nation* by Eric Schlosser and *The Omnivore's Dilemma* by Michael Pollan, and movies like *Food, Inc.*, consumers are beginning to understanding the nutritious, aesthetic and socio-economic differences between commercially engineered produce and small-farm, organic produce—and demanding the latter. As the need for organic produce increases, small chains are appearing that specialize in mostly locally grown, mostly organic produce and other goods. Farmers' markets have appeared where there hadn't been one in decades, or ever.

Larger retail stores that have minimal organic selection are scrambling to regain some of the organic market share without losing the efficiency of modern inventory tracking and the economy of scale. Farmer-owned cooperatives are working to meet these retailers halfway to create a win-win for retail, small farmers and consumers alike. One cooperative has grown in Eugene, Oregon's, Organically Grown Company. Produce is collected from hundreds of small vendors and delivered to non-exclusively organic grocery chains like Fred Meyer. Each of the participating farms would be too small to individually leverage a deal, but together they can.

Keep in mind that in order to plant a cash crop, you will probably have to front the money yourself—access to a loan or line of credit as a first-time farmer is limited at best. If you own farmland but cannot or don't want to work it yourself, lease it to a neighbor for crops or livestock. Make sure you both sign a clearly written agreement that delineates the terms of harvest, maintenance, and restitution for damage to your fences or other equipment.

A good way to make yourself more appealing to lending institutions is to get some work experience by volunteering or interning on a working farm. You will see if the lifestyle is something you embrace, and you'll learn by doing. One way to get experience is via an international organization called World Wide Opportunities on Organic Farms (WOOFF), which serves as a clearinghouse for farmers seeking help and individuals seeking hands-on experience.

Keep in mind that small farm operations only "pencil out" if you are not paying yourself. Not even $10 per hour. It is truly a labor of love.

Agri-Tourism

In the last ten years, Oregon's Hood River Valley has become a model of the phenomenon that I once saw characterized as "agri-tourism" in a magazine. The different farms have collaborated to market the entire valley, very successfully, as a tourist destination to nearby urban centers. Capitalizing on the idea that people want to visit farms, they have created events like "Blossom Fest," which is celebrated in the spring, when the apple and pear orchards are all in bloom. Visitors are given a map of the valley and participating farms, and then drive the "Fruit Loop," a circular route, to visit them.

You could have people come to you, instead of bringing your products to market. Consider a "U-Cut" Christmas tree lot, or a "U-Pick" orchard or berry field. A farm near us made most of its money between Memorial Day and Halloween: During the summer the farmers had a fresh-produce stand, which was more of a small store that carried lots of value-added products (I explain that below). In the fall, they offered hay rides, a petting zoo of farm animals, crafts and hot cider—when people go to pick out a couple of pumpkins, it turns into an half-day affair. Be sure to purchase ample liability insurance.

Tax Deferral

Many people who move to the country are intrigued by this little snippet of information they heard somewhere or another of getting out of paying taxes on their land by operating a farm or timber operation, no matter how small. "All you have to do is get a couple of horses," someone told me.

Not quite that simple. First of all, it's a deferral, not a deduction. That means that the taxes are still assessed; you postpone payment so long as you have a farm in operation. That means keeping good records, and showing a profit at least most of the time. Showing a profit differentiates you from someone doing what you do as a hobby. If at any time you cease to operate a farm-as-business, those taxes may come due. If you sell your farm and the new owners choose to not run an official farming operation, someone (most likely you) may have to pay the deferred taxes.

However, your operation truly doesn't need to be all that big. If you sell eggs, milk or cheese, and vegetables and flowers at the farmers market, you may be in good enough shape. Just make sure you're not spending $2,000 to save $1,000 in taxes. Check with a tax advisor who specializes in small farms, who has no conflicts of interest, for the details.

Employees

As the owner of a modest farming operation you will likely serve as CEO, foreman, bookkeeper and marketing department. Maybe you'll hire your accounting out. If you've got a big-for-this-book operation, it may be necessary to hire employees. If you are hesitant to hire undocumented workers for any of a multitude of reasons, you are going to struggle with this. It's one of those systems in the United States that is broken, and there is no clear path to fixing it.

U.S. agriculture makes the money that it does because of immigrants, many of whom are undocumented. People from Mexico, Guatemala and other Latin American countries come here to work because they can make a decent amount of money during the growing season and then go back home to their families for the winter.

This tradition began in the 1940s, during World War II. Just as "Rosie the Riveter" helped to compensate for the lack of men to work in factories, Mexican migrant men called *braceros* filled in to keep the farms going. As American men returned, took advantage of the G.I. Bill, and flocked to white-collar work, *braceros* continued to return to make good American wages during the summer months. This increased further in the 1980s, as American teenagers began to eschew work in the hot sun picking berries and corn, and looked for summer jobs in restaurants and shopping malls.

As the supply of American farm workers decreased and demand for migrant workers increased, some farm owners became more lax about registering their workers. Which leads us to today's predicament: undocumented workers are despised by much of the American public, but American agriculture (and other industries) are addicted to them.

If you find yourself in a position of needing workers, one option is to "borrow" a neighbor's workers. Friends who have a small farm live near a commercial orchard that hires full-time labor during the summer. However, there are down times for the laborers between tree-trimmings, so they're hired out for a day or two of weeding. This way, my friends don't have to deal with ensuring the workers are in the country legally; the orchard owners have already done so.

Finding good laborers is a bit like finding a good mechanic; most are advertised via word-of-mouth. Some farmers pay their laborers "under the table," in cash, which eliminates a taxable paper trail. This is not sustainable, however; I recommend keeping things on the up-and-up. This includes purchasing workers' compensation insurance.

Interns

Another echelon of worker, particularly with organic operations, are interns. Generally college-aged, interns are full of optimism, idealism and—most important to your operation—energy. They will work in the field for eight hours, haul produce to the farmers market and sell for three hours. Cheerfully. They will ask for little or no pay, plus room and board. Or you can pay them but deduct room and board. Interns are looking for "life experience" and the opportunity to learn about farming so they can open their own CSA in a couple of years.

The World Wide Opportunities on Organic Farms (WOOFF), which serves as a clearinghouse for farmers seeking help and individuals seeking hands-on experience, is a good option here as well. Be careful in whom you invite to your farm; I know of people who were "burned" by interns that trashed their living quarters and left without compensating them for repairs. I'm sure this is rare, but make sure you've vetted your applicants carefully.

Organic Certification

The battle around the word "organic" in commercial agriculture is pretty interesting. Large-scale farms ignored the pesky little dirty-hippie operations on the West Coast for years, until the tide began to turn and people other than hippies began to care how their food was grown and what chemicals were added to it. Nowadays, there is organic Prego spaghetti sauce; there are "green" cleaning products made by Clorox. In the free market, demand rules supply.

As interest in "organic" grew, different organizations vied to be the definitive word on what is organic. Graphic artists and publicists thrived as each organization came up with a logo and a promotional campaign. There were nuances: sustainably grown; permaculture; biodynamic. Meanwhile, agri-business tried to weaken the standards that make something organically grown, so they could put a logo on food that actually wasn't grown with any concern for consumers or for the environment. To them, it was simply a marketing tool.

There are numerous organic certifiers in the United States, the first of which was California Certified Organic Farmers. The heir-apparent to the Kingdom of Organicland seems to be Oregon Tilth. While agri-business is content with the watered-down U.S. Department of Agriculture logo, farmers across the United

States who really want to be respected for their practices go for Oregon Tilth certification.

Acquiring Oregon Tilth certification is exacting and expensive—a minimum of $850 per year (it goes up depending on your annual income). An inspector will make an annual visit your farm and walk the land with you to make sure you're not hiding anything. She will also go over your receipts.

Value-Added Products

Stop by any farm stand and you will find, in addition to the produce, moderately to expensively priced products. Think of the things that come in a bottle or a jar. These are called "value-added products," because the farmer has taken a commodity and processed it into something more expensive than the original commodity. The value-added products that bring the highest prices are gift items.

Value-added Ideas
- **Lavender:** Sachets, skin products, essential oil
- **Wool:** Dyed yarn skeins, knitted and felted clothing, hats, mittens, etc.
- **Bees:** Candles, skin products, honey
- **Fruit:** Pies, jams, gift baskets, dried fruit
- **Herbs:** Salad dressings, vinegars, dried seasonings, essential oil
- **Vegetables:** Pickled and canned vegetables, frozen soups
- **Meat/Fish:** Jerky, smoked meat or fish, skins, leather products
- **Crafts:** Can be made of anything, from corn-husk dolls to wooden toys to decorative items

If you have a shop on your property in which you sell value-added local products, consider adding a line of related retail items. For example, if you sell honey you could also sell mugs, honey-drippers and decorative knives. You could even sell pre-packaged tea, crumpets and English muffins! A farm stand near our house offered the requisite produce, as well as dish cloths that must have been crocheted by Grandma.

If you create products that are edible, you have more work to do than if you make lotion or candles. All food items must be produced in a commercial kitchen or other facility that is regularly inspected by the health department to meet certain standards for cleanliness and professionalism. And really, would you want someone selling food made in their own kitchen, with the dog hair and the kids sneezing and the spouse sneaking a taste when the cook isn't looking?

When starting out, it probably makes more sense to check with the local community college to see if they have a commercial kitchen that's available, or talk to a local restaurant to see if you can lease their kitchen (if, for example, they're closed on Mondays, perhaps you can rent it then). I know a woman who retrofitted an old school bus to make Bloody Mary mix. She decked it out in stainless steel, installed the requisite vents and water sources, and was in business.

If you sell you wares via an existing shop, keep in mind that you'll make half of the retail price—the seller will get the other half. Sometimes the shop owner will buy your product outright, and sometimes they will only consign it. Consignment means they carry the product but only pay you once it sells. Keep track of what you've given him or her, and check in regularly to see how the inventory is moving.

Other Opportunities

Check zoning restrictions in your area before pursuing these opportunities. Consider the logistics: Where are you going to put all these people's cars? Where will they go to the bathroom?

- **"U-Cut" Christmas trees:** This option plays out best in the Pacific Northwest, where Douglas fir trees can grow to harvest size in just five years. To make it an event, give away hot apple cider and cookies. Check into liability insurance, since people are going to be walking around with handsaws. The trees require some maintenance in the spring and summer to help them conform in shape and stifle surrounding growth.
- **"U-Pick" Fruit:** Giving people some buckets and turning them loose in your orchard or berry patch is a lot easier than picking the fruit yourself or hiring it done. Make sure you coach them about what "ripe" looks like before they go out—every unripe fruit that is picked is wasted. You need a fairly good-sized area to make money. If you are planting rather than buying an existing business, keep in mind that it will be a number of years before you can invite people in.
- **Farm Adventure:** People simply like to visit a farm—they used to be ubiquitous but are now a novelty. You can draw people to your farm with a pumpkin patch, a corn maze, a petting "zoo" (make sure you select extremely tame animals and monitor the area at all times), or tractor rides. One farm near our house had weekend events and school groups, and included story time and a craft table for kids to play with.
- **Writer/Artist Retreat:** Creative types love a getaway to work on a specific project. They will need a workspace (writer = desk with electricity and Internet; artist = large table that can get paint/clay/whatever on it and

311

running water). They will all want good lighting and, preferably, a view. If you really want to sweeten the deal, cook for them. Check with the visual artists about what chemicals they use; remember, their effluent is going into your land and groundwater.

- **Campground:** If you have a lot of open land, rent it out to campers. Major considerations include visual and audible impact on neighbors and wildlife, waste-removal, and law enforcement.
- **Fish Pond:** Stock a natural or human-made pond on your property with trout, and you're ready to start your U-Fish business! You can provide poles for all comers, or rent them out. The charge can be per fish or per hour.
- **Boarding:** Renting out your pasture (generally to horses) is fairly simple: It doesn't generate a lot of income but it doesn't require a lot of work, either. Because the fencing is on your land, installing and/or maintaining it is your responsibility.

    Actually boarding horses is a little more complicated: you'll have to have well-built and -maintained stalls and grooming areas. Ideally, you'll either have enough land for your tenants to ride on, or have nearby access to public land.
- **Goat Rental:** Some people loan or rent out their goats to neighbors and friends, so they will eat back an overgrown area, such as a briar patch. They need to be tethered to the area; otherwise, they'll migrate over to the sweet, green grass.

Bed-and-Breakfast

One often-successful strategy to integrate your life with your income is to, essentially, hire out your lifestyle by way of offering bed-and-breakfast lodging. City folks *love* to come to the country for a bite-sized piece of authenticity. They will coo over your animals, rave about the food you prepare, and walk around your property in blissful contemplation of The Things That Really Matter. You know—you're currently one of them!

If you're a social person and a good cook, this can be a brilliant way to bring the excitement to you, since your ability to leave the farm to find excitement is limited. One advantage to this type of business is that you can deduct just about anything you buy from your income taxes (keeping careful records, of course). Groceries, livestock feed, gardening supplies—it's all a part of feeding and entertaining the guests.

If you or your spouse is someone who needs "alone time," you'll have to either work that into your booking schedule, or have a building or area that is off limits to the guests. When you have guests, it will not be possible to get much done until at least 9 o'clock, since you don't want to disturb them.

In addition to welcoming regular people looking for a weekend getaway, you can also host events, such as birthday and anniversary parties, graduations, and family and school reunions. If you are really a glutton for punishment, you'll schedule weddings. These will eat you alive, but the season is short and people will pay a *lot* of money to have their Perfect Day at your establishment. The trick is, they really want the Day to be Perfect. "Perfect" takes a lot of work and organization, and the ability to act fast to accommodate last-minute requests (or, in some cases, demands). You'll have to coordinate with caterers, party-rental companies, transportation and other vendors, or decide to bring some of this in-house (i.e. buy a bunch of folding tables and chairs, and then charge the client to use them). When considering what to charge, keep in mind there is at least one day tacked onto the front and back of the wedding day for set-up and clean-up. As one man who hosts weddings on his property said, "Those paper napkins blow everywhere."

Chapter 25
Health Care

When retirees move to a small town, they want to know if the closest hospital has good heart- and cancer-treatment services. Sports fanatics want to know if the hospital has good orthopedic surgeons and physical therapists. Young couples want to know how the obstetrics department rates.

The best way to find out is to do some research. Schedule a walk-through and meet some of the staff. Get a feel for the place, and see if you're comfortable there. Don't assume that the health care providers are low-grade—some have come to the area for quality-of-life reasons, just like you.

That said, many rural areas are already keenly experiencing the shortage of medical personnel that the urban areas will eventually have. Our nation has been unable to train enough medical providers, especially nurses, to care for the population—this will become especially apparent as the Baby Boomers age and need more medical care.

Because today's young doctors come out of medical school tens of thousands of dollars in debt, they can't afford to set up a family practice in a small town—their salary wouldn't even cover their student loan payments. Instead, most move into a specialty and practice in a city. The government has tried to assuage this by forgiving a certain amount of student loans for doctors who spend at least five years in family practice in a rural area.

But, even this can't draw physicians to some parts of the country. The best that many communities can do is to have a nurse practitioner or physician assistant, or a traveling doctor who comes once per week in an RV outfitted with medical equipment. The former two are equally compassionate and sophisticated individuals as doctors are; they've simply had less schooling. Unless your condition is unusual or severe, a PA or an NP will be able to handle it.

A nurse practitioner is a registered nurse who independently provides health care in an expanded specialty role, such as family practice or mental health. He has a master's degree. A physician assistant works under the direction, supervision and responsibility of a doctor. She has completed specialized medical training and passed a licensure exam. In some communities, PAs are in partnership with a big-city doctor, who—via the wonders of the telecommunications age—can view photos and charts sent by your PA, and advise her on your treatment.

Other specialties, like dentists and ophthalmologists, you'll have to interview and tour their facilities before you can decide. Ask around for recommendations from friends and neighbors. Outdated décor is not necessarily a strike against someone—a doctor might put his money into paying his staff well or covering the debts of poor patients, rather than buying new carpeting for the waiting room.

Mental Health

Getting therapy in a small town is weird, there's no other way to say it. Think about it: in a city, you go to a stranger and tell him all about your innermost thoughts, feelings and fears. You tell him about your parents. You tell him about your partner and your sex life. You never expect to see him outside of his office. No one else, even family members, knows that you go to therapy unless you divulge that fact. The therapist may tell his wife about you over dinner but your name is not used, and she doesn't know you from Adam.

In the country, there are only a handful of therapists at best, maybe even one. She hears the innermost thoughts, feelings and fears of half of the town, and everyone knows it. (This role has also been filled by the town pastor; it's not a new phenomenon.) If you park in front of the therapist's building, anyone who recognizes your car knows what you're doing. If you and your spouse are both parked in front of her building, anyone who recognizes your cars knows you're not getting along. If the therapist tells her husband about you over dinner, she'll hopefully not use your name—but there are only so many people in town. Her husband will probably be able to figure it out.

The reason there aren't many, or any, therapists or clinical social workers is that country folks typically don't go to them. Being self-reliant is a strongly held value that would be compromised by asking for help. The prevailing mindset is something along the lines of: I'm not going to a doctor, especially for sissy-pants depression, of all things. Better to buck up and go mend some fence.

Reproductive Health
Obstetrics

Because of soaring malpractice insurance rates, many rural doctors are ceasing to provide obstetrics care, leaving women to have to drive further and further to deliver a baby. If you choose to go to a hospital to have a baby, be sure to ask them a lot of questions. Do they work with doulas, or midwives who perform home births? What is their emergency Cesarean section rate? What is their episiotomy rate?

A growing alternative is harkening back to the "old ways"—hiring a licensed practical midwife to deliver the baby at home. As OB docs give up their practices, midwives are stepping in, mainly with non-"at-risk" births (young, healthy mothers). As hospitals lack the wherewithal to provide obstetrics care, they are beginning to work in partnership with midwives—reversing a century of blanket sabotage of their reputation as professionals.

Infertility

Don't waste a lot of time with small-town physicians if you are struggling with fertility issues. This is such a new and unregulated field that even the most well meaning health care provider will not have the most up-to-date information and practices at her disposal. Go to a major city. If you're considering in vitro fertilization (IVF) and haven't moved to the country yet, I would recommend waiting. I did IVF while we lived in the country, which meant I had to drive seventy miles into Portland often, sometimes three times per week, so they could draw blood and perform other procedures. It was ridiculous.

Pregnancy Avoidance or Termination

If you have, or will have in a few years, a sexually active teenager, find out if RU-486 is dispensed at a local pharmacy—some communities refuse to on "moral" grounds. Birth control pills and condoms should not be a problem, but check to be sure.

Abortions are legally accessible to any pregnant woman in the United States. But, how accessible is accessible? Not very. If you or your daughter choose to end a pregnancy, you may have to travel hundreds of miles to find a doctor who will perform the procedure. And, legislation exists in some states that requires two visits a certain number of days apart—one for counseling and one for the procedure. This means a multi-day stay in a foreign city, or two trips. Making the decision to have an abortion is never easy; the logistics of acquiring one add to the difficulty.

End-of-Life Care

As with any health care, make sure that you are comfortable with both the facility and the staff of an assisted-living facility, nursing home, or hospice. Hospice providers in rural areas make "house calls": that is, they endeavor to enable a terminally ill person to decline at home. Many people—urban and rural—don't realize that hospice care is a free service for everyone, either paid by one's private insurance, Medicare, or by the hospice itself as part of its mission as a not-for-profit organization. Be extra cautious around the burgeoning group of for-profit hospices—they aren't necessarily nefarious but tend to be more in it for the money than a nonprofit is.

State death-with-dignity laws often come up against similar roadblocks in rural areas as abortion-rights laws: the only people in the area who can administer the drugs refuse to because of their personal beliefs.

Every year, a number of people take advantage of the Country Death-With-Dignity policy—walking out to the woods with a loaded rifle.

Alternative Medicine

The popularity of naturopathy, acupuncture and massage therapy has grown steadily in the last decade, and will continue to make inroads in the years to come. While you won't have as many choices as in a metropolitan area, your town may have a few. People who visit these practitioners usually build long-term relationships.

Because naturopaths are few and far between in rural areas, many also dispense their prescriptions. Some even brew up their own medicines using purchased extracts. The true hard-core naturopath wild-harvests his own plant material. Naturopathy can be controversial because, while most of the treatments offered are hundreds or thousands years old, there are no checks-and-balances on this system. The main reason this is the case is that the Food and Drug Administration is heavily influenced by the pharmaceutical industry, which can't make money on natural compounds (although they're trying to change that) and doesn't want the competition. So, they won't fund dosage trials that would lead to FDA approval and regulation of the medicines.

Acupuncture is also an ancient art. Modern American acupuncturists have taken the premise of acupuncture and tried to soften it for their consumers, who are more pain-adverse than traditional acupuncture patients. There is generally an emphasis on relaxation and a spa-like atmosphere. Unless you are in a rural area in the Western United States, particularly California, chances are your local acupuncturist will be of this non-traditional school of thought.

Some massage therapists take the day-spa approach, even selling lotions and other products in the lobby, while others choose a more medical path, usually sports medicine. As you would do in the city, interview each practitioner and make sure you feel comfortable with her technique and facility, and check to see if she bills insurance for service (most won't or can't), or if there is a discount for paying cash.

Studios and Gymnasiums

There is usually some kind of gym or studio in even the smallest town. The Curves franchise, which offers a thirty-minute workout aimed at women, is currently popular across the country.

Yoga and tai chi have captured the imagination of Americans of nearly all stripes, small towns included. Not only can you take yoga classes, you can probably teach them if you're so inclined. If there isn't already a studio in operation, you can open one in town or in your home (be sure to purchase extra liability insurance if you run the business out of your home). Or, you might be able to use the local gym or senior center.

Safety

Urban people don't take personal safety as seriously as country people do, because they don't need to. If you are mowing your lawn in flip-flops and have an accident, an ambulance will be there in minutes to take you to get your toes sewn back on. In rural areas, it can be a little different. If you bought your place because you like the fact that it's thirty minutes out of town and twenty minutes up a gravel road, you won't like it as well when your spouse puts his hand in the wood chipper and it takes the ambulance an hour to get to you. And that's in the summer; imagine when there's snow on the road.

I recall a story of a sixteen-year-old in remote rural Oregon who was tending irrigation lines. His sleeve got caught in the machinery, which tore off one arm at the elbow. Being a level-headed country kid, he picked up his arm and ran to the nearest barn, where there was a four-wheeler. He drove it one-armed toward the neighbor's house but got it caught in a ditch; he ran to the nearest shed to the crash site and got another four-wheeler, which he drove until he crashed it as well. Then, he got up and ran the rest of the way. He was "Life-Flighted" (ambulance helicopter) to Bend and then to Portland, where his arm was eventually reattached (not restored completely, but not bad given the circumstances!).

The first line of defense is to have everyone in your family take a first-aid class so you know the basics of CPR and wound care. Then, make sure you have first-aid supplies and hardcore painkillers if you can get a hold of them, maybe extra pills from a previous injury or surgery. I have friends who are rock-climbers; they have Vicodin stashed away in their bags in case they've hiked in a ways and someone takes a fall. Have an epinephrine auto-injector, too, even if no one in your family is allergic to bee stings—a visitor might be. If you have a working farm with employees, there will be state guidelines about where and how many first aid stations to have.

If you're working alone in the field or woodlot where no one can see or hear you, carry a cell phone or walkie-talkie. My friend Chris was pruning canes in her vineyard when she accidentally pruned her palm, which split wide open and started gushing blood. She stayed calm and used her walkie-talkie to contact her son, who was making breakfast in the kitchen. "Bring towels," she said. He drove her to the emergency room.

A neighbor of mine wasn't so lucky—he was found face down in his apple orchard, dead of a heart attack. A friend's neighbor actually drowned inside his septic tank while he was cleaning it out. Now, that is a bad way to go.

If you are really out in the boonies you might consider "Life Flight" insurance if it's available. This provides guaranteed service for no charge other than a monthly membership fee. This is a growing business; companies in different areas are building reciprocity agreements to extend the coverage area for their members.

Keep extra medications on hand, especially in the winter, in case you are unable to get to town to replenish. This is true of food and water as well. Stock that pantry! Buy in bulk! The worst feeling is to wake up Sunday morning to two feet of snow after you had the chance to go to the grocery on Saturday and decided not to. The best feeling is to wake up that same Sunday after having gone to the grocery and thinking to yourself, "Bring it on! We're ready."

Abuse

Dealing with domestic or child abuse is tricky anywhere, but especially in the country because everything is such a crucible already. If you're witnessing an actual assault, calling 911 is pretty straightforward. However, most abusers are smarter than to beat up their spouses on Main Street in the middle of the day.

Each state has its own requirements about mandatory reporting of abuse when it is observed or suspected. Generally, law enforcement officers, school employees, health care workers and counselors are all required to report. If you're not a mandatory reporter and are afraid of the repercussions of reporting, document the situation for possible future use in an investigation.

And then, not all abuse results in black eyes—there is also sexual, emotional and financial abuse. Approximately 85 percent of abuse is of women. If you suspect an adult is being abused, give them opportunities to tell you about it. Ask if they're all right; offer to help if they need it. Don't pressure them; they have to decide to make a change. But let them know you're there if they need it.

Deciding to make a change can be extremely difficult. I can't say it any better than the National Coalition Against Domestic Violence:

> "Rural battered women face lack of resources, isolation, small-town politics, few if any support agencies, and poor or little transportation and communication systems in addition to the other complications of intimate partner violence that is intensified by the rural lifestyle…The patriarchal 'good old boys' network, fundamentalist religious teachings, deep-rooted cultural traditions and commonly accepted sexual stereotyping can form a chorus of accusations that the battered rural

woman is unfaithful in her role as a woman, wife and mother. The act of leaving the home place, land and animals that could depend on her may be emotionally wrenching, leaving the battered rural woman surrounded by walls of guilt and self-abasement."

And it's even harder for rural same-sex victims. Imagine finally gathering up the courage to go to the police, and the officer tells you to go back home. Or threatens to deport you:

> "Battered immigrant and refugee women in the United States have further complications by issues of gender, race socioeconomic status, immigration status and language in addition to those complications of intimate partner violence. A battered woman who is not a legal resident or whose immigrant status depends on her partner is isolated by cultural dynamics that may prevent her from leaving her husband, seeking support from local agencies that may not understand her culture or requesting assistance from an unfamiliar American legal system. Some obstacles may include a distrustful attitude toward the legal system, language and cultural barriers (that may at the least be unknown and at the worst hostile), and fear of deportation."

If the suspected victim is a child, report the abuse to the proper authority, which may be the sheriff and may be a state department of human services. There are also national hotlines. You may report anonymously. You will not be given any follow-up information about the case.

If a child confides in you, stay calm and let the child lead the story—don't interrogate or jump to conclusions. Don't make reactions that betray disgust or shock, as the child might interpret that as judgment of him. Depending on the situation, you'll most likely have to return the child to his home. But report the abuse.

Parenting is stressful, and everyone has bad days and occasionally does or says something they regret. That's not abuse. Abuse is systematic, manipulative and compulsive.

Chapter 26
Vehicles and Driving

Nothing says "city" like a Volvo station wagon. Country people buy American rigs: Ford. Chevrolet. Dodge. The possible exception is Sports Towns, in which Japanese SUVs and Subarus are also common. I'm just saying. When in Rome, drive what the Romans drive unless you want to stick out.

Bicycles are generally the domain of those who have lost their licenses to excessive DUI convictions. There may be some bike lanes in the vicinity of a school, but other than that, try to stay off the main roads, for safety.

In the city, drivers are hyper-aware because hazards abound—stop signs and signals on nearly every intersection; other drivers and pedestrians darting out in front of them; bicyclists sneaking up from behind. In the country, there is rarely any cross-traffic but there are other hazards. The biggest ones are complacency and speeding; since the roads are fairly clear people feel they can drive fast, which is fine if they're paying attention, but over time many lose their sense of danger about it. Some even cut across centerlines on purpose (what my neighbor called "straightening the curves").

At night, drivers use their brights or fog lights to better illuminate the road (most country roads do not have streetlamps). Dim them if a car is approaching, or if you approach another car from behind. Sometimes, an oncoming car's lights will not dim, or it is a tall pickup or SUV and its regular lights are blasting right into your eyes, and you are blinded. Not fun! If this happens, look down and to the right, and keep the fog line (the white, solid line on the right) in sight until the vehicle has passed. Flashing your brights at them to "send them a message" may feel satisfying but endangers both of you, especially if the other driver is intoxicated.

Roads are made for travelers, yes, but in the country they are also access roads for the farms that are adjacent to them. If you are driving and come across a tractor or herd of animals in the road, yield. You may pass them, but do it carefully, slowly and courteously. Farm equipment and animals have the right of way.

If you're coming up on someone, you may find them moving toward the shoulder slightly. This is a courtesy; they are signaling that it's safe to pass, and making your line of sight clearer so you can see for yourself. Do make sure yourself that it's safe, and then pass with care.

Traffic safety is a little different in the country. In addition to farmers occasionally using the roads as their personal property, you also have to be on the alert for people pulling out in front of you. Not because they're rude, but because the previous fifty times they pulled out at that intersection there was no one there. They are accustomed to not having to wait for any cars to pass before entering a roadway, and get a titch lazy and don't feel like stopping. Once you live there long enough, you'll find yourself doing the same thing. Drive defensively.

You might even see two people going opposite directions stopped in the middle of the road, talking. Be patient; one might be your neighbor, or the fella you're on your way to have a job interview with.

Animal Collisions

As I mentioned in the Animals Section, deer cause thousands of vehicle accidents every year. The most likely months for such collisions are October and November because of the following:

- Deer are in rut and chasing each other around.
- Deer are generally more active at dusk, and the autumn's short days put that time right around when people are driving home from work.
- Drivers who are leaving work are tired (less alert), and speeding in order to get home as soon as possible.

To avoid deer collisions: Use your brights, which illuminate the sides of the road, when possible. If you see one deer cross the road, slow down immediately—there are likely others following it. There is no evidence that deer whistles and other repellants have any effect.

One of the worst things driving down a winding country road is to encounter a group of deer, which you successfully pass by, only to see someone approaching at full speed from the other direction. A common means of warning someone is to flash your brights but, as I mention above, this can just add danger to danger.

Despite a driver's best efforts—slowing his speed and watching carefully—he might still hit a deer because of the animal's propensity to leap from cover, virtually appearing out of nowhere. "Insta-deer" my friend calls it. It may be impossible to avoid.

If you see an animal in the road, don't swerve. Let me say that again: Do not swerve. Many people are injured when their car flips off the road or hits another vehicle, while the animal trots off to live another day. Most accidents can be avoided just by braking—not slamming on the brakes, which can cause you to lose control of your car, but even, steady braking. If you feel like you have the car under control and have checked the roadway for other vehicles, you can steer carefully around the animal.

If a collision is imminent, get a good grip on the steering wheel, break as cleanly as possible and try to relax, which can help to minimize injury. If you injure the deer rather than kill it do not approach it; it can spring up and hurt you. If your car is functional, try to note where the collision occurred using mileposts and landmarks, go home and phone your sheriff's or wildlife-control office (not 911, unless there is a major human injury). And, of course, phone your insurance agent.

Waving

Driving around, you may notice people waving to you as you pass. This is normal; rural folks wave whether they know each other or not. If you are on a country road and a pickup truck is approaching, do you wave? It depends on how remote you are; if you haven't passed a vehicle in a while, I'd wave. If it's a populated state highway, you don't need to. If it's a gravel road, definitely wave. If there are road workers with orange signs, wave. I prefer to wave and not have it reciprocated than the other way around.

It's not really a wave, more of a salute. People have their hands near the top of the steering wheel and pick up their fingers on one hand. If it's a really cool dude, he might just raise one finger. Either that, or it's a Country Diss, like "Yeah, I'll wave, but I don't know you. Stranger."

Open Range

Once, I was driving south of Burns, Oregon, on my way to visit the Malheur Wildlife Refuge. The road was stick-straight and flat—I was going 70 miles an hour and felt like I could safely speed twice as fast. There was absolutely nothing to hit. Miles ahead, I saw some cattle grazing on the side of the road. One enormous black bull was walking, which I love to see since cattle are usually just standing there. He was going at a pretty good clip. He was walking toward the road. As I was coming up on him, I thought "Wow, he's going to have to slow down or he'll run into the fence." Then the "Livestock" sign I had passed twenty minutes before popped into my head. I slowed just in time to be able to swerve around him—he had charged out onto the asphalt with absolutely no concern about the metal "bull" speeding toward him.

"Open range" means there are no fences, or the only fences built are to keep cattle out of an area, not in it. And, as I've mentioned, farm animals and equipment have the right of way, so if you happen to smash into a cow and kill it, you have to pay the rancher for the damages.

Unpaved Roads

Many roads in a rural area are gravel. Driving on a gravel road that's in good condition requires a slower speed and a little more caution on curves, but they're otherwise very passable. Most rural people drive down the middle of a gravel road unless there is a blind rise or curve. If you're approaching a gravel driveway from a paved road, or the road is going from paved to gravel, do your breaking on the paved road or you may skid. Watch for other hazards, such as potholes, washboard (ridges in the gravel) and "soft shoulders."

A friend of mine was once a passenger in a truck; the driver was showing her a dammed river in our area because she was writing an article about the dam (which produced electricity) and its affect on the environment. As he pointed out features of the dam, he got a little too close to the edge of the road. The gravel on the shoulder was soft, meaning there wasn't a fortified underlayment to it, and it collapsed under the right side of the vehicle, pitching it over. The embankment of this road happened to drop off at a serious angle—the only thing that stopped them from rolling about ten times to the bottom of the ravine was, ironically, an electrical pole. They managed to escape unharmed but quite shaken.

Some roads are dirt, basically scraped into the surface of the Earth. Dirt roads require even less speed and more care, and may be impassable during the winter (unplowed) and spring (mud).

You'll quickly learn why you don't want to follow directly someone on a gravel or dirt road: cars kick up an astonishing cloud of dust when they're going more than about 30 miles per hour. It's fun to see one in the distance—it looks like a comet. Not so fun up close—shut your windows and switch your heater's air intake to "recirculate."

Snow

If you've never driven on snow before, the basic tenet is to slow down and plan ahead, further ahead than if you were on dry pavement. "It's easy to go fast on snow," my Dad used to tell me when I first started driving, in Minnesota. "It's stopping that's hard."

Before you get into a vehicle that you plan to drive on snow, you need to know two things: Does it have anti-lock brakes? Is it two- or four-wheel-drive, and if two wheels, front or back?

If your vehicle has conventional brakes, you will pump your brakes gently when slowing or stopping. So: braaaaake, release, braaaaaake and so on. This will hopefully keep you out of a skid. If you have anti-lock brakes, you simply depress the brake pedal; it is designed to pump for you. You may hear it when this happens—a kind of rattling sound under the car that can freak you out, but stay calm and leave your foot on the brake. And keep in mind that the first way to slow down is to simply stop accelerating. Amazing how many people have their foot either on the gas or brake at all times, one or the other. Drivers with a manual transmission can also use it to decelerate.

A front-wheel-drive car is more stable on snow than a rear-wheel-drive car for a couple of reasons: The latter is pulling the front end rather than pushing it, and it has the weight of the engine to hold the tires down. A four-wheel-drive car is even more stable (but not invincible—I have an anecdote here that involves my husband overconfidently driving our Subaru, but for the sake of my marriage I will refrain from including it). The most stable is a heavy truck that has two 4WD gears—high and low. Four-wheel low will get you out of nearly anything.

The main thing to do when driving on snow is to not panic. When people panic, they slam on their brakes and steer sharply, either of which will land you in the ditch (or worse, if you're in the mountains). However, even if you're driving in a perfectly composed manner, you can still get into a skid. If this happens, take your foot off the gas but not necessarily on the brake yet. Steer gently into the skid so that the car is going forward and not sideways, and then try to steer it back in the direction you want to go.

Remember that roads are, for some reason, slipperier when the temperature hovers just above freezing, and when it gets down near zero Fahrenheit, which can produce an effect known as "black ice." While gravel roads are a little more slippery when it's dry, they can provide a bit more traction than pavement when the roads are wet or snowy.

Chapter 27
Urban Connections

It's exciting to move to the country but hard to leave the city, and your network, behind. When I announced that I was moving to a friend who had lived in the country during the 1970s and returned to "civilization" a few years later, the first thing out of his mouth was a warning: "Your friends won't come to visit you."

This was not entirely true, but there was certainly a tug sometimes because of the things we either missed or had to go to great lengths to participate in. Some of our friends came out more than once because they enjoyed the rural respite (and, Mike cooked his ass off when we had visitors) or, bless their hearts, offered to help us on the land. Some never came because they had small children or were otherwise sidetracked every week. Some couldn't imagine why we had done such a fool thing in the first place, and were certainly not going to accommodate us by joining us in the sticks.

You may move far from the city in which you've established a community. We were only seventy miles away, which made it possible to continue our relationships with city friends, even if we didn't see them as often. Things like email and social networking sites help to close the gap. Sharing anecdotes and photos via the Internet can make you feel less isolated.

Visitors

Soon enough, you will have settled in and someone will come out to see if this crazy fantasy of yours is real. It is then that you will realize that country life has changed you.

I remember being at my friend's house in Trout Lake one summer, when Mike and I still lived in Portland but were interested in rural life. Tara was out of town for a week and had invited me up to have a secluded writing retreat. She even more kindly allowed Mike to bring two friends up, who were visiting from Minneapolis and whom we hadn't seen in a few years. I went up first, and later in the week Mike brought our friends.

I was overjoyed when they pulled in the muddy drive—so excited to show them how the broccoli plants were up and the deer tracks I had found, and to enjoy a nice evening with them in front of the fire. I rushed out in my sweatshirt, grungy jeans and rubber boots. They stepped gingerly out of the car and froze—both had gotten black mud on their pristine, white Adidas shoes. Both had short hair dyed a peroxide blonde. Both were wearing white shirts and white jeans. I'm not kidding. They peered at me and the house through fifty-dollar sunglasses, afraid to take another step for fear of soiling something else. Culture shock on both ends.

Events

When we lived in the country, our Portland friends sometimes invited us to their barbeques. Whether to go was a major decision, as it cost about twenty dollars in gas and resulted in the loss of an entire day of gardening and land-maintenance. One of our friends has still not forgiven us for missing her daughter's first birthday party; we'd had a tree fall during a windstorm and needed to deal with it.

Or, it was a nighttime party, or a live music show or literary event. If we went we had to drive home late, and with a beer or two in the system. Neither fun nor particularly safe.

Friends were always inviting us to stay over when we came into the city, which we occasionally did. But usually not—if we stayed, there would be a leisurely breakfast, and chatting, which would be lovely but meant that we'd be missing yet another land-maintenance day.

Index

power, 91–92, 96–98

    see also country living; fuel; green power and alternatives; wood heating

preservation, food

    canning, 228–32

    dehydration, 234–35

    freezing, 232–34

    see also fruits and vegetables, growing and preparation; gardening

prior appropriation water rights, 41–42

pythons, 164

quail / partridge, 175–76

rabbits

    butchering, 187, *189*

    care and handling, 152–53

    and fencing, 65, 67

    and gardening, 212

    see also livestock, raising animals for profit

raccoons, 66, 172, 213

rammed earth, building material, 105

raptors, 174

rats and mice, 171

Reagan, Ronald, 293

real estate, buying

    airspace, 37

    buying, 26–28

    and development, 32

    "dividable," 27

    driveway, 32

    easements, 36, 37–38

    environmental issues affecting, 35–37

    inspections, 77

    internet, telephone, television, 92–93, 96, 101, 292, 299, 326

    land contract, 28

    mineral, timber rights, 36

    and noise, 37, 38–39

    outbuildings, 111–12

    public works projects, impact on, 35

    septic system, 40, 44–45, 81, 106

    surveys, 37–38

    taxes, 33–34

    topography of, 28–32

    utilities, 39–40, 45–47

    views, 32–33

    water features on property, 29–31

    and water quality, 41, 43

    zoning, 34–35

    see also community amenities, services; houses and residences; permits; rights; seasonal issues; town personalities; water

recycling, 46–47

    see also waste disposal

rights

    mineral, 36

    riparian, 41–42

    timber, 36

    water, 29, 30, 31, 40–41

    see also real estate, buying

"right to farm," laws, 34–35

rodents

gophers, 208–11

    mice and rats, 171

    owls and, 175

    voles, 213

    see also animals

Rotary International, 284

rural culture

    cash for services, 79